CRITICAL INSIGHTS

Alice Walker

CRITICAL
INSIGHTS

Alice Walker

Editor
Nagueyalti Warren
Emory University

SALEM PRESS
A Division of EBSCO Publishing
Ipswich, Massachusetts

Cover Photo: © Bonnie Schiffman/Corbis

Editor's text © 2013 by Nagueyalti Warren

∞ The paper used in these volumes conforms to the American National Standard
for Permanence of Paper for Printed Library Materials, Z39.48-1992 (R1997).

Library of Congress Cataloging-in-Publication Data
Alice Walker / editor, Nagueyalti Warren.
    p. cm. -- (Critical insights)
  Includes bibliographical references and index.
  ISBN 978-1-4298-3730-9 (hardcover)
  1. Walker, Alice, 1944- 2. Authors, American--20th century--Biography. 3.
African American authors--Biography. I. Warren, Nagueyalti.
  PS3573.A425Z538 2013
  813'.54--dc23
  [B]
                                    2012014427

PRINTED IN THE UNITED STATES OF AMERICA

Contents_____

Resources

About This Volume

Nagueyalti Warren

Contributors to this volume present not only a summary of the life and work of poet, essayist, novelist, short story writer, and activist Alice Walker; they analyze her most important works and offer new insights in Walker scholarship. Sally Wolff King discusses Walker's career, life, and influences in a short biography that introduces this volume. The critical context in which Walker's works have emerged is detailed in Lillie P. Howard's essay on the critical reception of such works as *The Color Purple*, her other novels, the essays in *Living By the Word*, her first collection of essays, *In Search of Our Mothers' Gardens*, and her poetry. Howard concludes that the "critical reception of Walker's works—by literary scholars and the public in general—has been richly mixed, reflecting the complexity of Walker and her controversial, ever-evolving vision."

Napolita Hooper-Simanga's essay "Five Critics on Alice Walker" presents a critical lens through which critics Susan Willis, Robert Butler, Trudier Harris, Gale Keating, and Lynn Pifer examine Walker's important early novels *Meridian*, *The Color Purple*, and *The Third Life of Grange Copeland*. Hooper-Simanga declares that Walker's body of work transcends boundaries, blurs "the difference between traditional Southern and African American literary conventions while carving space for literary critics to uncover the seemingly endless themes and developments" in Walker's works.

Carmen R. Gillespie provides the social and historical background from which Walker's works evolve. Her essay begins in 2011, with the end of the *Oprah Winfrey Show*, and works backward to the time of Walker's birth in 1944. World War II and the historical events preceding this cataclysmic change in the world provide the context from which Walker draws her activism as well as her creativity. Gillespie outlines Walker's development through 2011, and her involvement in the mission on board *The Audacity of Hope*, a ship that attempted to sail from Greece to Gaza to protest the treatment of Palestinians by Israel and the Israeli blockade of Gaza.

Ciara Miller compares and contrasts Walker's most famous novel, *The Color Purple*, with Sapphire's novel *Push*. The female protagonists Celie and Precious are similar in their situations of abuse; however, the contrast is apparent in the ways in which each author resolves the problems that the young women face. Walker's resolution is life affirming and optimistic, whereas Sapphire's is excruciatingly dark.

Eleven scholars provide new critical readings of Walker's works. For the most part, these essays are arranged chronologically from Walker's first novel to her last. The arrangement of the works in the order in which Walker wrote them enables the reader to see her development as a writer and to compare her mature work with the early works. In what is perhaps his final essay, the late Rudolph P. Byrd examines Walker's first novel, *The Third Life of Grange Copeland*, from a masculinist perspective. Byrd, who defined *mannism* just as Alice Walker defined womanism, writes in *Traps: African American Men on Gender and Sexuality*, that mannism derives from the folk hero High John the Conqueror. In "The Tradition of John: A Mode of Black Masculinity" Byrd wrote that mannism is a mode "for Black men who are committed to the abolition of emasculating forms of masculinity; a mode of masculinity for Black men who are committed to the abolition of racism, sexism, homophobia, and other forms of ideological traps" (1). Thus, in his essay included here, "'But where was the *man* in me?' Alice Walker's *The Third Life of Grange Copeland*," Byrd interrogates the masculinist mode represented by the first life of Grange Copeland and the wasted life of his son Brownfield.

In "*Meridian* and *We Are the Ones We Have Been Waiting For*: Alice Walker's Evolving Vision of the Spiritual Warrior," Shirley Toland-Dix argues that Walker began "her still evolving concept of the spiritual warrior" with the protagonist Meridian in the novel of the same name. Toland-Dix focuses on the questions posed in Walker's second novel, which are: "When is it acceptable for the spiritual warrior to use violence? What are the costs?" Within the context of the novel, Walker's answers vary. In the later work *We Are the Ones We Have Been Waiting For: Inner Light in a Time of Darkness—Meditations* (2006), Walker encourages trust in a universe that will teach us how to be in the world.

In "Looking for God: Alice Walker's *The Color Purple* and Gloria Naylor's *Mama Day*" Paula C. Barnes compares and contrasts Walker's third novel published in 1982 with Gloria Naylor's third novel published in 1988. Barnes posits that Walker is to Naylor what Zora Neale Hurston is to Walker, a literary foremother to whom Walker writes within the contours of her texts. Naylor writes back to Walker and revises the nature of God as it appears in *The Color Purple*. Barnes writes that *Mama Day* enters into the theological debate with the novel in the same way that *The Color Purple* engages *Their Eyes Were Watching God.*

"Walker's Womanist Agenda" by Brenda Young examines Walker's first collection of essays, *In Search of Our Mothers' Gardens* (1983). In particular, Young considers Walker's definition of womanism contained in the collection and discusses the feminist/womanist position in selected essays. Explaining why there was a need for the term *womanism*, Young writes, "Walker found dissatisfaction in the narrow and exclusive stance of the feminist movement of the 1970s—a social movement that had as its major objective the abolishment of the sexual, political, and economic oppression of women, a movement which tended to subsume the intricate realities of non-Anglo women within it, thus rendering them invisible." The term *womanism* has been widely adopted and has proven especially useful for black women theologians.

Deborah Plant uses Walker's statement from the book *Anything We Love Can Be Saved*, "What is happening in the world more and more is that people are attempting to decolonize their spirits. A crucial act of empowerment, one that might return reverence to the earth, thereby saving it, in this fearful-of-Nature, spiritually colonized age," to examine Walker's political activism and her most recent literary works *Sent by Earth: A Message from the Grandmother Spirit* and *We Are the*

Ones We Have Been Waiting For as well as the classic works of the 1980s. Plant concludes that by decolonizing the spirit one is able to see the world from one's own perspective, to enable a natural activism, joy, and laughter so necessary for a healthy life.

"The Myopic Eye in Alice Walker's 'The Flowers'" by Antoinette Brim discusses Walker's often overlooked short story about the loss of innocence and the inability to see beauty in a world riddled with racism and violence. Brim points out that the ability to see beauty, especially in one's self, is a recurring theme in Walker's work. Examining Walker's essay "Beauty When the Other Dancer Is the Self," Brim compares Walker's own blinding with the image of the lynched man in the short story. She concludes the essay by comparing the story to the events captured in the book and website *Without Sanctuary*, a collection of picture postcards that contain photographs of lynched bodies. Neither Walker after her blinding nor the child Myop in "The Flowers" is able to see the beauty they once took for granted.

In "Sexuality and the Healing of the Self: *The Color Purple, Possessing the Secret of Joy*, and *By the Light of My Father's Smile*," Karla Kovalova has selected what she admits might be Walker's three most polarizing and controversial novels. Her essay concludes that in these novels Walker "challenges us to create new rituals to restore the sacredness of sexuality and with it, our original bond with nature, divinity and Creation, and egalitarian way of being in the world."

Toni Wynn in "Living Spaces for Learning in Alice Walker's *The Temple of My Familiar*" presents Walker's womanist spiritual beliefs as expounded upon in *The Temple*. Walker's temple is the physical space that her characters occupy and Wynn's essay "tours these 'temples,' moving the reader through them and their connection with the characters in *The Temple of My Familiar*." In doing so, Wynn offers readers another way to read the novel. She makes a compelling argument that space and place represent ways in which our environment extends and informs us.

In her essay "Participant, Witness, Activist: Alice Walker's Novels in Historical Context," Donna Winchell looks at *The Third Life of Grange Copeland*, *Meridian*, *The Temple of My Familiar*, *Possessing the Secret of Joy*, and *Now Is the Time to Open Your Heart* from a historical perspective, casting Walker as historian. Winchell writes that Walker's interests have broadened such that she has become a historian of "humankind." Walker's works are grounded in the history of the times they represent but expand from the agrarian South in which *The Third Life of Grange Copeland* is set, to the Southern civil rights landscapes that anchor *Meridian* to the political landscapes of Africa found in both *The Temple of My Familiar* and *Possessing the Secret of Joy*. *Now Is the Time to Open Your Heart* includes the landscapes of South America and Winchell posits that Walker draws from her experiences as participant, witness, and activist in order to ground her fiction.

The poet Opal Moore examines Walker's poetry in the essay "Possessing the Secret of Metaphor: Alice Walker's Poetics of Self-Recovery." Using the novel *Possessing the Secret of Joy*, Moore frames the study of Walker's poetics using Tashi, the novel's protagonist, "as metaphor—a figure of speech where the tangible *difference* provides the strategy for unveiling the intangible likeness." This essay covers Walker's stance during the Black Arts Movement as well as her current activism in travel, her blog on issues that concern her, and the continuing evolution of her poetry.

Gerri Bates presents still another view of Walker's poetry in the essay "Euterpe's Daughter: Ecological/Political/Sociological Poetics of Alice Walker." Bates presents an extensive exploration of the influences on Walker's poetry, listing writers from antiquity to the twentieth-century poets Langston Hughes and Gwendolyn Brooks. Bates discusses Walker's eight volumes of poetry and concludes that because of its exoteric nature it has not received the attention from critics that it might have if her forms had been more complex. She writes: "Some critics react indifferently to Walker's craftsmanship. They find her use of language stilted and her messages fused with a kind of naïveté. They want her to be more grand and eloquent; simplicity to them is ineffective. However, Walker's poetry covers more than four decades of devotion to free verse. Her poetry underscores many of the complexities of life. She not only writes love poetry but also composes poetry with ecological, social, and political themes, demonstrating a humanely noble approach to her aesthetics."

The concluding essay in this volume discusses Walker's prose. In "Alice Walker's Essays, Speeches, and Conversations" Donna Akiba Sullivan-Harper analyzes Walker's nonfiction voice, a voice characterized by a fearless, outspoken quest for truth regardless of the consequences. This essay delineates Walker's development as an essayist from the time she won a contest in 1967 for writing "The Civil Rights Movement, What Good Was It?" to the 2008 establishment of her blog, which proclaims that with the election of Barak Obama as president of the United States, the world has indeed changed.

A chronology of Alice Walker's life is a useful resource included in this volume as well as a listing of all her major works and an extensive bibliography for those readers looking to conduct further research. Whether or not Walker has written and published her last novel or prose fiction, as she has claimed, remains to be seen. However, should she not produce any more works of fiction, this volume provides an excellent and comprehensive overview of her contributions to both the twentieth and twenty-first centuries. Few writers have provoked such ire and awe as has Alice Walker in her quiet and unassuming way of exposing the world as she sees it.

CAREER, LIFE, AND INFLUENCE

On Alice Walker

Nagueyalti Warren

"The universe is made of stories, not of atoms"
(Muriel Rukeyser, *The Speed of Darkness*, 1968)

Alice Walker's works are more relevant today than ever. With war, climate change, economic crisis, failures in public education, racism, sexism, and homophobia all still part of current events, Walker is not only a creative writer but an activist engaged in doing what she can to save the earth that so many people appear bent on destroying. Hers is a neoteric approach in a society still mired in a patriarchy that still, for the most part, worships an anthropomorphic male god who punishes evil doers and rewards those lucky enough to please him, judges human actions but does not intercede, and lives apart from and looks down on his creation. Walker brings a mature rendering of divinity, one that incorporates the best from all spiritual traditions; one that sees God in creation as creation, a loving, nonjudgmental presence in us and within the earth. In her corpus the earth and all that is in it is holy. People have the holy obligation to take care of all the earth and each other.

Not only does her work expose the sexism embedded in Western theology, she has declared that organized religion is "an elaborate excuse for what man has done to woman and to the earth" (*World Has Changed* 90). Her writings address ethical issues that people need to consider seriously in order to lead better lives. For instance, her novels demonstrate the impossibility of living a choiceless life. As human beings we have choices and the decisions that we make or do not make affect not only our lives but the lives of others. Connected to choice is outcome—cause and effect, karma, or the reaping of what one has sown. People often do not appear to recognize how their choices affect the lives of others as well as the planet, and some give in to the belief that they actually have no choice.

Excuses, regardless of circumstances, never suffice. Walker's no-excuses posture caused criticism from some African American writers who seem to believe that she is especially unaware of the debilitating effects of racism in the lives of black men in particular. Her no-excuses philosophy possibly stems from her study of the works of Albert Camus and other French existentialist philosophers while a student at Sarah Lawrence College ("Albert Camus"). The philosophy is uncomplicated. People are responsible for their own lives, for the decisions that they make, and for their reactions to external circumstances. People cannot shift blame to God, society, or social conditions. This philosophy coincides with the New Thought belief that people are responsible not only for themselves and the way they react to the world, but ultimately are accountable for the way the world is. Walker forces readers to confront what they believe about themselves and about others. *The Color Purple* (1982) in particular calls into question our belief in God. Do we accept what we have been told as children or do we use our intelligence and intuition to come to our own mature understanding? What exactly is this earth that we live on? Do we believe that it is alive, sacred? Are we? For many people these issues simply are not frequently contemplated; for others their scrutiny challenges traditional mythmakers—an act of sacrilege.

Walker's writings force an examination of relationships: woman to man, woman to woman, parent to child, child to parent, and man to man. However, relationships do not end with human beings but include all the seen and unseen, animate and inanimate, sacred and profane. Her work challenges the reader to move through the fog of other people's opinions and dogma in order to find out what it is one truly thinks. Consequently, Walker has made as many enemies as she has friends. Her severest critics have charged that her work is a New Age (California) fad, a "pantheistic plea, lesbian propaganda, past-lives chronicle black-pride panorama" (Wolcott 30). Richard Bernstein says that the ideas presented in *By the Light of My Father's Smile* (1998) are tendentious New Age clichés. Actually, her works are more closely aligned with New Thought and existentialist questioning. *The Color Purple* raises the following existential questions: why do we suffer, why do we need love, why are we men or women or black or white? Where do children come from? Why are we here in the first place? What lies beyond this life as we know it? These issues are of concern to all people, except, of course, for those who think they already know the answers. For people who have been spoon-fed other people's opinions, Walker's works challenge all that they have been told. She forces the reader to examine her or his philosophy of life. Her later works beginning with *The Temple of My Familiar* (1989) pose what-if questions. What if what you have been taught is wrong? What if what you believe is incorrect? Questioning creates existential doubt, and for some people doubt is uncomfortable. Doubt is nothing but the capacity to be uncertain, which often translates into being honest. Uncertainty appears to be part of the human condition and reasonable doubt is part of the US justice system. There is a gap between supposition and certainty, and doubt is what fills the gap (Storz 77–81). When critics complain that Walker is rewriting history in regards to her romance of 500,000 years (*Temple*), in fact she is creating doubt.

In a 2006 interview with Amy Goodman, Walker declared herself a pagan, a worshipper of the earth. For some people her declaration meant that she was an atheist. Far from being a nonbeliever, Walker sees the presence of God or the Great Spirit in the earth and in all of creation. In 1983 she told Claudia Tate that she was in the process of replacing the oppressive image of God with "everything there is, so you get the desert, the trees; you get the birds, the dirt; you get everything. And that's all God" (Tate 179). As early as 1970, Walker made clear her relationship to the earth when she wrote in "The Black Writer and the Southern Experience" that "in the cities it cannot be so clear to one that he is a creature of the earth, feeling the soil between the toes, smelling the dust thrown up by the rain, loving the earth so much that one longs to taste it and sometimes does" (*In Search* 21). She was responding to her "northern brothers," the militant urban members of the Black Arts

Movement who would have been happy to have Southern black writers characterize all whites "as a vast malignant lump" and blacks (especially the men) "as a conglomerate of perfect virtues" (*In Search* 19, 20). To her credit, Walker did not fall prey to the prevailing trend but sought rather to write the truth as she knew and experienced it.

In response to a poem written for her by former don (college teacher at Sarah Lawrence College) Muriel Rukeyser, Walker dedicated "Pagan" (1990) in which she acknowledges that pagan "was our religion / all along" (10–11) to her former mentor. She honors both African and Native American traditional belief systems in her embrace of paganism. Perhaps Walker's poem was prompted by Rukeyser's description of Ireland's pagan Puck Fair in *The Orgy: An Irish Journey of Passion and Transformation* (1965). Walker's prompt is not clear. However, what is clear is her effort to push beyond the traditions of institutionalized religions and embrace traditions of people of color, the African for whom there was no dichotomy between the sacred and the secular, the Native American who honored the earth, and to include all traditions prior to the introduction of organized, hierarchical, and materialistic religions. Organized religions are often dogmatic and encumbered with rules and regulations; hierarchy is patriarchy—male rule and male godheads, priests, and preachers telling people what to do and how to think. Materialism is expressed in the production of buildings from cathedrals to storefront edifices in order to worship the unseen, while ignoring that which is seen and holy: trees, sky, stars, and the salutation of Celie's finale when she finally sees the light. Walker ends "Pagan" with the following: "Scripture like chains. / Dogma like flies. / Smiles like locks / and lies" (21–24). She forces a confrontation with unquestioned assumptions.

For many critics *The Color Purple* is Walker's paean to Spirit, and indeed it is. However, her third novel simply makes clear what her work points to from its beginning. *Once* (1968), the collection of poems she wrote while still a college student and her first publication, indicates her predilection for addressing issues of the land and Spirit. In

"South: The Name of Home" she writes: "the earth is red / here—/ the trees bent, weeping / what secrets will not / the ravished land / reveal / of its abuse?" (18–24) Walker's concern for people and land might have begun in the geography of the South but soon expands to knowing that H-O-M-E is here on mother earth.

As a young girl Walker saw the sacred in the ordinary. She recalls her memory of losing sight in her right eye after her brother, Curtis, shoots her with his BB gun as they are playing cowboys and Indians. "There is a tree growing from underneath the porch that climbs past the railing to the roof. It is the last thing my right eye sees. I watch as its trunk, its branches, and then its leaves are blotted out by the rising blood" (*In Search* 364). As an eight-year-old, what sticks in her memory amidst all the pain is the grandeur of the tree. Trees become for Walker symbols of love and creativity. Indeed in 1984 she named her now defunct publishing company Wild Trees Press.

Walker's works not only challenge preconceived ideas, they encourage people to examine their inner lives. Kate Nelson Talkingtree in *Now Is the Time to Open Your Heart* (2004) is a primary example of engaging one's inner life by going on spiritual retreats, examining dreams, and spending time in meditation. The cultivation of self-knowledge inherent in Walker's writing emerges in those characters that are able to transform and to find some semblance of peace, and the lack of self-awareness in characters renders them as villains. Brownfield in *The Third Life of Grange Copeland* (1970) is the prototype of an unredeemed, un-self-actualized person. His ignorance leads to the abuse of his family and murder of his wife. Meridian in the novel of the same title is becoming whole through a process of self-understanding. Other characters that transform include Grange in his third life, Albert after Celie leaves him, and Celie after Shug leaves her. Self-reflection leads to transformation, a central theme in Walker's works. Preston McKever-Floyd has called *The Color Purple* a theology of transformation. Not limited to *The Color Purple*, a theology of transformation is a dominate feature in Walker's corpus. Another important aspect in Walker's fiction demonstrates the logic and necessity of self-forgiveness and forgiveness of others.

All of Walker's novels, many of her short stories and poems, as well as her essays wrestle with the issue of forgiveness. What does it mean to forgive? Walker has confronted the issue of forgiveness in her personal life beginning with the incident that left her blind in her right eye. Her brothers, fearful of the punishment they would receive for hurting their sister, concocted a lie about what happened. Walker goes along with the explanation that she knows is untrue. Consequently, not only does she have to forgive Curtis, the brother who shot her, but she must also forgive herself for not telling the truth. The anger over what she saw as her disfigurement, and the shame of lying about it, produced a depression that led her to contemplate suicide. Fortunately, writing would prove to be the therapy she would need in order to save her life. In the essay, "Saving the Life That Is Your Own: The Importance of Models in the Artist's Life," Walker writes: "It is, in the end, the saving of lives that we writers are about" (*In Search* 14). Following the publication of *The Temple of My Familiar* Walker, in an interview with Claudia Dreifus for *The Progressive*, says: "I started out writing to save my life" (*World Has Changed* 79). As is the case with many of her characters, Walker eventually confronts her mother about what came to be known in her family as "Alice's accident," and her mother apologized for how the incident had been handled. Walker accepted the apology.

In her fictional works apologies are not always accepted. When Grange asks his son Brownfield for forgiveness, Brownfield refuses, but his refusal leads to his own demise. Lack of forgiveness produces illness, as with Meridian, who needs to forgive herself. Albert, who must ask for Celie's forgiveness, must also forgive himself. In *The Temple of My Familiar* Fanny has the formidable task of forgiving racist whites. In *Possessing the Secret of Joy* (1992), Tashi goes insane because she is unable to forgive herself; unable to forgive the *tsunga*, or circumciser, Tashi murders her. Similarly unhappy outcomes appear in

By the Light of My Father's Smile (1998), where the Robinson sisters' unwillingness to forgive produces estrangement from their parents and from each other. Failure to live in the present moment is still another issue that Walker connects with the inability to change or to forgive. Blaming one's childhood, as June, the oldest sister in *By the Light,* does is impossible if one lives in the present moment. Being beaten by her father and separated from her lover made pain unavoidable, but her suffering is optional. Forgiveness eliminates suffering and so does the act of creating.

In Walker's own life as well as in the lives of her characters the act of creating is therapeutic. The making of pants is more than just a way to earn a living for Celie in *The Color Purple*. Sewing becomes a balm for the sickness she feels when Shug leaves her for Germaine, a new young lover. Robert Towers in his review of the book notes certain "improbabilities," one being that in the 1930s Celie "would have found fulfillment in designing and making pants for women" (35). He misses entirely the symbolic meaning of the pants and the freedom they represent. The folk pants are a trope for female liberation and because the pants are unisex they signify freedom for the men as well. In *The Temple of My Familiar* (1989) Hal heals his blindness by painting and whenever he stops the blindness returns. Zedé in the same book is able to retain her sanity through the art of creating lovely feathered capes. In terms of Walker's own healing, she has said that focusing on the act of creating enables "a kind of spiritual alchemy that happens and you turn that bad feeling into something that becomes a golden light. . . . The point is to heal yourself" (*World Has Changed* 80). The point also is to heal others. When asked how people can heal from so many miseries and whether or not psychotherapy might be the answer, Walker replied that it does not have to be a therapist and that it could be "a novel" (*World Has Changed* 88). Psychiatrist and Jungian analyst Jean Shinoda Bolen believes that when one writes from a soul level and the reader comes along she or he can be touched and healed by the spirit of the work.

Walker is a Southern writer in the same tradition as William Faulkner, Eudora Welty, Margaret Walker, Flannery O'Connor and Richard Wright. What characterizes her as a Southern writer aside from the fact that she was born and grew up in the Jim Crow South is the poignant sense of place she creates in her early works. Her publications prior to *The Temple of My Familiar* contain clear descriptions of the Southern landscape. The red clay dirt, rural farms, cotton fields, and grape arbors in *The Third Life of Grange Copeland* re-create a sense of the Southern physical world. The porch in the short story "The Child Who Favored Daughter" (*In Love and Trouble*) the flowered roadside, and the dirt dauber produce the peculiar locale of the rural South.

Another element of Walker's corpus that situates her within the Southern tradition also places her within the African American folk tradition. Trudier Harris in "Folklore in the Fiction of Alice Walker: A Perpetuation of Historical and Literary Traditions," observes that Walker uses African American folk material in her novels in sometimes subtle ways as with the storytelling that occurs between Grange and his granddaughter Ruth. The most obvious way in which Walker engages the African American folk element is through the re-creation of African American folk speech in her characters, beginning with *The Third Life* and culminating in a perfect rendering of folk expressions in *The Color Purple*. The language of the rural Southerner is distinct from the language of urban African Americans. Walker, more perfectly than any other writer, captures the nuances of the black Southern tongue.

Walker herself believes that a deep sense of community also characterizes the South, at least the South of her childhood, and in her early works she attempts to capture this collective concern for community members. This communal element finds its way into almost all of her fiction. Rudolph Byrd has noted that after the publication of *The Color Purple* Walker's writing underwent a shift from the geographic and cultural South to encompass a more expansive and universal view, including Africa and the world at large. Works that follow *The Color Purple* do not contain folk speech, nor for the most part are they set in the rural South. *The Temple of My Familiar* begins in South America, then moves to San Francisco and to Baltimore, Maryland, to Europe, and Africa, and returns to the United States, where it focuses on relationships to the neglect of the deep sense of place that exudes from the early works.

Walker has been criticized for the didacticism in her fiction, for telling as opposed to showing. Alice Hall Petry has written that Walker possesses a "disinclination for exposition . . . [and] a marked preference for 'telling' over 'showing'" (Petry "Alice Walker" 12–27). Petry concludes that Walker distrusts her readers or her texts or both (22); however, Walker, I believe, does not harbor such distrust as much as she follows a different cultural standard. Within African American culture storytelling is precisely what it says, *telling*—and not story showing. Walker has stated on numerous occasions that her writing, particularly the short stories, comes from the tradition passed on from her mother who was a consummate storyteller. In this tradition stories often have a moral that is stressed in an oral tradition that appears imperious in the written word. Telling is what Walker does best. Her truth telling enables the reader to agree or disagree with her conclusions. Telling enables her to examine her own thoughts. Therefore it is not surprising that Walker would write "You have one / weapon / & / one weapon / only: // Use it. // It is / your / ability / to / teach" ("Told" 22–32; *Hard Times* 107–8). Furthermore, she has stated that for her, writing is not about audience. "It's about living. It's about expanding myself as much as I can and seeing myself in as many roles and situations as possible" (Tate 185). Therefore, whether or not her works conform to the standards of Western fiction is a moot issue.

Walker has not produced an autobiography per se. She has written autobiographical works, some more so than others. *Anything We Love Can Be Saved: A Writer's Activism* (1997), *The Same River Twice: Honoring the Difficult* (1996), and *Sent by Earth: A Message from the Grandmother Spirit after the Bombing of the World Trade Center and the Pentagon* (2001) are clearly autobiographical. But in so many ways all of her work is autobiographical. *The Way Forward Is with a Broken Heart* (2000), a memoir of her marriage, consisting of personal facts and imagination, is an example of autotherapy—a way to heal old wounds. Other works also have been deeply grounded in the writer's lived experiences, and this is one reason criticism of her subject matter is so irrational. The frame for the story of *The Third Life of Grange Copeland* stems directly from an event that took place in the writer's hometown of Eatonton, Georgia. A woman was murdered by her husband and there was cardboard in her shoe as they were too poor for good shoes or even for shoe repair. One of Walker's sisters, a beautician who styled the dead woman's hair, took the young Walker with her to the mortuary to see the woman who had been killed by her husband. The image was seared into Walker's consciousness, and the woman became the character Mem in *The Third Life.* By the time Walker wrote the novel, she had come to know that Mem represented all women and their vulnerability to male violence especially if they adhered to patriarchal religions and customs. Grange Copeland is patterned after her paternal grandfather who became a better human being as he grew older. Of course, the content in *Meridian* is based upon Walker's firsthand knowledge of the civil rights movement. She has stated that she is not Meridian because Meridian is better than she was. In the Tate interview Walker confessed that Meridian "is an exemplary person; she is an exemplary, *flawed* revolutionary because it seems to me the revolutionary worth following is one who is flawed" (184). The second reason Walker is not Meridian is her own middle-class lifestyle, whereas Meridian owned nothing.

In the short story, "The Child Who Favored Daughter" (from *In Love and Trouble*), one that Petry describes as "marred by having the father kill his daughter because he confuses her with his dead sister named 'Daughter'" ("Walker" 204), Walker reveals that she wrote it "out of trying to understand how a black father would feel about a daughter who fell in love with a white man" (Tate 186–87). Walker had recently ended her relationship with David DeMoss, a white man to whom she had been engaged and for which she had encountered her father's rancor (White 242). Again her writing is a useful therapeutic. "The Revenge of Hannah Kemhuff" from the same collection of short stories is based on an event that happened to Walker's mother during the Great Depression in the 1930s. Walker, commenting on her short story collection *In Love and Trouble: Stories of Black Women* (1973), stated that "To Hell with Dying" was her most autobiographical story. She says that "the way autobiography works for a writer is different from what you'd think of as being autobiographical. It's autobiographical though, in fact, none of it happened" (Tate 187). But in fact some of it did happen. While Walker was in college in New York, an elderly man whom she had loved as a dear friend died. She could not afford to attend his funeral and so she wrote the story as a way of bidding him farewell. As is probably the case with so many writers, the germ of fiction is rooted in the facts of lived experiences.

Walker's own experiences with poverty and depression have led her to not only use creative writing as therapy for her own healing and well-being but to offer examples of how people can heal and transcend deep emotional wounds and despair. In each of her novels, for instance, and in many of her short stories, there are characters that suffer from guilt, shame, rage, and poverty. Poverty, the great enervator, pervades Walker's first novel, *The Third Life*. The economic scourge of the Southern sharecropping system does not have to be the determining factor in a person's life, as Walker illustrates with the characters Grange and Brownfield. The choices presented in the novel are to leave the South as Grange gathers the courage to do; to acquire enough money to purchase one's own farm, as Grange does when he returns to the South; to become educated as Brownfield starts to do when he allows Mem to teach him to read and write—although he eventually forgets what he has learned and slides back into the darkness of ignorance; or to join a movement that will dismantle the system of oppression represented by the Jim Crow laws in the South. Walker introduces this option with the civil rights workers at the end of the novel. The choice that each character makes leads to either positive or negative consequences. Grange is able to overcome poverty and leave a legacy of property and financial security for his granddaughter, Ruth. Josie, the prostitute in the novel—and both Grange and Brownfield's other woman—is an example of what happens to people, especially women, when they are either unwilling or unable to value themselves, and when their self-worth is tied to others, such as a spouse, children, or parents. Josie is never able to heal from her abuse because she is unable to name, speak about, or tell what has happened to her. When she visits Sister Madelaine, Josie is unable to do the one thing that the psychic fortuneteller instructs her to do, and that is "call his name . . . you will be cured" (49). Naming the pain opens the door to releasing the shame and the guilt as well as the attendant anger, emotions that Josie numbs with food and sex. Josie's inability to heal because of her choices leaves her vulnerable to the abuse of Grange and Brownfield. Brownfield is anxious to improve his circumstances but unwilling to improve himself.

Reflecting 1800s New Thought rather than 1970s New Age, Walker's oeuvre reflects the philosophies of both Ernest Holmes and James Allen, respectively. Holmes believed that there is a power in the universe that can be used to live a productive and joyous life. Allen wrote that, by virtue of the thoughts we choose and encourage, we create our world; our mind is the master weaver, "both of the inner garment of character and the outer garment of circumstance, and that, as [we] may have hitherto woven in ignorance and pain [we] may now weave in enlightenment and happiness" (Allen 9). Each person has access to this power through thoughts and actions. Walker says, "You will see / living as you do / in the Aquarian / Age / when it is / at last / possible / for mere / thought / to quickly / transform / the world— / nothing / will / ultimately separate / us" ("Meeting You" 24–39). In actuality, elements of both New Age and New Thought philosophies find expression in Walker's works, but whereas New Age has been recognized in her oeuvre, New Thought has not.

Each work contains an example of healing. Grange is healed in his third life. In *Meridian* the central character heals herself through the choices that she makes. Celie is a shining example of how the creative acts of writing, telling, and then creating pants enable her to transcend despair. *The Temple of My Familiar* presents a collage of wounded characters. By the end of the novel, each one has recovered by embracing some lost part of herself or himself. Through her remembrance of a childhood encounter with racism, Fanny is able to forgive so that she can heal herself from the destructive emotion of hatred. Carlotta is able to forgive her mother and husband for what she sees as their ultimate betrayal of her by becoming sexually involved with each other. Suwelo is able to forgive his mother for remaining with his father, her alcoholic husband, and allowing him to kill her and himself by driving drunk. Suwelo's anger is deeply embedded in his treatment of women, but through his engagement with Lissie he is healed. In *Possessing the Secret of Joy* Tashi is healed not by any of the therapists that she sees but as a result of deciding to kill the tsunga and willingly accepting the consequences of her decision. In *By the Light of My Father's Smile* Walker offers an unorthodox view of healing that takes place in the afterlife of the characters. The Robinsons heal as they examine the lives that they have lived and view people, including their children, whom they have hurt. Perhaps this is Walker's way of saying that it is never too late to make amends, never too late to forgive. In *Now Is the Time to Open Your Heart* Kate Nelson Talkingtree is the consummate example of the self-actualizing person who examines her life and makes choices that enable her to grow.

Walker has been criticized for practically every position she has ever taken. When she took a stand to stop violence against women, critics claimed she was male bashing; when she spoke out against female genital mutilation, some told her to mind her own business, while others charged her with cultural imperialism. But the most bizarre critique she has received has come from those who are opposed to vegetarianism. Journalist Ellen Bring in an interview asked Walker what she thought of "the argument that vegetarianism violates cultural traditions and rituals and, therefore, is racist or imperialist" (*World Has Changed* 75). Walker's response was more thoughtful than the question itself. She compared the slaughter of animals for human consumption to slavery. While white enslavers were satisfied with what they saw as Southern culture, their position failed to take into account the desire of the enslaved who wanted to be free. In the same way, Walker believes that animals do not want to be eaten. Her short essay "Am I Blue" from *Living by the Word* created a firestorm in California, resulting in the banning of the essay from the California Learning Assessment System (CLAS) test by the State Board of Education in 1994. Parts of *The Color Purple* and the short story "Roselily" also were banned.

To break the hypnotic spell of so-called authority, the power of the herd that dictates what to eat, wear, and think, Walker uses her sacred imagination and invites her readers to do likewise. Her works give the power back to the people and insist that we are the ones with the ability to transform ourselves and the world. One of Walker's intentions for writing is to achieve wholeness. She has stated that she is committed to "the spiritual survival, the survival *whole*, of my people" (O'Brien 192). One could assume, as many have done, that Walker is referring to African Americans as her people. And perhaps she was at the time of that early interview. But within the context of her collected work, it becomes clear that Walker is concerned for the wholeness of all people and of all things—the wholeness of the planet.

Although she has been critiqued for the sometimes didactic political stances of her characters, Walker insists on writing what she knows, and she seems to know, as Toni Cade Bambara wrote, that "revolution begins with the self, in the self. The individual, the basic revolutionary unit, must be purged of poison and lies that assault the ego and threaten the heart" (Bambara 133). All of her political and spiritual creative efforts urge a transformation of the self for the highest good of all. The solution to every problem she knows is within us. In 2006, Walker reminded us that "we are the ones we have been waiting for" (*We Are the Ones* 251).

Works Cited

Allen, James. *As A Man Thinketh: James Allen's Original Masterpiece.*1902. Rockville, MD: Arc Manor, 2007.

Bambara, Toni Cade. "On the Issue of Roles." *The Black Woman: An Anthology.* Tony Cade Bambara, ed. New York: Washington Sq., 1970.

Bernstein, Richard. Rev. of *By the Light of My Father's Smile. New York Times.* New York Times Co., 7 Oct. 1998. Web.

Bolen, Jean Shinoda. *Giving Birth, Finding Form: Three Writers Explore Their Lives, Their Loves, Their Art.* Sounds True, June 1993. Audiocassette.

Harris, Trudier. "Folklore in the Fiction Alice Walker: A Perpetuation of Historical and Literary Traditions." *Black American Literature Forum* 11.1 (1977): 3–8.

Holmes, Ernest. 1938. *The Science of Mind: A Philosophy, A Faith, A Way of Life.* New York: Penguin, 1998.

McKever-Floyd, Preston. "'Tell Nobody but God': The Theme of Transformation in *The Color Purple.*" *Cross Currents* 57.3 (2007): 426–433.

O'Brien, John, ed. *Interviews with Black Writers.* New York: Liveright, 1973.

Petry, Alice Hall. "Alice Walker: The Achievement in Short Fiction," *Modern Language Studies* 19.1 (1989): 12–27.

_____. "Walker: The Achievement of the Short Fiction." *Alice Walker: Critical Perspectives Past and Present.* Eds. Henry Louis Gates Jr., and K. A. Appiah. New York: Amistad, 1993. 193–210.

Rukeyser, Muriel. *The Orgy: An Irish Journey of Passion and Transformation.* 1965.

Storz, Margaret. "The Honesty of Doubt." *Science of Mind.* 83.6 (2010): 77–81.

Tate, Claudia, ed. *Black Women Writers at Work.* New York: Continuum, 1986.

Towers, Robert. "Good Men Are Hard to Find," *New York Review of Books,* 12 Aug. 1982, 35–36.

Walker, Alice. "Albert Camus: The Development of His Philosophical Position as Reflected in His Novels and Plays," Sarah Lawrence College, n.d. Papers Box 88, Folder 19.

_____. *Anything We Love Can Be Saved: A Writer's Activism.* 1997. New York: Random, 1998.

_____. *By the Light of My Father's Smile.* New York: Random, 1998.

_____. *The Color Purple.* 1982. New York: Mariner, 2006.

_____. *Hard Times Require Furious Dancing: New Poems.* Novato, CA: New World Lib., 2010.

_____. *Her Blue Body Everything We Know: Earthling Poems.* Orlando, FL: Harcourt, 1991.

_____. *In Love and Trouble: Stories of Black Women.* Orlando, FL: Harcourt, 1974.

_____. "Meeting You." *Hard Times Require Furious Dancing.* 92–95

Meridian. 1976. New York: Simon, 1986.

_____. *Now Is the Time to Open Your Heart.* New York: Random, 2004.

_____. *Once: Poems*. Orlando, FL: Harcourt, 1968.

_____. "'Outlaw, Renegade, Rebel, Pagan': Interview with Amy Goodman from *Democracy Now!* (2006)" *The World Has Changed*. 268–79.

_____. "Pagan." *Her Blue Body*. 420–21.

_____. Papers. Subseries 2.4E: College Papers, 1961–1966. Manuscript, Archive, and Rare Book Library (MARBL)–Emory University Lib., Atlanta, GA.

_____. *Possessing the Secret of Joy*. Orlando, FL: Harcourt, 1992.

_____. *The Same River Twice: Honoring the Difficult*. New York: Scribner, 1996.

_____. *In Search of Our Mothers' Gardens*. Orlando, FL: Harcourt, 1983.

_____. *Sent By Earth: A Message from the Grandmother Spirit After the Bombing of the World Trade Center and the Pentagon*. New York: Seven Stories, 2001.

_____. "South: The Name of Home." *Her Blue Body* 101.

_____. *The Temple of My Familiar*. San Diego: Harcourt, 1989.

_____. *The Third Life of Grange Copeland*. 1970. New York: Harcourt, 2003.

_____. *The Way Forward Is with A Broken Heart*. New York: Random, 2000.

_____. *We Are the Ones We Have Been Waiting For: Inner Light in a Time of Darkness Meditations*. New York: New Press, 2006.

_____. *The World Has Changed: Conversations with Alice Walker*. Ed. Rudolph P. Byrd. New York: New Press, 2010.

White, Evelyn C. *Alice Walker: A Life*. New York: Norton, 2004.

Wolcott, James. "Party of Animals" Rev. of *The Temple of My Familiar*. *New Republic*. 200.22 (1989): 28–30.

Biography of Alice Walker

Sally Wolff

Multiple award-winning author and activist Alice Malsenior Walker was born in a small community outside Eatonton in Wards Chapel, Putnam County, GA, on February 9, 1944. She was the last of eight children born to sharecroppers Willie Lee Walker and Minnie Lou (Tallulah) Grant Walker (Bates 2; White 11–13; *World Has Changed* xi). In anticipation of Walker's arrival, her parents hired a midwife, Miss Fannie; the occasion was the first time they had the money to do so. Walker, however, was born before Miss Fannie arrived (White 11–13).

Walker started first grade at age four, a year earlier than usual, because her mother was forced to work to support the Walker family and had no one to watch her young, curious, and highly independent child. Walker was enrolled in the class of Miss Reynolds at East Putnam Consolidated—a school that Walker's father had helped to establish in 1948—with the hope that a strong education would keep young Walker from facing a future in which she would be forced to toil in the fields to support herself. From very early on, Miss Reynolds noted Walker's interest and intellect in the classroom (White 14–15; *World Has Changed* xi).

Towards the end of the summer in 1952, at the young age of eight years old, Walker suffered the eye injury that would change her views, both literally and figuratively. While she was playing cowboys and Indians with her brothers Bobby and Curtis, Curtis shot her in the right eye with a BB gun by mistake. The injury left her blind in one eye (Bates 3; *World Has Changed* xi). Immediately realizing the trouble they would be in with their parents, Walker's brothers entreated her to claim she sustained the injury from stepping on a wire. The boys later admitted the truth to their parents and received only a tepid scolding.

In an effort to help an ailing Walker, her father Willie Lee and brother Jimmy caught the attention of a white man driving down the highway and entreated the man to help them transport Walker to a hospital.

The man declined to help, so the Walkers were forced to care for their daughter on their own using natural folk remedies. Eventually, after realizing their daughter required modern medical treatment, the Walkers raised the $250 necessary to send her to a white doctor in Macon, Georgia. According to the Walkers, the doctor simply gave Walker a bottle of eye drops and told her that eyes are sympathetic and therefore she would likely become blind in her left eye as well.

The injury indelibly altered Walker's personality and her perspective on the world. Her schoolwork suffered, as did her self-esteem. Once a self-assured young girl, she became much less so after the injury (Bates 3–4). This disorientation was compounded by her family's move to Milledgeville, Georgia—a town known as the location of Flannery O'Connor's farm Andalusia—and her enrollment in a new school. Eventually, Walker was allowed to return to Ward's Chapel, where she lived with her father's father Henry Clay Walker and his wife Rachel—Walker's prototype for Celie in *The Color Purple*. The return home, however, did not improve Walker's malaise. She withdrew into the world of literature and began to write. Later, Walker would come to see the incident as one that had alienated her from the rest of her family. She felt her brothers and her parents had betrayed her, and she began to realize that people can cause their loved ones intense pain. She also became more fully aware of the negative consequences of lying (White 33–40).

Walker graduated from Butler-Baker High School as valedictorian in 1961. Though she considered attending Savannah State University, Walker matriculated at Spelman College, in Atlanta, Georgia. Her attendance was financed by a "rehabilitation" scholarship she received from Spelman as well as seventy-five dollars she received from the members of the community in Eatonton. In August of 1961, she left her home for Atlanta with a suitcase, a sewing machine, and a typewriter (Bates 8–9; White 63–64; *World Has Changed* xi–xii). Walker felt increasingly out of place at a school she felt did not offer adequate support for students who advocated social change. She decided to withdraw in December 1963 (White 95; *World Has Changed* xii). In the first months of 1964, she enrolled (on a full scholarship) at Sarah Lawrence College, an all-female college located in Bronxville, New York (Bates 10; White 99–100). Though she felt more at home intellectually at Sarah Lawrence, Walker could not help but notice the extreme wealth and privilege of her classmates (White 101). While at Sarah Lawrence, Walker met poet Muriel Rukeyser, who played an integral role in introducing Walker's work to a larger audience (Bates 10; White 108–9).

Walker travelled to East Africa in the summer of 1965 (Bates 12). She returned to school pregnant and decided to have an abortion. Her decision, however, would be easier formulated than executed—at that time, abortions were still illegal in the United States, and women looking to terminate unwanted pregnancies faced traveling abroad for the procedure or undergoing the procedure secretly and at a high price. Seeing little hope in her situation, Walker decided to commit suicide if she could not obtain an abortion (White 113–14). A friend at Sarah Lawrence located a doctor who performed the procedure for two thousand dollars. Walker was able to secure the money from friends and terminated the pregnancy (White 115–17; *World Has Changed* xii). In the aftermath of her turmoil, Walker wrote a number of poems and a short story titled "To Hell with Dying," which she gave to Rukeyser (Bates 11). She graduated with honors from Sarah Lawrence in January 1966 (White 118–19; *World Has Changed* xii).

On March 17, 1967, at the New York City Family Court, Walker married a young civil rights lawyer named Melvyn R. Leventhal, whom she had met while working for the NAACP Legal Defense and Educational Fund in Mississippi the previous summer They moved back to Mississippi to continue their work for the civil rights movement (White 154; *World Has Changed* xii–xiii). Later that year, Walker won the *American Scholar* essay contest for her submission "The Civil Rights Movement: What Good Was It?" (Bates 16; White 156–58). She became a consultant in black history for the Friends of the Children of Mississippi, a part of the Federal Head Start Program, where she encouraged the black women she worked with to write their autobiographies (White 161–62).

Once, Walker's first collection of poetry, was published in 1968, and sold in stores for $4.50. Langston Hughes selected "To Hell with Dying" for publication in *The Best Short Stories by Negro Writers*, published in 1967. Rebecca Grant Leventhal was born at 7:06 p.m. on November 17, 1969, at Jackson University Hospital. In the margins of the birth certificate appears the penciled-in note "correct," referring to the racial status of the parents being listed as: "Mel White" / Alice "Negro" (White 181–82). Only three days before the birth of her daughter, Walker had placed the finishing touches on her first novel, titled *The Third Life of Grange Copeland* (1970) (Lazo 60).

In March 1971, Walker received the fellowship from Radcliffe (*World Has Changed* xiii) and she journeyed to Cambridge, Massachusetts with Rebecca that September. In 1972, Walker was hired to teach at Wellesley College, where she conducted what is considered to be the first class in black women's literature (Bates 16; White 222; *World Has Changed* xiii). She applied for and received an extension of her fellowship at Radcliffe and decided to stay in Cambridge.

In Love and Trouble and *Revolutionary Petunias* were published in 1973; both works drew new attention to Walker and her work (White 231). The same year, after a long fight with emphysema, diabetes, and pneumonia, Willie Lee Walker died on January 26. His death forced Walker to come to terms with their troubled relationship.

Walker and Leventhal left Mississippi in 1974 and moved to New York where she became an editor at *Ms.*, a magazine to address the concerns of women across the globe. *Revolutionary Petunias* was nominated for a 1974 National Book Award in poetry. Walker, along with fellow nominees Audre Lourde and Adrienne Rich, prepared a joint acceptance speech to be read if one of them won the award. Rich won and accepted the award "in the name of all the women whose voices have gone and still go unheard in a patriarchal world, and in the name of those who, like us, have been tolerated as token women in this culture." (Rich). Walker published her promised children's book, *Langston Hughes: American Poet* in 1974, and attended Yaddo, a writer's colony in Saratoga Springs, New York, where she made finishing touches to *Meridian*, her second novel (White 277). Despite her success with her work, she felt her relationship with Mel was becoming strained, and by 1976, the couple had separated and filed for divorce (White 278–80).

In 1977 Walker published *Meridian*, a novel dealing with the sacrifices that individuals make towards a shared humanity as they engaged in the struggle for civil rights. The novel focuses on the conflicts among blacks in the struggle (White 285). Walker said of the themes in *Meridian*: "Part of our legacy is to maintain [the elders'] values so that our children will be able to see the beauty of their ancestors' faces" (White 291). The novel also represented a departure from a traditional narrative format and revealed the impact of Jean Toomer's *Cane* (White 292).

Walker received a Guggenheim Fellowship in 1977 (*World Has Changed* xiv; White 310) and decided to leave New York for San Francisco to be with Robert Allen. They settled in the small town of Boonville, three hours outside San Francisco (*World Has Changed* xiv; White 308–11). Here Walker began working on the novel that became *The Color Purple*.

In 1979, Walker released two new works: a collection of poems titled *Goodnight Willie Lee, I'll See You in the Morning* and a collection of essays on Zora Neale Hurston titled *I Love Myself When I Am Laughing . . . and Then Again when I'm Looking Mean and Impressive* (*World Has Changed* xiv; White 319). The essays on Hurston were Walker's effort to resurrect the work and reputation of the woman with whom Walker felt she had much in common (White 320–21). In 1981, Walker released a second short-story collection titled *You Can't Keep a Good Woman Down*, in which she focused on black women who had been tested and tried, but never beaten (Walker xiv).

The Color Purple, published in 1982, grew out of a Walker family story originating from Walker's grandfather's life-long love for Estella "Shug" Perry, even though he was married to Rachel (White 18, 334). The novel was written in black folk English and the epistolary style (composed of ninety letters). Even though her publisher warned against her reliance upon the epistolary format, Walker would not yield on what she felt had been passed down to her from her ancestors (White 341). The project garnered much attention in the literary world even before it was officially released, and Walker's friends fought for her work—most notably Gloria Steinem, who dedicated a cover story in *Ms.* to Walker (White 341–42).

Once the book finally was released, it began to draw much attention. Many felt that *The Color Purple* represented the strongest manifestation of the themes that Walker had considered. The result was emotionally and technically impressive (White 348–49). Regardless of how people reacted to the novel, they read it and debated it. This attention reached its apex when Walker won the Pulitzer Prize in fiction on April 18, 1983. Walker was the first black woman to win the prize (351; 352–57). That year, Walker's novel also received the National Book Award (Walker xiv; 21). In her response to the awards, Walker deferred the honor to the joy her characters must be feeling—she seemed only to care that the people who inspired her work were widely recognized and valued (White 358–61). The novel sold more than six million copies, and Walker, true to form, declined to attend the Pulitzer celebration in New York (White 362–63; *World Has Changed* 21).

In Search of Our Mothers' Gardens (1983), released six months after *The Color Purple*, sold very well in the wake of her Pulitzer Prize (White 370). The book, a collection of short pieces, focused on black women as they relate to other black women, the black community, and themselves (White 373). The titular essay further advances the study of black women's literary theory, much as her Wellesley course did (White 373–78). Walker was featured in the *New York Times Magazine* cover story "Novelist Alice Walker: Telling the Black Woman's Story" (White 380–81).

Together with her companion Robert Allen, senior editor of the *Black Scholar*, and her friend Belvie Rooks, Walker launched Wild Trees Press in 1984. Situated on her newly purchased land in Mendocino County, Wild Tree was inspired by Virginia Woolf's Hogarth Press, and the new publishers were dedicated to "publish[ing] only what [they] love" (White 388). Walker then issued *Horses Make the Landscape More Beautiful*, her fifth volume of poetry, in 1984 (Bates 52). The collection received a positive response from readers and critics alike (White 390).

Quincy Jones and Steven Spielberg approached Walker about making a film version of *The Color Purple*, which would be financed by Peter Guber (White 393). After some hesitation (spurred by the portrayal of black characters on screen in the recent past), Walker met with Jones and Spielberg and agreed to the film. She was motivated to make the film especially for her mother, the aging and ailing Minnie Lou Walker; Mrs. Walker was unable to read the novel, so Walker saw the film as a way to share her story with her mother (White 400–401).

If Walker's Pulitzer Prize–winning novel stirred controversy, the film reignited that kind of reaction as well. The Hollywood chapter of the NAACP and groups like the Coalition Against Black Exploitation (CABE) offered up their criticisms of the film (White 414–15), which was released on December 18, 1985 (416). Walker and Robert attended a private screening of the film in San Francisco, where Walker realized that much had been changed from her novel, most notably, the relationship between Shug and Celie (417).

Ruth Walker, Alice Walker's sister, began the work necessary to have *The Color Purple* premiere in Eatonton at the Pex Theater and to establish The Color Purple Scholarship Fund (White 424–25). The film was shown in Eatonton to the delight of Walker's hometown, especially Mrs. Walker (425–26). Soon after, the film was nominated for eleven Academy Awards (427). It received none.

Walker published *The Temple of My Familiar* in 1989. The novel, inspired by a vanilla bean pod, followed the stories of three couples trying to find peace with themselves and the world (White 445–46) and borrowed much from magical realism, myth, and fantasy (446). As the follow up to *The Color Purple* and in its departure from her previous work, *The Temple* received lukewarm reviews (446–49).

Finding the Green Stone, a children's book, and *Her Blue Body Everything We Know*, a poetry collection, were published in 1991 (White 466). The following year, Walker published *Possessing the Secret of Joy*, a novel that takes up the topic of female genital mutilation. With director Pratibha Parmar, Walker produced a documentary film on the same topic entitled *Warrior Marks* (1993) (459).

Walker has continued to write, adding two more novels, three volumes of poetry, and four collections of nonfiction to her oeuvre. In 2007 Walker placed her archive at Emory University ("Walker, Alice 1944–"). Alice Walker's Garden is her official website and hosts her blog (Alicewalkersgarden.com). As committed to humanitarian activism as ever, Walker joined the Freedom Flotilla II to Gaza aboard *The Audacity of Hope* in the summer of 2011 to deliver "letters expressing solidarity and love" to the people of Palestine (*Guardian*).

Works Cited

"Alice Walker." *Emory News Center*. Emory University, 19 Mar. 2012. Web. 21 Mar. 2012.

Bates, Gerri. *Alice Walker: A Critical Companion*. Westport, CT: Greenwood, 2005.

Fitzgerald, Stephanie. *Alice Walker: Author and Social Activist*. Minneapolis: Compass Point, 2008.

Lazo, Caroline Evensen. *Alice Walker: Freedom Writer*. Minneapolis: Lerner, 2000.

Rich, Adrienne. "National Book Awards Acceptance Speeches: Adrienne Rich, Winner of the 1974 National Book Award for *Diving Into the Wreck*." 18 Apr. 1974. *National Book Foundation*. National Book Foundation, 2007. Web. 21 Mar. 2012

Walker, Alice. "Walker, Alice 1944– : Alice Walker Papers, Circa 1930–2010." *Emory Libraries: Emory Finding Aids*. Emory University Manuscript, Archives, and Rare Book Library, 2010. Web. 21 Mar. 2012.

_____. *Alice Walker: The Official Website.* Alicewalkersgarden.com, 2010. Web. 21 Mar. 2012.

_____. "Alice Walker: Why I'm Joining the Freedom Flotilla to Gaza." *The Guardian.* Guardian News and Media, 24 June 2011. Web. 21 Mar. 2012.

_____. *The World Has Changed: Conversations with Alice Walker.* Ed. Rudolph P. Byrd. New York: New Press, 2010.

White, Evelyn C. *Alice Walker: A Life.* New York, London: Norton, 2004. 11–13.

CRITICAL
CONTEXT

Alice Walker: Critical Reception

Lillie P. Howard

Poet, novelist, "womanist," activist, spiritualist, animist, and Pulitzer Prize winner Alice Walker has been called a "lavishly gifted writer" (Watkins qtd. in Gates and Appiah 16) with "an astonishing versatility" that demonstrates that she is "equally at home with poetry and fiction . . . and as an essayist alone . . . would be a noteworthy presence in American letters" (Gates x). "Few twentieth-century American writers," adds Ikenna Dieke, "have left their imprint on several generations of readers as Alice Walker has. From the time she emerged on the literary scene in 1968 with the publication of her first volume of poetry, *Once* (1968), to the present, Walker appears to have been imbued with an insistent, almost dour and sacrificial determination to tell the truth, a truth that has insistently and consistently evoked contradictory feelings in her readers" (2). In *The Way Forward Is with a Broken Heart* (2000), Walker admits that in the fine tradition of the acclaimed women of her "Sisterhood"—Toni Morrison, June Jordon, Ntozake Shange, and others—she is a "shameless" writer who says of herself, "I honestly like living on the edge, wherever it is; that is where I feel most alive and most free" (47).

Following in the footsteps of Zora Neale Hurston, the literary foremother she helped to reclaim in the mid-1970s, Walker has not been afraid to be herself and to demonstrate unabashedly through her writings that she is firmly committed to evolving fully into that self. Her description of Shug of *The Color Purple* (1982) as "completely unapologetic" and accepting of herself "as outlaw, renegade, rebel and pagan" (*World Has Changed* 275), then, is an apt description of Walker herself and of the themes she explores in her writings. Indeed, Alice Walker's "incorrectness," coupled with her unerring determination to always do exactly as she pleases, is, arguably, one of her most valuable and provocative attributes as a writer.

In "'Writing to Save My Life': An Interview with Claudia Dreifus from *The Progressive* (1989)," Walker adds that "[w]hat I'm doing is literarily trying to connect us to our ancestors. All of us. . . . I see the ancient past as the future . . . ; if we can affirm it in the present, it will make a different future . . . . it's really fatal to see yourself as separate. You have to feel . . . more or less equal and valid in order for the whole organism to feel healthy" (*World Has Changed* 85).

Given the above, what one finds in all of Walker's writings is a "collective oneness" (51) meant to encourage the "spiritual survival, the survival *whole*" (40) of a people—black people, particularly black women, in the South in her earlier writings, all people everywhere in her later writings—who understand that they are capable of a "higher consciousness" (41) that can lead to solutions to oppression and other world problems, particularly if people perceive "all of creation as living" (41) and realize that it is "imbued with spirit" and thus deserves to be honored, respected, and protected. Such a holistic, all-inclusive perspective, Walker believes, can lead to a "healthy" and "whole organism" (85) that understands the interconnectedness of all of creation—people, plants, animals, Earth, the universe. Her writings thus lead her readers toward a future where everyone and everything can "bloom" (84) into their fullest potential, into their very best selves, into the (Walker's) ideal universe.

In addition to clearly delineating the thematic foci and compelling interconnected vision of her works, Walker has also encouraged her readers to think of her writings as occurring in two distinct periods or phases: an early period from 1968 to 1988, when she was writing from what she described as a womanist—i.e., "a black feminist or feminist of color" (xi)—perspective about "the oppressions, the insanities, the loyalties, and the triumphs of black women," (250) a perspective upon which Walker expounds in her well-received collection of essays, *In Search of Our Mothers' Gardens: Womanist Prose* (1983), and a more "mature" period, introduced with the publication of *Living by the Word: Selected Writings 1973–1987* in 1988, when she was writing from the perspective of a spiritual seer whose understanding of life, the world, and spirituality had greatly expanded beyond black women and black people in general to embrace all people, the environment, all plants and animals, and the universe in general. Walker's awareness of the advent of her mature period corresponded with the approach of her fortieth birthday when, as she reports in *Living by the Word*, she wrote in her journal that "next month, I will be forty. In some ways, I feel my early life's work is done, and done completely" (95). In *The Same River Twice: Honoring the Difficult* (1996), Walker further identifies the beginning of her mature period with the "experience of making a film of my work," which, for her, became "an initiation into the next, more mature, phase of my life" (32).

The period between the release of Spielberg's film of *The Color Purple* in 1985 and the beginning of Walker's "more mature phase" had also been influenced by the debilitating illness of Lyme disease, which brought with it what Walker describes in *The Same River Twice* as frequent

> dreams, visions and spiritual revelations of extraordinary power. . . . There were things I just suddenly seemed to know, about life, about the world. As if my illness had pushed open an inner door that my usual consciousness was willing to ignore. I found myself in easy contact with the ancestors . . . and I seemed to spend long, delightful seasons in a time before this one. I recorded some of the experiences in my book *Living by the Word*, and in the novel I wrote after *The Color Purple*, *The Temple of My Familiar*. (32)

In *Living by the Word*, Walker also acknowledges that she had come to terms with the sobering fact that her ancestors were not only black; they were also Native American, and white. In her more mature phase, then, she revises and expands her sense of who she is and whom she represents to encompass all of her ancestors, and, by extension, the oneness-with-the-earth sensibility characteristic of a Native American consciousness.

Readers of *Meridian* (1976), a novel from Walker's first phase, will, of course, note the similarities between Walker's experiences during her illness as she transitions to her new phase and the "out of body" experiences of Meridian throughout the novel and those Truman Held prepares himself to experience near the end of the same novel. And, of course, it is not easy to forget Celie's epiphany near the end of *The Color Purple* where instead of writing just to God as she has done from the first page of the novel, she now addresses the whole of creation as "Dear God. Dear stars, dear trees, dear sky, dear peoples. Dear Everything. Dear God" (286), acknowledging an understanding of the interconnectedness of all things. Clearly, then, Walker had already flirted with such transcendent feelings in her early phase of writings, though those feelings certainly found fuller expression in her later, more mature phase where she gives stronger voice to themes of spirituality, optimism and hope that the world she envisions can become a reality. Walker's own characterization of her work as "linear" and thus cumulative, then, is an apt description of the progression and growth in her writings through both phases of her writings, with the second phase occurring on the same continuum as the first, building upon and adding new dimensions to the earlier one, and affirming that Walker's literary and world vision is continuously evolving, is ever "under construction."

Writing: A Calling and Craft

According to her mother, Walker knew from an early age that writing was her calling, for as chronicled by Rudolph Byrd in his introduction to *The World Has Changed: Conversations with Alice Walker* (2010), Walker began to write "well before she began to walk," using "a twig" to " 'write' in the Sears, Roebuck catalog" (*World Has Changed* 2). In Gloria Steinem's interview "Alice Walker: Do You Know This Woman? She Knows You" Walker admits that she kept a notebook from the time she was eight years old, one that she filled with "horrible poems, but they were poems" (Steinem 294) Years later, at Sarah Lawrence College, Walker, celebrating the fact that she had not committed suicide because of an unwanted pregnancy, began to write a series of poems that she would nightly slip under the door of professor and poet, Muriel Rukeyser. Rukeyser shared the poems with others, including Harcourt Brace Jovanovich, who would become Walker's long-term publisher, and, by so doing, helped to introduce Walker to her first public audience. Walker published her first short story, "To Hell with Dying," when she was twenty-three, her first book of poetry, *Once* (1968), when she was twenty-four, and her first novel, *The Third Life of Grange Copeland* (1970), when she was twenty-six. Today, Walker's much-acclaimed output includes nine volumes of poetry; seven novels; five collections of short stories; fifteen volumes of nonfiction; five volumes of children's literature; and numerous presentations, interviews, and other publications.

Not surprisingly, Walker has been very conscious of her craft, very deliberate in the selection of themes for her writings, very generous in sharing the influences that guide her works, and very persistent in directing the reader to her messages. She explains in an "Interview with Jim O'Brien," for example, that "I am trying to arrive at that place where black music already is; to arrive at that unself-conscious sense of collective oneness, that naturalness, that (even when anguished) grace" (*World Has Changed* 51); that "I am preoccupied with the spiritual survival, the survival *whole*, of my people. But beyond that, I am committed to exploring the oppressions, the insanities, the loyalties, and the triumphs of black women" (40); that "the white women writers that I admire, Chopin, the Brontës, Simone de Beauvoir, and Doris Lessing, are well aware of their own oppression and search incessantly for a kind of salvation. Their characters can always envision a solution, an evolution to higher consciousness on the part of society, even when society itself cannot" (41); and that "If there is one thing African Americans have retained of their African heritage, it is probably animism: a belief that makes it possible to view all creation as living, as being inhabited by spirit" (41). In an "Interview with Claudia Tate" Walker adds that her "whole program as a writer is to deal with history just so I know where I am," explaining that she needed "to write a story like *The Third Life of Grange Copeland . . .* so I could, later on, get to *Meridian*, to *In Love and Trouble*, and then on to *The Color Purple*. I can't move through time in any other way" (*World Has Changed* 67).

Critical Reception

Regardless of whether one accepts that Walker's writings occur in two distinct phases or continue without discernible interruption from one phase to the next, it is irrefutable that for five decades Walker's writings have attracted considerable ongoing literary attention from scholars around the world, resulting in numerous awards, reviews, critical essays, books, interviews, and other expressions of passionate high regard or befuddlement, with most of her critics, admirers and detractors alike, including the general public, focusing on her womanist-period themes of oppression, degeneration, rebellion, regeneration, and surviving whole, primarily as expressed in her fiction. It is also irrefutable that critical responses, including those of the general public, to *The Color Purple* and the film that followed, marked a turning point in Walker's life and her career, a demarcation that was at first marked by poignant silence and heightened by her struggles with Lyme disease as she delved more deeply inside herself, calling on all of her ancestors to help her survive whole, and then by a resurrected, seemingly transformed Alice Walker who was now ready to embrace and hold sacred not only black people, but all people and all manner of things in the universe.

In spite of the rich literary landscape offered in Walker's entire corpus of work across both periods, then, critics have been most captivated by her earlier works, by those written before her fortieth birthday, during her womanist period. The vast majority of scholars writing about Walker's works from this period—Gates, Appiah, et al., in *Alice Walker: Critical Perspectives Past and Present*; Dieke, et al., in *Critical Essays on Alice Walker*; Howard, et al., in *Alice Walker and Zora Neale Hurston: The Common Bond*; Bates, et al., in *Alice Walker: A*

Critical Companion—have focused on themes or motifs that they have described as "the regenerate self, the belief by Walker that it is possible for human beings to transform themselves"; the "sense that human life is a journey, a continuing process of growth and discovery"; the "forbidden in society . . . as a possible route to truth"; the "ubiquity of pain"; an exploration of the "subliminal ego . . . the collective unconscious" of her characters; and an "emphasis on the unity and interconnectedness of all life—human, vegetable, animal" (Dieke 3–5). That is, most scholars have been apt and devoted Walker pupils and have focused on those themes that Walker herself has identified as most characteristic of her writings; these critics have praised Walker for both her courage and her versatility, her use of folk idioms and economy of language, and her character development. Trudier Harris, for example, acknowledges that Walker "knows the language of the folk, knows the forms in which they communicate with each other" (Howard 31). Barbara Christian describes Walker's works as "quilts—bits and pieces of used material rescued from oblivion for everyday use. She takes seemingly ragged edges and arranges them into works of functional though terrifying beauty" (Gates and Appiah 50). Others (Reed, Milloy, et al., qtd. in Bobo) have criticized and condemned Walker for focusing too relentlessly, too unforgivingly, on the oppressions that black people visit upon other black people, particularly black men upon black women, resulting, some critics vehemently claim, in a stereotypical depiction of black men.

Karla Simcikova speculates in her book, *To Live Fully, Here and Now: The Healing Vision in The Works of Alice Walker*, that "most critics did not welcome the publication of *Living by the Word*," and thus the advent of a new period and consciousness in Walker's writings, "with much praise largely because the collection was different from Walker's previous works; it did not fit the womanist 'parameters'" (14). Rather, says Simcikova, Walker's mature period offers "an entirely new way of seeing the world—through the lens of Native American consciousness (14), a consciousness that leads to hope and optimism about 'human capability' and that requires . . . that *all of us work together*" (141). This view of hope and optimism about human capability, of course, is also consistent with similar themes of Walker's earlier works, including her very first novel, *The Third Life of Grange Copeland*, *Meridian,* and *The Color Purple.*

Simcikova acknowledges Derrick Bell and Donna Haisty Winchell among the few scholars who have made the transition from woman-ist scholarship to the spiritualist scholarship required of Walker's later writings (26), and suggests that the vast majority of Walker scholars have avoided the works from Walker's mature period either because they simply overlooked the transition in her works marked by the pub-lication of *Living by the Word* and the acknowledgment of the pres-ence of a "Native American consciousness," or did not understand that transition which seems to move away from Blackness; or perhaps they simply resented such movement as inconsistent with the perspec-tive they had come to laud and admire in Walker's works, and chose to ignore it. Gerri Bates' critical volume, which offers essays about works from both of Walker's literary periods, is a notable exception. It is also possible, of course, that scholars realized, as stated earlier, that Walker's Native American consciousness was not unique to her mature period, for it permeates the majority of her works across both the ear-lier and later periods of her writings.

Poetry

Though Walker made her debut on the literary scene as a poet and has continued to publish volumes of poetry throughout her long career, few scholars have focused on her poetry. Those scholars (see below) who have focused on Walker's poetry acknowledge that her poems are impressive and reflect a voice that speaks knowledgeably and coura-geously about a vast array of topics ranging from the deeply personal to the highly political, neither of these necessarily exclusive of the other. DeWitt Beall, writing a review of *Once* for the *Chicago Daily News,* and quoted on the back cover of *Revolutionary Petunias and*

Other Poems (1973), said of Walker's poetry that "at last there is a black poet I find really exciting. Her name is Alice Walker is not hung up on anybody's course in Modern Poetry or anybody's dogma about the Black Revolution. She just calls 'em the way she sees 'em and that, in this dogmatic age, is refreshing. Miss Walker is quick, direct, witty, pungent, and in her book *Once* she impresses me as the best young woman poet I've read, black or white."

Muriel Rukeyser described *Once* as "[b]rief slashing poems—young, and in the sun"; and a reviewer for the journal "Poetry" described Walker as "[a] sensitive, spirited, and intelligent poet. Feeling is channeled into a style that is direct and sharp . . . Wit and tenderness combine into humanity" (*Once* back cover).

Because Walker's poems are personal and written about her own experiences from her point of view—they may be seen, says Hanna Nowak in "Poetry Celebrating Life" (Gates and Appiah 180), as the "best access to the personality of Alice Walker." Nowak believes that in her early poems, Walker expresses her "deep concern for all human beings, optimism, and affirmation of life, the feeling of continuity, and a highly personal vision" (179). Thadious Davis, writing in the same volume (275–78), adds that "Walker's expressed particularities encompass Southern segregation, American racism, family violence, macho expressionism, female reproduction, and more." Davis continues: "For Walker, poetry is the experience of emotional purging, a release of emotion in expressions usually brief, but occasionally extended over several moods encapsulating one dominant idea, the development of which takes place in the longer fictional pieces." Davis concludes that though Walker is "the premiere African-American and Southern author of her generation," and has produced fiction that has "accelerated in acclaim with the publication of *The Color Purple* . . . her poetry . . . has yet to attract a critical audience." Davis suggests several possible reasons for the absence of a critical audience for Walker's poetry: that perhaps Walker is simply more engaging and clearer in her messages as a fiction writer; that perhaps Walker's exploration of themes, including "racial deprivation" and the pain that women suffer, are more muted in Walker's poetry and are thus less accessible to the reader; that perhaps "few readers choose these days to curl up with a book of poems after a long day or week of multiple assaults on the senses. Or perhaps, as a cynic might think, it is simply bad poetry" (275). Davis leads the reader to believe that Walker's poetry is not "bad poetry," but is instead a necessary precursor to her fiction, and thus the medium through which Walker constantly seeks, resurrects, and reclaims a self that finds fuller expression in her fiction.

Jeffrey L. Coleman (in Dieke) takes exception to what he considers Davis' rather limited view of the importance or literary purpose of Walker's poetry as simply a "preface to fiction," and argues that Walker's "revolutionary stanzas" about the civil rights movement and human rights in general, as captured in *Her Blue Body Everything We Know: Earthling Poems, 1965–1990* (1991), a compilation of poems from Walker's previous four volumes of poetry, deserve deeper study. Coleman offers such a detailed exposition in his essay, arguing that his "reflections on Walker's work not only make clear the scope of her literary and cultural productions, but also delineate her far-reaching concerns for civil and human rights in America and those geographic regions outside the realm of the United States" (98–99). These observations of Coleman, Davis, and Nowak actually complement one another and, together, offer a more complete picture of Walker's poetry.

The Color Purple and Other Works of Fiction

Usually "when one hears/reads the name Alice Walker," says Jeffrey Coleman in "Revolutional Stanzas: The Civil and Human Rights Poetry of Alice Walker," it is not Walker's poetry or nonfiction that "comes immediately to mind"; rather, "it is the genre of fiction, most likely . . . *The Color Purple*" (83). Though a prolific and masterful writer across all genres, then, as stated earlier, it is primarily Walker's fiction that defines her as a writer in the minds of many literary scholars around the world. And while many of the works from her womanist period have received critical attention, as Coleman notes, it is *The Color Purple*, winner of the Pulitzer Prize and the National Book Award, which has generated the most attention. That novel, and the Steven Spielberg film that followed, generated not only high praise and critical applause, but also such a hue and cry from both scholars and the general public that Walker felt she had to leave the country to find peace.

The critical acclaim Walker received for her epistolary novel *The Color Purple* (1982) culminated in 1983 when she became the first African American woman to be awarded the Pulitzer Prize for fiction and her status as a literary writer reached a rare, exalted level. When Steven Spielberg's film of the same name was released in 1985, garnering eleven Oscar nominations, it affirmed the importance, status, and stature of both Walker and her novel, while also providing an irresistible forum for the public to assess and assail the film, as well as the book and its writer. Because the "black man as oppressor" theme that Walker had so relentlessly explored, to mixed critical reviews, in *The Third Life*, found fuller, unrelenting, and even more compelling expression in *The Color Purple*, many of Walker's readers, particularly black men—scholars and laymen alike—were livid about what they perceived as stereotypical, unnecessarily cruel depictions of black men, depictions that they felt threatened relationships between black women and black men. As Jacqueline Bobo reports in "Black Women's Responses to *The Color Purple*," African American writer Ishmael Reed called the book and film a "Nazi conspiracy"; Courtland Milloy, writing for *The Washington Post*, called the book "demeaning," adding that he "got tired, a long time ago, of white men publishing books by Black women about how screwed up Black men are"; talk show host Tony Brown, using the theme, "Purple Rage," devoted a full week to a discussion of the novel and the film; representatives from the NAACP had "hostile views" about the film; and the Coalition Against Black Exploitation picketed the opening of the film in Los Angeles (Bobo). Even some black women critics, adds Bobo, denounced the book and the film for its stereotypical and excessively negative portrayal of black men, and the happy ending that some readers found unrealistic. Such strident, public, and prolonged criticism overwhelmed the positive responses to the book and the film.

Walker recalls the critical reception to both the novel and the film best:

> The attacks, many of them personal and painful, continued for many years, right alongside the praise, the prizes, the Oscar Award nominations. . . . It was said that I hated men, black men in particular; that my work was injurious to black male and female relationships; that my ideas of equality and tolerance were harmful, even destructive of the black community. That my success, and that of other black women writers in publishing our work, was at the expense of black male writers who were not being published sufficiently. (White 23–24)

Furthermore, Walker was "'accused' of being a lesbian, as if respecting and honoring women automatically discredited anything a woman might say"; stalked by a black male writer who attacked her in his lectures, interviews, and books for over ten years; and was targeted by her local paper's editor and publisher for "hostile, inflammatory comments" (23–24) in her community north of San Francisco. Feeling "exposed and vulnerable," Walker temporarily moved to Mexico in order to be able to live and work in peace. "By then," she said, "I had grown used to seeing my expressions taken out of context, rearranged, distorted. It was a curious experience that always left me feeling as if I had ingested poison" (24).

In her 1989 interview with Dreifus, Walker would share her disappointment in critics of *The Color Purple*, explaining that she would never have expected that black men "had no identification with the struggle of women!" She said,

> If you have in your cultural background Paul Robeson, Martin Luther King, W.E.B. DuBois, all these people, how then can you really totally

ignore a progressive movement like the women's liberation movement? So that when you read my work, you read it without any acknowledgment that my work, especially *The Color Purple*, is in the context of a struggle for liberation that women all over the world are engaged in. . . . I wish that men could have more of an appreciation of gentleness in men and not find it so threatening. (*World Has Changed* 79).

In spite of the negative criticism of *The Color Purple*, however, the novel endures as Walker's most compelling and critically heralded work. Not only was the Spielberg's film a box office hit, earning more than $142 million on a budget of $15 million, but the novel has since been made into a Broadway musical, winning a Tony Award in 2006. *The Color Purple*, then—book, film, and musical—may have had the last word with its public, transcending its negative criticism to claim its place in history as one of the most important works of all time. Writing in the preface to the tenth anniversary edition of *The Color Purple*, Walker again reflected on criticism of the novel:

Whatever else *The Color Purple* has been taken for during the swift ten years since its publication . . . . [t]his is the book in which I was able to express a new spiritual awareness, a rebirth into strong feelings of Oneness . . . ; a chance for me as well as the main character, Celie, to encounter That Which Is Beyond Understanding But Not Beyond Loving and to say: I see and hear you clearly, Great Mystery, now that I expect to see and hear you everywhere I am, which is the right place. (xi–xii)

The public was not done with Walker, however, for as she later captured in *Alice Walker Banned*, a collection of poetry, fiction, and prose, the California State Board of Education tried to censure her works by banning two of her short stories from the statewide exam, "Roselily" for being "anti-religious," and "Am I Blue" for being "anti-meat-eating"—ironically at the same time that the governor of the state was inducting Walker into the California Hall of Fame (2).

Nonfiction

As indicated above, Walker's nonfiction, including collections of essays and interviews, offers valuable insight into her psyche, often clarifying the motivations behind her relentless and recurring themes, and offering clues as to how her works might best be read and understood. In fact, many of her nonfiction works might be seen as companion documents to her poetry and fiction, offering a running commentary on her writings and her life, and giving Walker recurring opportunities to provide "corrective" interpretations of her works and repeated public forums to express disappointment in her critics. *In Search of Our Mothers' Gardens,* the seminal work from Walker's womanist period, introduces the term *womanist* and its various definitions, to the public for the first time, and offers a poignant structural framework from which to view the works from that period. *Living by the Word,* as already discussed above, offers similar insights into Walker's mature period.

Conclusion

In sum, critical reception of Walker's works—by literary scholars and the public in general—has been richly mixed, reflecting the complexity of Walker and her controversial, ever-evolving vision; such criticism has also been enormously enriched, in the best of the call-and-response tradition, by Walker's running commentary on her critics and by her own self-expositions. Most critics would agree that she is the quintessential writer, standing free within herself, "Rebellious. Living. / Against the Elemental Crush. / A Song of Color / Blooming / For Deserving Eyes. / Blooming Gloriously / For its Self" ("The Nature of This Flower" 1–7).

Works Cited

Bates, Gerri. *Alice Walker: A Critical Companion.* Westport, CT.: Greenwood, 2005.
Beall, DeWitt. "Once." *Chicago Daily News,* 1973. Reprinted on back cover of Alice Walker, *Revolutionary Petunias and Other Poems.* New York: Harcourt, 1973.

Bobo, Jacqueline. "Black Women's Responses to *The Color Purple*." *Jump Cut: A Review of Contemporary Media.* 33 (1988): 43–51.

Byrd, Rudolph. Introduction. *World Has Changed* 1–34.

Christian, Barbara. "Novels for Everyday Use." Gates and Appiah 50–104.

Coleman, Jeffrey L. "Revolutionary Stanzas: The Civil and Human Rights Poetry of Alice Walker."

Davis, Thadious. "Poetry as Preface to Fiction." Gates and Appiah 275–83.

Dieke, Ikenna, ed. *Critical Essays on Alice Walker*. Westport, CT: Greenwood, 1999.

Gates, Henry Louis, Jr. Preface. Gates and Appiah ix–xiii.

Gates, Henry Louis, Jr., and K. A. Appiah. *Alice Walker: Critical Perspectives Past and Present.* New York: Amistad, 1993.

Harris, Trudier. "Our People, Our People." Howard 31.

Howard, Lillie P. *Alice Walker and Zora Neale Hurston: The Common Bond.* Westport, CT.: Greenwood, 1993.

Nowak, Hanna. "Poetry Celebrating Life." Gates and Appiah 179–92.

Rukeyser, Muriel. "Review of *Once*." *Once: Poems by Alice Walker.* New York: Harcourt, 1976. Back cover.

Simcikova, Karla. *To Life Fully, Here and Now: The Healing Vision in The Works of Alice Walker.* New York: Lexington, 2007.

Steinem, Gloria. *Outrageous Acts and Everyday Rebellions.* 1983. Paperback 2nd edition. New York: Holt, 1995.

Walker, Alice. *Alice Walker Banned.* Introduction by Patricia Holt. San Francisco: Aunt Lute, 1996.

_____. *The Color Purple.* 1982. New York: Harcourt, 1992.

_____. *In Search of Our Mothers' Gardens: Womanist Prose.* New York: Harcourt, 1983.

_____. "Interview with Claudia Tate from *Black Women Writers at Work* (1983)." Bird 58–69.

_____. "Interview with John O'Brien from *Interviews with Black Writers* (1973)." Bird 35–57.

_____. *Living by the Word: Selected Writings, 1973–1987.* San Diego: Harcourt, 1988.

_____. *Meridian.* New York: Harcourt, 1976.

_____. "The Nature of This Flower Is to Bloom." *Revolutionary Petunias and Other Poems.* 1971. New York: Harcourt, 1973.

_____. *Once.* New York: Harcourt, 1968.

_____. *The Same River Twice: Honoring the Difficult.* New York: Scribner, 1996.

_____. *The Third Life of Grange Copeland.* New York: Harcourt, 1970.

_____. *The Way Forward Is with a Broken Heart.* New York: Random, 2000.

_____. *The World Has Changed. Conversations with Alice Walker.* Ed. Rudolph P. Byrd. New York: New Press, 2010.

Watkins, Mel. "The Color Purple (1982)." *The New York Times Book Review.* 25 July 1982.

White, Evelyn C. *Alice Walker: A Life.* New York: Norton, 2004.

Critical Lens: Five Critics on Alice Walker_____

Napolita Hooper-Simanga

Alice Walker has generated a body of work that transcends boundaries, blurring the line between traditional Southern and African American literary conventions while carving space for literary critics to uncover the seemingly endless themes and developments in her work. Critical analysis of Walker's work has ranged from discussion of the womanist voice in her fiction to her inclusion of spirituality in both essay and verse. Indeed, Walker's multiple voices and themes have caused an overlapping of criticism and encouraged readers to reimagine African American culture, women, the American South, and humankind in general.

Five critics who have detailed some of Walker's strongest themes (that of self-actualization, redemption, woman as outsider artist, and folk tradition as social commentary) are Susan Willis, Lynn Pifer, Robert James Butler, Gail Keating, and Trudier Harris. These critics' examinations of Walker's publications open dialogue about Walker's unique ability to present varied themes and responses to social, political, and cultural issues.

In Susan Willis' "Walker's Women," she examines female characters in three of Walker's novels—*Meridian* (1973), *The Color Purple* (1982), and *The Third Life of Grange Copeland* (1970). Yet it is her discussion of *Meridian* that best examines the emphasis on language and motherhood in the lives of Walker's black female characters. Specifically, Willis draws parallels between the transformation of the protagonist, Meridian, from a college student at Saxon College who struggles with the expectations of her black bourgeois academic community to that of a self-actualized woman who eventually leaves to join another black community—one that consists of the small Southern towns "for whom the Civil Rights movement passed too quickly to transform embedded racist and sexist practices" (Willis 85).

Moreover, Willis focuses on the use of language in *Meridian* to examine Walker's many layers of meaning and context. In particular, Willis asserts that the character Wile Chile (also known as The Wild Child) is self-destructive as seen through not only her behavior (she's a thirteen-year-old orphan who eats out of garbage cans and lives on the streets) but her language as well. She contrasts Wile Chile with Meridian, positing that the orphan is Meridian's social antithesis. Wile Chile farts and swears to communicate with others, expressing herself through obscene yet natural methods. She is unabashed, essentially free of social norms that undermine her self-actualization, despite the outsider status she is forced to endure.

Paradoxically, Meridian, a college student in search of her own identity despite very defined expectations of the surrounding academic community, is challenged by the notion of self-determination for black women (Willis 82). That is, she feels pressured to adhere to gender norms influenced by white European culture, which results in isolation from class and community (Willis 83). These gender norms include the fulfillment of motherhood among other things. According to Willis, Walker addresses the role of motherhood as representative of oppression for black women. Moreover, Meridian's and Wile Chile's lives overlap on one point—the possibility of being made pregnant. However, Wile Chile succumbs to the oppression of motherhood whereas Meridian initially struggles against it in her journey toward self-discovery.

Furthermore, while both are isolated from community, Meridian and Wile Chile represent opposing stages in black female development. Walker suggests that black women have effectively used language (as well as rejected it) during these conflicting stages, revealing painful but successful navigation in a racist patriarchy. Indeed, Wile Chile's nontraditional articulation and Meridian's academic speech inform readers of the black female marginalized experience. In fact, Willis asserts that *Meridian* makes a clear statement about the black female and language: "The question of language is not meaningful except in relation to the community" (Willis 85). Thus, Meridian and Wile Chile reflect very meaningful ideals about language usage as it relates to communal inclusion and exclusion. Willis further argues that Meridian's desire to speak as an individual who chooses her own community mirrors Walker herself—a writer who recognizes and appreciates the need for the space between self and community.

Willis finds further evidence of the importance of language in *Meridian* through the character Louvinie, a slave woman from West Africa with special storytelling skills. Readers learn of Louvinie's magic at a storytelling event in which her master's "weak-hearted" young son dies in the middle of one of her tales (Willis 83). When the master cuts out her tongue, Louvinie becomes symbolic of the silence black women have historically endured. She is forced to bury her tongue under a magnolia tree in the middle of the Saxon College campus that eventually grows into the largest magnolia in the county. Willis states that the tree is in opposition to the two social institutions: the plantation and the university. It is language that helps to uncover the particulars of the black female experience on the plantation and as well as the campus. When written, it provides testimony to the atrocities suffered by black women. When spoken, it provides immediate affirmation of their experiences. And when altered or translated, it resounds with the perceived threat of the black female presence to the dominant culture.

Both the plantation and the university seek to silence the resistance put forth by black women, as seen through Louvinie and Meridian. Named The Sojourner, the tree resurrects the lives of black women who used language in their struggle for freedom; this ultimately empowers Meridian (Willis 84). Again, we are brought back to the notion of community as integral to self-discovery and determination. Walker's characters typically return to the community, but it is their ability to reconcile conflicting personal and social expectations along with radical self-actualization that allows this to happen. In Meridian's case, language requires negotiation to avoid total submergence within the community and proficiency to work with it (Willis 85).

The issue of language and one's capacity to voice one's opinion—speak oneself into the social discourse—is also discussed in "Coming to Voice in Alice Walker's *Meridian*: Speaking Out for the Revolution" by Lynn Pifer. Pifer's essay focuses on Meridian's silence and ultimate transformation/self-actualization. She states, "Because of her refusal to participate in authorized discourse, Meridian fails to fit in with a succession of social groups—from her church congregation, to those at the elite college she attends, to a cadre of would-be violent revolutionaries. She begins a process of personal transformation when she sets out alone to fight her own battles, through personal struggle and Civil Rights work" (51). Meridian's transformation involves forgiveness of her perceived failings, learning to love and respect herself and see the moments of silence as subversive measures aimed at a system that refuses to recognize her. This realization is important as she would otherwise be forced to view those silent moments as evidence of disappointing those who love her (Pifer 53). In addition, Pifer sees the importance of the rejection of motherhood and dependence on folk tradition in Meridian's life. These prove to be invaluable as the protagonist makes choices that are both empowering and socially unacceptable.

Pifer discusses the contrast between Meridian and The Wild Child through language and communal roles. Pifer writes, "There is no survival for the unrestrained independent female" (57). In fact, the girl is killed when she attempts to flee Meridian's well-intentioned efforts to help clothe and shelter her (she runs into the street and is struck by a speeding car). The administration in charge of the academic community refuses to acknowledge the girl's death; thus, her body is not allowed on campus, even as a corpse. She represents the very essence of what the academic community resists—the education of the students' minds (Pifer 58). When the school refuses to hold funeral services on campus for the girl, Meridian and her classmates are compelled to respond. In fact, their initial reactions include throwing their jewelry on the ground, which, according to Pifer, is representative of a rejection of forced ladyhood. They also stick out their tongues, an act that could be considered childish were it not for Louvinie's legacy. Astonishingly, the girls rebel against the most beloved part of the campus: The Sojourner. The girls chop down the tree, despite Meridian's protest.

Pifer insists that folklore is a vital part of Walker's narrative, as it is embedded in the novel in various places. She believes Meridian turns to folk traditions such as songs, dances, and stories for expression and inspiration as she makes her way through a journey of self-discovery (Pifer 53). Because she does not want to depend on her own words, Meridian depends on the stories of strong, rebellious women who lived before her. Pifer points out the distinct similarities between the girls in the academic community and the slave women of the plantation upon which the college was built. This connection makes for a compelling history from which Meridian is able to draw as she looks for strength and communal affirmation. She states that the girls are kept on the campus surrounded by an ornate gate just as the slaves were forced to stay on the plantation; all of the students are expected to spread the name of the college just as their ancestral mothers were forced to increase the stock of slaves and thereby spread the names of their masters. Perhaps the single most important example of folk tradition available to Meridian is The Sojourner, for it represents the history of the dominant culture and black female resistance, which has always fought against it.

Because the tree has been the subject of stories handed down for generations at the campus, it is meaningful to Meridian. Pifer states that "Louvinie and the conjured image of Sojourner Truth serve as positive examples of women who use their tongues as weapons in the struggle for liberation" (54). However, she also believes that Master Saxon's response to Louvinie is equally important, for Meridian learns that the consequence for speaking against racist patriarchy could be permanent silence. Thus, when she must "reproduce patriarchal discourse" (e.g. a patriotic high school speech), she chooses to be subversive. Unlike black women who choose to speak out against racist patriarchy, Meridian draws inspiration from Louvinie's severed tongue by choosing to remain silent.

Folklore, then, is a major part of the novel's development. In fact, Meridian participates in creating folklore when she travels to Chicokema, a segregated town besieged by racism. Meridian learns of the town's practice of separating black and white workers at the guano plant, which has led to negative socialization on the part of the town's black children (Pifer 55). Believing themselves to be inferior, the black children assume that they can never rise above the class and caste in which they have been placed. It is Meridian's heroic act, however, that challenges these children's self-perceptions. She lines them up to see an exhibit on a "whites only" day, clearly defying the social norms of the town. She waits for the police, then takes the children to the exhibit. The townsfolk are left to stare at her without taking action, despite the intimidating tank parked in the town square.

Like other critics who have examined *Meridian*'s theme of motherhood and self-identity, Pifer concentrates on Meridian's response to motherhood and reads her actions as both self-affirming as well as conforming. She states that Meridian does not object to having children. Indeed, she reaches out to the orphaned Wile Chile and sympathizes greatly when she learns of her pregnancy. To better understand Meridian's position, Pifer turns to the mythical Black Mother as discussed by feminist critic Barbara Christian. According to Christian, this myth assumes that a mother should forfeit her personality and interests in order to provide for her children. This mythical role casts a long shadow over black women in particular because of the added burden of enduring motherhood under a system of slavery that forced them to renounce their own children for those of their masters. If Meridian and other black women deny the role of motherhood, they also sever ties to the millions of black women who survived the indignities of slavery.

Meridian's self-centered feelings about motherhood, then, are understandable and seen as heroic in some ways. Although she does become a mother, it is important to note that she is the victim of sexual violence and does not enjoy sex with her boyfriend. She conforms to social expectations by becoming a wife and mother, but she spends her time contemplating suicide instead of doting on her child. Meridian eventually escapes her domestic life but must learn to shed her guilt, which impedes her from seeing and moving freely (Pifer 63). She does become the traditional mother like her own mother, who Pifer points out is unhappy due to the suppression of her own emotions to conform to tradition. Nor does she become trapped between childhood and motherhood like Nelda, her childhood friend who desired to attend college but never finished high school due to an unplanned pregnancy at age fourteen. As Pifer states, she becomes the "worthless minority of mothers excluded by the tradition" (62).

Meridian's journey ends with the acceptance of a church community, one that is unconventional nonetheless. Pifer states, "In order to survive, Meridian must see through the mystique of martyrdom, learn to value her own life, and find a community to live with, rather than a company of names to be listed among" (65). Unlike her childhood Baptist church, this church has a stained-glass image of blues musician B. B. King, a preacher who encourages members of the church to be self-determining, and music that contains empowering lyrics. The congregation is allowed to remember the past and mourn together, something that Meridian never experienced in previous spiritual or academic communities. Whether through folklore or spiritual community, Meridian manages to survive her journey of self-actualization and resist cultural norms that have traditionally resulted in the death of soul and spirit of those who defy them.

Deeply rooted in Southern black culture, Walker's work often reflects the challenges as well as the autonomy resulting from her characters' ability to survive complex and dangerous social constructs. In "Alice Walker's Vision of the South in *The Third Life of Grange Copeland*," Robert James Butler asserts that the novel "best expresses Walker's powerful ambivalence toward Southern life" (90). Through the three main characters—Brownfield, Ruth, and Grange Copeland—

Walker is able to portray the triumphant human spirit despite the generational plight of racism and classism.

Butler analyzes the novel's multiple narratives, beginning with Brownfield's, which Butler states is "all that is negative about Southern culture: He is cruelly victimized by the extreme racism and poverty of the Georgia backwoods world in which he is born and raised" (91). Butler includes a discussion of Brownfield's name, stating that it clearly suggests blighted growth. Images associated with this character include symptoms such as head sores and boils, which imply that Brownfield has been infected and, eventually, "destroyed by a racist world [that] systematically deprives him of human nourishment" (Butler 91).

Brownfield's story is one of Southern servitude that results in his being "cheated out of land and morally dispossessed of a human foundation for his life" (Butler 92). Even his marriage to the loving Mem is eventually ruined by his inability to accept her love and devotion. His neurotic jealousy leads to degradation as he attempts to recover part of his ego through his superiority over her. "Brownfield murders Mem because a social environment that strips him of manhood cancels out his love for her" (Butler 92). Eventually, Brownfield comes to accept and love the South as he "develops a perverse love of the world which dehumanizes him" (92).

Butler thinks that if Brownfield is the book's most degraded character, then Brownfield's father Grange is able to give Ruth, Brownfield's daughter, a nourishing environment to ensure her growth and development. Grange takes Ruth in when her mother is murdered and becomes her surrogate father. "From the moment of her birth, Grange sees Ruth as unique and beautiful, someone who almost magically appears in the midst of an environment which is harsh and ugly" (Butler 94). Grange provides a new home for Ruth along with the love and support she needs to prosper beyond her parents' lives and ambitions. He also nourishes her mind and soul, forbidding her from working in the cotton fields and even arranging for her to attend school. He also tells her folktales to explain the trickster figure and its relevance to black history. Now the

South is a place of folklore and music (Grange also sings blues music), a place of tradition. Because Grange has grounded his granddaughter in the life-affirming South and its traditions, he has also endowed her with the values which will ultimately lead to her survival in the racist world to which other characters fall victim (Butler 94).

Grange is able to redeem himself through his support of Ruth. Though he abandoned Brownfield during his childhood, Grange is the source of love for Ruth during hers. When Ruth decides to leave the South, she is prepared because of Grange's help. "It becomes increasingly clear to Grange that the only way to protect Ruth from Brownfield is to encourage her to leave the South, for the full weight of Southern law is in favor of returning her to Brownfield" (Butler 95). After the court orders Ruth to be taken away from him, Grange shoots Brownfield and is shot and killed by police, thus sacrificing himself to save Ruth. According to Butler (96), Grange's death provides her with possibilities she otherwise would not enjoy.

Just as Walker's work explores themes of self-actualization and redemption, it also demonstrates Walker's belief in the importance of female-centered communities and groups. Walker's literary and critical work and her insistence on a womanist perspective changed the feminist dialogue concerning women of color and the complexities of their lives, thus challenging preconceived notions of generic women's literature and criticism. Her work encouraged scholars in both literature and women's studies to reimagine the portrayal and relevance of African American female characterization throughout American and international cultural/literary history.

Through essays, poetry and fiction, Walker's inclusion of female relationships and communities reveals the need for such relationships and communities for African Americans. Gail Keating discusses Walker's inclusion of woman-centered narrative and woman outsider artist in "Alice Walker: In Praise of Maternal Heritage." Keating states that Walker "acknowledges the great contributions women have made to our culture and traces the power of women through her own matri-lineage" (101).

Starting with Virginia Woolf's beliefs about women and art, Keating states, "Woolf points out that the reason why so many women writers are not successful is because they allow unimportant, unnecessary, irrelevant distractions to take precedence over their work" and that "a woman, in order to be successful, must remove herself from the distractions that prohibit her having the time to create" (102). However, Keating moves her attention to Walker's response to this notion of art and women's limited time, pointing out Walker's statements in the essay "In Search of Our Mothers' Gardens." In this groundbreaking essay, Walker suggests a new consideration of what constitutes art. She moves from a male-centered definition that includes specific artist types such as novelist, essayist, and poet, to other artistic expressions such as gardening and quilt making.

Keating points to Walker's short story "Everyday Use," the essay "In Search of Our Mothers' Gardens," and her novel *The Color Purple* for evidence of Walker's acknowledgment of these outsider artists. In the short story, the mother and one sister (Maggie) live simply in the rural South. They spend time quilt making and collecting the quilts of their female relatives. Though another sister (Dee, a.k.a., Wangero Leewanika Kemanjo) wants to take the quilts and hang them as a celebration of her folk heritage, Maggie and her mother are confused and angered by such a display. Keating states, "What Dee (Wangero) doesn't realize is that her mother and sister are doing just fine . . . they have found a very natural outlet for their creativity which society has just begun to appreciate, but is not a part of it" (105). Women, according to Walker, have always been expressive and creative. Remarkably, they have often existed as outsider artists whose work remains unappreciated and unrecognized by elite artistic communities and institutions.

In the essay "In Search of Our Mothers' Gardens," Walker discusses the love her own mother, Minnie Tallulah Grant Walker, had for gardening. Walker recalls her mother's commitment to her garden and the comfort and pleasure it provided her family. People came to her for cuttings and praised her ability to work with the worst soil (Keating 107). Keating asserts that Walker makes us realize that the time has come to acknowledge the tremendous emotional weight that so many women have been forced to carry, especially black women. Indeed, Walker reminds us that we should honor the work they have done as cultural stabilizers.

In *The Color Purple*, Walker uses quilt making and sewing as creative outlets for women that, though largely ignored, provide a source of strength for her characters. Celie, the novel's protagonist, is the victim of sexual and domestic abuse. She is "thin and dark and ugly" with "so little going for her in life except for her natural ability and creativity displayed in her quilt-making and sewing" (Keating 107). By the novel's end, Celie is able to use her talent for her personal recovery, giving meaning to her life and enabling her to become a self-aware and self-actualized woman. In fact, she is able to socialize with others as an adult woman because of her creativity.

Furthermore, Keating perceives Celie's quilt making as a bonding exercise with other women in her community who are separated by their own personal challenges and histories. In fact, Celie's skills unite her with other women. This leads Celie to share her art with others. "Art for a woman like Celie is not a luxury to be admired and enjoyed. Art is an integral part of daily life" (Keating 109). In fact, Celie is able to use her sewing skills to support herself after she leaves her abusive husband. She becomes famous for her pants, which she details for each customer. Keating points out the importance of Celie's progression with this skill. She asserts that Celie's art develops to maturity and that her pants transform into beautiful creations (111). She further states, "Celie's creations are a labor of love. She designs these pants with the same precision and diligence and inspiration an architect would use in designing a building, a painter in painting a landscape, a composer in writing an opera, a writer in writing a novel" (112).

Finally, Trudier Harris discusses Walker's work within a literary black folk tradition in "Folklore in the Fiction of Alice Walker: A Perpetuation of Historical and Literary Traditions." Harris asserts that "[a] close look at the fiction, especially the shorter pieces, of Alice Walker reveals that she employs folklore for purposes of defining characters and illustrating relationships between them as well as for plot development. By so doing, she comments on the racial situation in the United States and, in some instances, chastises her black characters for their attitudes toward themselves" (3). Harris likens Walker's use of folklore to that of Charles Chesnutt's and Zora Neale Hurston's, which dates back to the late nineteenth century.

Harris begins with Walker's short story "The Revenge of Hannah Kemhuff" from the short story collection *In Love and Trouble: Stories of Black Women* (1973). In this story, Walker relies on the theme of conjuration and the figure of the conjure woman. Walker's character Tante Rosie is compared to Chesnutt's character Aun' Peggy. Both women possess conjuring abilities that empower them within their respective communities. Harris points out that Tante Rosie's powers are not as supernatural as are Aun' Peggy's. In fact, the destruction "of her victim is more psychological than physical. The victim *believes* in the potential threat to her physical well being and thereby emotionally destroys herself" (4). This portrayal of the conjure woman within the black community exposes the limited access to the legislative system blacks had (and still have).

As for portrayal of the lifestyle of the conjure woman, Harris draws parallels among Walker and Hurston. She notes, "Walker puts her narrator in the position of apprentice to Tante Rosie and, even though she mentions that she is still learning the trade, the narrator does tell what she knows. Her fervor in carrying out Tante Rosie's orders is reminiscent of the enthusiasm of the youthful Hurston" (4). In the story, Hannah Kemhuff goes to Tante Rosie to seek the death of a woman who destroyed her family. Hannah's husband convinces Hannah to join the welfare lines to receive handouts while he continues to see another woman. He leaves Hannah and their children for this woman, and years later the children die and Hannah becomes a prostitute and drunk. Harris points to the difference in food supplied to the black recipients compared to that given to the white recipients. Blacks were given less desirable food, revealing blatant racial discrimination. Harris writes, "In the face of such oppression, conjuring becomes Hannah's only viable means of protest; it is the only weapon she has when religion fails. She cannot turn to the law and courts because the system has set up the inequality. Therefore, Walker allows Tante Rosie to take on the cause for social justice" (6). Thus, the conjure woman is the only choice for Hannah, reflecting Walker's understanding of social injustice but acknowledgment of the folk alternatives that have served the black community in spite of such injustice.

Harris identifies Walker's use of folk tradition, though limited, in *The Third Life of Grange Copeland*. She states, "Folk material becomes significant in defining the relationship between Grange and Ruth, his granddaughter. It is a way to seal the bond between them and to identify their unity against a hostile and un-understanding world" (7). Grange tells Ruth folktales to entertain her, but Harris is quick to point out that Grange is "not a mindless teller of tales solely for the sake of entertainment" (7). For Harris, Walker's depiction of Grange as one capable of analyzing and reinterpreting folktales indicates that "Walker does not view the folk culture as something separate from life, but as an integral and useful part of one's existence" (7).

Alice Walker's work has expanded the parameters of Southern literature and detailed particular facets of black Southern life. Scholars continue to track various themes in her work that express the depth and complexity of not only black Southern culture, but the human experience in general.

Works Cited

Bloom, Harold, ed. *Alice Walker: New Edition*. New York: Chelsea, 2007.

Butler, Robert James. "Alice Walker's Vision of the South in *The Third Life of Grange Copeland*." Bloom 89–100.

Harris, Trudier. "Folklore in the Fiction of Alice Walker: A Perpetuation of Historical and Literary Traditions." *Black American Literature Forum* 11.1 (1977): 3–8. Web. 10 July 2011.

Keating, Gale. "Alice Walker: In Praise of Maternal Heritage." Bloom 101–14.

Pifer, Lynn. "Alice Walker: The Achievement of the Short Fiction." Bloom 51–67.

Willis, Susan. "Walker's Women." *Modern Critical Views: Alice Walker*. Ed. Harold Bloom. New York: Chelsea, 1989. 81–95.

Cultural and Historical Context_____

Carmen R. Gillespie

When she ended her talk show in May of 2011 after twenty-five years, Oprah Winfrey paid brief homage to the film version of Alice Walker's best-known novel *The Color Purple*. Oprah noted that success in life is about knowing one's inner self and using that information as a talisman against whatever narratives the world may create about you. Winfrey showed the famous clip from the film where Miss Celie, played by Whoopie Goldberg, delivers her curse to her abusive husband, Mister. "Until you do right by me, everything you even think about gonna fail." Then Miss Celie leaves her abusive husband with the line "I'm poor, black, I might even be ugly, but dear God, I'm here. I'm here." This re-iteration of Walker's words, unadulterated from her novel, marks a fundamental change in the public perception of African American women, a change perhaps most publicly wrought by the persistence of women like Oprah Winfrey, but also deeply and foundationally rooted in the transformative activism and artistry of writers like Alice Walker.

By the time Winfrey retired her show in May 2011, President Barack Obama had been in office for over two years. During the particular tumult of 1944, Alice Malsenior Walker was born on February 9. She was the eighth child of Willie Lee and Minnie Lou Grant Walker who were sharecroppers in the small Georgia town of Eatonton, Georgia. At the time of Walker's birth, the possibility that an African American could reside in the White House as President of the United States and leader of the free world would have seemed remote at the very least and probably did not even occur to most people, whether they were black or not.

Walker's understandings of the world were affected by the circumstances of her birth as well as by the histories of her family, community, and nation. On the national front, in 1944 the United States found itself in the midst of the world's most cataclysmic war to date. During World War II, more than sixty million people lost their lives. The war in Europe ended shortly after Walker's birth. African American participation in the war lent strength to the fight in African American communities for the recognition of equal citizenship that had eroded since the establishment of the Fourteenth and Fifteenth Amendments. The systematic growth of racial segregation occurred in the United States through the creation of laws based on the principle of separation of blacks and whites. This set of laws emerged as the dominant system policing racial interactions. That system, based upon the construct of separate but equal, was formalized in the 1896 Supreme Court decision *Plessy v. Ferguson*, and became known, particularly in the Southern United States, as Jim Crow. In the year of Walker's birth, the distinguished African American historian Rayford W. Logan edited the volume *What the Negro Wants*. With essays from African American intellectuals such as Mary McLeod Bethune, Sterling Brown, W. E. B. Du Bois, Langston Hughes, A. Philip Randolph, and Roy Wilkins, Logan's volume is an important iteration of the problems African Americans faced at the time and was a consistent and persuasive argument against segregation and its consequences.

World War II was in many ways a watershed moment in African American history. Segregation was the law of the land and African Americans throughout the country, but ubiquitously in the South, had to employ public facilities, including transportation, schools, libraries, and other facilities, that were inadequate and substandard. As previously mentioned, in the Southern United States, this system of separation was often referred to as Jim Crow. The term *Jim Crow* refers to both the laws that enforced racial segregation in the American South between 1877 and the 1950s and the resulting attitudes and lifestyle in the South, in which African Americans and whites could not mingle in most public arenas, forcing blacks into degrading and insulting social roles.

The name *Jim Crow* had its origin in a stereotypical black minstrel show character. The segregation laws under Jim Crow were a reaction by Southern whites against Reconstruction, which the federal government implemented in the South after the Civil War until 1877. Many

Southern whites were angered and frightened by the freedoms granted to African Americans—almost all of them ex-slaves—under Reconstruction. Unwilling to live in a society where blacks were their equals, the Southern state legislatures began to pass laws that forced the two races apart and took back from blacks most of their rights as US citizens.

Jim Crow laws led to daily insults and violations to African Americans. Because the message of Jim Crow was an endorsement of white racial superiority to blacks, many whites felt free to take advantage of the injustice. Black women could be raped by white men without legal recourse, black sharecroppers could be cheated of their money by white landlords, and black shoppers could be publicly insulted by white shopkeepers. At its worst, Jim Crow victimized blacks with white mob violence and lynchings.

It was not until shortly after World War II, following Alice Walker's birth that the constitutionality of Jim Crow was seriously challenged. In 1950, the Supreme Court ruled that because the state did not offer equal education, the University of Texas's law school had to admit a black man. Just four years later, with *Brown v. Board of Education of Topeka, Kansas*, the Supreme Court found segregated educational facilities were unconstitutional. African Americans and their white allies used boycotts, sit-ins, and court challenges to fight Jim Crow.

Although they had valiantly served their country during both World Wars I and II, veterans returning from the war often faced discrimination and violence. Protests by African American veterans were at the heart of the 1946 riots in Columbia, Tennessee, riots in Chicago, and post–WWII violence in Redwood City, California, and Munroe, Georgia. In 1947, President Truman created the Committee on Civil Rights, which generated public conversations about the issues of discrimination and racial inequality. The committee released a report entitled *To Secure These Rights.* The report suggested, among other recommendations, the review of the policies of racial segregation within the military (Saxe 178–79).

Of course, these arguments against legalized segregation were not limited to the world outside Walker's immediate community and family. The Eatonton African American community predominated slightly outside the main town, in the neighborhood known as Wards Chapel. In this neighborhood, Walker attended Wards Chapel AME Church. Walker's parents were community activists and ensured that their children all attended school, despite pressure to keep them working in the fields. Walker's mother and father were instrumental in the formation of the black school East Putnam Consolidated, where Alice began her education at the age of four (Bates 2–3). The Walker family story of activism predates Walker's parents. Walker's great-great-great-great-grandmother, May Poole, was, according to family oral history, said to have walked from Virginia to Georgia carrying two small infants in her arms. Walker includes a photograph of Poole at the beginning of her collection *Anything We Love Can Be Saved* (1997), with the inscription, "A precious heritage." Walker has said that it is Poole's story that has persuaded her never to change her last name. These stories, coupled with the larger context of African American social activism, infused Walker from a young age with a sense of possibility and a determination to right wrong and to battle oppression.

Walker was a bright child who was adored by her family and particularly by her older sister, Ruth. According to Walker's official biographer, Evelyn C. White, Walker's relationship with Ruth would later affect her relationship with her father. Willie Lee was abusive towards Ruth as she matured. His expression of a sexual double standard towards his male and female children led Walker to an elementary understanding of gender discrimination and its consequences. Another pivotal and formative event in Walker's young life occurred in 1952 when she was wounded in her right eye by one of her brothers by his BB gun. Walker gives her account of these events in her 1983 collection of essays *In Search of Our Mothers' Gardens*. Throughout her writings, Walker alludes to her blinding as a multilayered trauma. She was overwhelmed by the physical pain of the injury, but the incident was perhaps equally compounded by its psychological impacts. Walker withdrew from her previous level of social engagement, became quiet and introverted in school, and retreated to the imaginative worlds of reading and writing. Shortly after the incident, Walker was sent to live with her grandparents, and she remained there for a year. The relocation compounded her sense of alienation and exile (*Gardens* 384–94).

Walker's family has a story of Alice beginning to read and write when she was only three years old. It seems that from the beginning of her life, she has always been engaged with the tools, pleasures, and agency of narrative. The world of words created a kind of haven from the occasional violence endemic to her immediate family and contained in her family's history. The distinctions between the experiences of and the stories about this violence created a bridge between Walker's lived reality and her developing identity as a creative writer. Many members of the Walker family were accomplished storytellers, and Alice grew up listening to the tales of and about her immediate and extended family. One of those stories was the narrative of her grandmother who was murdered by a man with whom she was having an affair (*World Has Changed* 19). Walker's father, Willie Lee Walker, saw his mother's murder. These and other stories Walker learned from her family would later find their way into her novels and short stories.

Walker attended Spelman College from 1961 to 1963. At Spelman she became engaged in civil rights activism. Atlanta in the early 1960s could almost be described as a headquarters of the civil rights movement. The Southern Christian Leadership Conference (SCLC), one of the primary organizations responsible for civil rights activities, was based there. Dr. Martin Luther King Jr. was born and raised in Atlanta and graduated from Morehouse College before continuing his studies at Boston University. In 1960 King returned to Atlanta to be co-pastor, along with his father, Martin Luther King Sr., at Ebenezer Baptist Church. In 1962, Martin and Coretta King invited the freshman Walker to their home to celebrate her selection to attend the World Festival of Youth and Students in Helsinki, Finland (Bates 10; White 465). While attending the festival, Walker met her lifelong friend and partner in struggle, feminist activist Gloria Steinem.

The civil rights movement of the late 1950s and early to mid-1960s was largely based upon the integrationist school of thought elaborated by men and women such as Frederick Douglas, Anna Julia Cooper, Frances Ellen Watkins Harper, W. E. B. Du Bois, Walter White, Septima Clark, Diane Nash, and Martin Luther King Jr. Through slavery and until the first half of the twentieth century, the black church was the stronghold and organizing center of African American communities. Although legally begun by various experts within African American political organizations such as the NAACP in the early decades of the twentieth century, the civil rights movement of the 1950s and 60s took place largely through the actions and support of black Christian churches. The main strategy of the movement was to confront racist and segregationist laws and practices with nonviolent direct action. This strategy manifested in boycotts, sit-ins, and other nonviolent protests that forced confrontation with the practice of Jim Crow segregation in public life, housing, schooling, and voting practices.

In the mid-to-late 1960s, there occurred a major schism in the civil rights movement between those who favored integration and those who abandoned the ideals of the movement. This ideological split marked the beginning of the disintegration of integrationism and nonviolent direct action as the movement's dominant strategic tools. The actions of the individuals involved in the civil rights movement brought about the aforementioned 1954 Supreme Court decision *Brown v. Board of Education*, which rendered illegal segregated schooling; the various voting rights acts; the 1961 Interstate Commerce Commission's ban on segregation in public transportation; and the Civil Rights Act of 1964.

Alice Walker was deeply involved in the civil rights movement from her days as a student at Spelman College. The philosophies of her writings are grounded in the principles and strategies that guided the movement. Her novel *Meridian* is most explicitly about the struggles of the movement and the human toll activism took on those who dedicated their energies, and sometimes their lives, to moving the United States forward. Walker ultimately found Spelman's environment too conservative for her. She also reports that she was molested by a respected male person at the college for whom she was working ("Saying Goodbye to My Friend Howard Zinn"). This dissatisfaction and abuse was at the heart of Walker's decision to transfer to Sarah Lawrence College in New York in January of 1964 (*World Has Changed* 7).

Despite her transfer, Walker has returned to Spelman many times as a guest lecturer. In one of her lectures, "Oppressed Hair Puts a Ceiling on the Brain," reprinted in *Living by the Word: Selected Writings, 1973–1987*, she says to Spelman students gathered for a 1987 Founder's Day celebration:

> As some of you no doubt know, I myself was a student here once, many moons ago. I used to sit in these very seats (sometimes still in pajamas, underneath my coat) and gaze up at the light streaming through these very windows. I listened to dozens of encouraging speakers and sang, and listened to, wonderful music. I believe I sensed I would one day return, to be on this side of the podium. I think that, all those years ago, when I was a student here and still in my teens, I was thinking about what I would say to you now. (69)

Although ambivalent about her experiences there, Walker seems to accept her time at Spelman as an intrinsic and definitive part of her intellectual journey.

At Sarah Lawrence, Helen Lynd, mother of one of her Spelman professors and mentors, Staunton Lynd, served as Walker's faculty advisor. She also gave Walker money for winter clothes and a blanket upon the student's introduction to the brutality of northern winters ("Saying Goodbye"). Walker has noted Lynd's role in making Western philosophy accessible. Sarah Lawrence expanded Walker's creative and intellectual universe. While there, Walker again traveled overseas, this time to Africa to study in Kenya and Uganda. Walker also found writing mentors at Sarah Lawrence who proved pivotal to her transition to professional writing. The poets Muriel Rukeyser and Jane Cooper encouraged Walker's aspirations to become a creative writer.

Muriel Rukeyser was a poet, novelist, essayist, creative writing teacher, and an early champion of Walker. She circulated to publishers the manuscript of Walker's first published poetry collection, *Once: Poems* (1968). Rukeyser also sent Walker's story "To Hell with Dying" to Langston Hughes, who enthusiastically included it in the collection *The Best Short Stories by Negro Writers* (1967). Walker dedicated her 1979 essay "One Child of One's Own" to Rukeyser. As Walker gained prominence, the relationship between the two women became strained, but Walker continues to acknowledge the assistance she received from Rukeyser (*We Are the Ones* 156). Another important early influence was the poet Jane Cooper.

Cooper was a prolific and well-respected poet, essayist, and teacher. Cooper taught at Sarah Lawrence College from 1950 until 1987 and worked closely with Walker. Cooper consistently praised the freshness and clarity of Walker's prose and recommended her for a writing fellowship grant at Harvard University's Radcliffe Institute. Walker dedicated her anthology of short stories *In Love and Trouble: Stories of Black Women* (1973) to Cooper. The women remained friends until Cooper's death in 2007.

Upon graduation from Sarah Lawrence in 1966, Walker determined to use her newly acquired credentials in the service of others. For several months, she remained in New York and worked at a welfare office in the city, but was drawn back to the South by her receipt of a grant from the Legal Defense and Educational Fund of the National Association for the Advancement of Colored People (NAACP). The grant took her to Mississippi where she worked with Marian Wright Edelman, who eventually founded the Children's Defense Fund. During the next decade or so and in the violence of the 1960s and 1970s in Mississippi, Walker continued her activism and her writing while married to Mel Leventhal. Before divorcing in 1976, the couple had their daughter Rebecca Grant Leventhal in 1969. Now known as Rebecca Grant Walker, she has become an activist and writer herself.

Walker's public stature changed permanently as she transformed her identity as a respected writer of two novels and short story and poetry collections into that of an internationally known, bestselling author with the publication of her third novel, *The Color Purple* (1982). *The Color Purple* is simultaneously Walker's most acclaimed and reviled work. While the novel earned the first Pulitzer Prize for Fiction awarded to an African American woman and also received the National Book Award, among other honors, it was also the target of scathing rebukes from quarters of the African American public and academic communities, the substance of which centered on accusations that the novel presents black male characters in negative ways.

One of the criticisms Walker has received is grounded in the perception that her allegiance to the second wave of the feminist movement trumps her concerns as an African American. The second wave of American feminism, as it emerged in the 1950s and 1960s was largely focused on the political, social, and economic interests of white, middle-class, heterosexual women. The beginning of the second wave movement is associated with women's changing role in American life during World War II, about the time Walker was born. With the male labor force largely involved in the military, women, particularly white middle-class women, worked in ways that previously had been largely prohibited. The second wave of feminism began for the most part as an intellectual movement with books such as Simone de Beauvoir's 1949 *The Second Sex*, Betty Freidan's 1963 *The Feminine Mystique*, and Erica Jong's 1973 *Fear of Flying*. Although different in focus, each book was an important influence on generations of women who recognized within the texts truths about the inequalities women experience and how that lack of equality limited their opportunities.

Important central issues of the second wave of American feminism were: acknowledgment and resolution of pay inequities; access to birth control; legalizing abortion; and ending violence, domestic abuse, and sexual harassment against women. Important institutions developed that worked to advance the fight for women's equality, including the National Organization for Women, founded in 1966 and *Ms.* magazine, cofounded by Alice Walker's close friend Gloria Steinem in 1971. A major objective for many of those involved in the second wave of feminism was passage of the Equal Rights Amendment. Second wave feminists also confronted issues of women's sexuality and tried to amend restrictive gender-specific cultural practices through awareness, education, and legislation. Women studies programs developed in American colleges and universities, and feminist theoretical inquiry became a common tool for intellectual analysis.

The second wave of feminism, like the first, was forced to confront issues of class and race. Minority and poor women articulated their concerns that the major voices in the feminist movement did not include their perspectives and that they remained invisible and voiceless in the struggle for women's equality. This belief led to the formation of feminist groups that were identity specific, such as the National Black Feminist Organization founded in 1973. Alice Walker was a central figure in the generation of second wave feminists and was particularly involved in articulating the schism between black and white feminists. Walker's integration of women of color, sexual plurality, sensuality, and spirituality into public understandings of female experience was widely embraced as a framework that destigmatized women's liberation for many by integrating the race, class, and gender struggles of a variety of women. *The Color Purple* reflects the complexity and multiplicity of her intersectional identity and advocacy. Its longevity affirms and vindicates the transcendent power of the narrative.

In 1985, Steven Spielberg released the film version of Walker's Pulitzer Prize–winning novel. Menno Meyjes wrote the screenplay for the film. Walker had written a screenplay version of *The Color Purple* that Spielberg chose not to use. Walker has written extensively about her involvement in the production of the film version of *The Color Purple* in her book *The Same River Twice: Honoring the Difficult—A*

Meditation on Life, Spirit, Art, and the Making of the Film, The Color Purple, *Ten Years Later* (1996). Walker includes in that book her original version of the screenplay, entitled *Watch for Me in the Sunset.*

Walker details in the account her sense of the distinctions between the novel and the film, which include Spielberg's emphasis on the brutality of Mister without the counterbalance of the story of Nettie and Celie's real father, the depiction of Mister and Harpo's incompetence as buffoonish and comic, and the distillation of the intimacy between Celie and Shug to a single kiss. Many of the same voices that objected to Walker's novel on the grounds that its depictions of black men were prejudicial found the same flaws in the film. The resonant narrative Walker created with her novel *The Color Purple* also found expression as a musical. The story line of the musical is largely the same as the Spielberg film version of *The Color Purple* except that the lesbian relationship between Celie and Shug is not hidden or subverted. Walker was not directly involved in the creation of the musical.

The same year she won the Pulitzer Prize, Walker published what is, arguably, her most important collection of essays, *In Search of Our Mothers' Gardens* (1983), an anthology of Walker's nonfiction written between the years 1967 and 1982. The anthology features thirty-six essays, letters, speeches, reviews, and previously unpublished pieces and is best known for its opening pages where Walker provides an outline of her term *womanist*, a concept she variously defines as "a black feminist or feminist of color," "a woman who loves other women, sexually and/or nonsexually," a lover of music, dance, the moon and self, among other open-ended possibilities, and concludes with the statement that "[w]omanist is to feminist as purple to lavender" (xi–xii).

According to Walker's definition of womanism, feminism is inappropriately narrow for black women, as well as for others who wish to embrace an inclusive and humanist vision of the world. Although womanism shares commonalities with feminism, it represents an expansion beyond its traditional concerns and definitions. The introduction of womanism spawned a debate over its implications. Womanism has become an important theoretical movement that has influenced scholars to analyze literature in womanist terms by relying on analyses of self-affirmation, female tradition, and matrilineal inheritance, among other themes. Walker's definition transformed the field of black women's studies.

The success of *The Color Purple* did not diminish Walker's productivity. She followed *In Search of Our Mothers' Gardens* with the publication of her poetry collection *Horses Make a Landscape Look More Beautiful* in 1984 and the cofounding of an independent publishing company Wild Trees Press, which continued operations until 1988. Walker also became more public about her bisexuality. The late 1980s also saw the publication of Walker's children's book *To Hell with Dying* (1988) and *Living by the Word* (1988), an essay collection featuring reflections on crafting *The Color Purple* and other contemporary themes. Walker's fourth novel, *The Temple of My Familiar* (1989), was a follow-up work to *The Color Purple* and featured some of the earlier novel's characters and themes. The novel is an ambitious foray into the complexities of nothing less than human history itself.

In the 1980s and 1990s, Alice Walker expanded her role as an activist to include the antinuclear and anti-apartheid movements. Alice Walker has supported the antinuclear movement by lending her name, presence, and art to various expressions of protest. Of particular concern to her is the safety of workers in various industries associated with nuclear energy and weaponry, as well as the preservation of a nontoxic environment in and around households in relatively close proximity to nuclear facilities. She has taken part in many public protests and her fiction and nonfiction writings frequently have as their major themes the struggle against nuclear power and weaponry, as well as environmental preservation generally. Walker is deeply committed to fighting against nuclear proliferation and energy; she sees them as inevitably linked to the destruction of humanity and the earth.

During these years, Walker's political concerns broadened as well. The term *apartheid* refers to the legalized system of segregation and discrimination practiced against blacks in South Africa from 1948 until 1991. Anti-apartheid movements in South Africa, led most prominently by the African National Congress (ANC), were the central voices opposing the system of apartheid. Alice Walker and many other writers, intellectuals, and celebrities contributed their time, money, and art to the efforts to end apartheid.

In 1991, in the midst of these activist engagements, Walker published her third children's book, *Finding the Green Stone*, and her sixth poetry collection, *Her Blue Body Everything We Know*, followed the next year by her fifth novel, *Possessing the Secret of Joy* (1992). Like *Temple of My Familiar*, the novel references incidents and characters from Walker's *The Color Purple*. The novel is, in part, the tale of a central character's struggle with female genital mutilation. Walker became an advocate in the movement to end the practice. As a consequence, Walker and British-Indian filmmaker Pratibha Parmar produced *Warrior Marks* (1993), a documentary and a companion book on female genital mutilation.

Walker's mother, Minnie Tallulah Grant Walker, died in 1993. The next year, Walker changed her middle name from Malsenior to Tallulah-Kate to honor the women from whom she is descended. Following the 1994 release of *Alice Walker: The Complete Stories*, an anthology of all of Walker's previously published short fiction, Walker published *The Same River Twice: Honoring the Difficult* (1996). The book focuses on Walker's responses to the various controversies surrounding the novel and film versions of *The Color Purple*. Continuing her explorations in nonfiction, Walker penned and published the highly personal collection of essays, letters, and reflections on political activism she entitled *Anything We Love Can Be Saved* (1997).

Entering her fifth decade as an author, Walker proved as prolific as she was during the first four. Between the years 1998 and 2008 Walker produced the novel *By the Light of My Father's Smile* (1998); a new collection of short stories, *The Way Forward Is with a Broken Heart* (2000); a short book, *Sent by Earth: A Message from the Grandmother*

Spirit (2001), in which she examines the national and global impact of the September 11, 2001, World Trade Center and Pentagon attacks; two new poetry collections, *Absolute Trust in the Goodness of the Earth* (2003) and *A Poem Traveled Down My Arm* (2003); an audio recording with ordained Buddhist nun Pema Chödrön, *Pema Chödrön and Alice Walker in Conversation: On the Meaning of Suffering and the Mystery of Joy* (2005); the essay collection *We Are the Ones We Have Been Waiting For* (2006), featuring a tribute to revolutionaries of the past such as Dr. Martin Luther King Jr. and Fidel Castro and suggesting the need for contemporary activist strategies; and the children's books *There Is a Flower at the Tip of My Nose Smelling Me* (2006) and *Why War Is Never a Good Idea* (2007).

Reflecting the transformation in publishing, communications, and social media that has taken place during her years as a public figure, in 2008, Walker began a website and blog entitled Alice Walker's Garden (Alicewalkersgarden.com). On the site she notes the origins of the new venue as a consequence of having turned sixty. Walker reveals that the chronological milestone freed her from the need to connect writing with the construction of a public identity and that she is attracted to the dynamic nature and democracy of the webpage. After her birthday she anticipated spending the rest of her life wandering and meditating and, although she did not expect to want to share those experiences publicly, she has been drawn to do so because of the power of those experiences and also as a result of her excitement about the 2007 political campaign and the candidacy of Barack Obama, whom she endorsed. In addition to the home page, the website includes an official biography, photos, audio, interviews, poems, bibliographic materials, public appearances, press releases, and her blog.

The year 2010 also proved prolific for Walker. In that year she published the short volume *Overcoming Speechlessness: A Poet Encounters the Horror in Rwanda, Eastern Congo, and Palestine/Israel*; a poetry collection, *Hard Times Require Furious Dancing*; and a series of interviews entitled *The World Has Changed: Conversations with*

Alice Walker, edited by her friend, the late Emory University professor Rudolph Byrd. In 2011, *The Chicken Chronicles*, another nonfiction collection, was published and received warm reviews. Walker has also made news as a result of her involvement with the Israeli/Palestinian conflict. In the summer of 2011, Walker joined a group of American activists and journalists aboard a ship called *The Audacity of Hope*. The group was joined by a coalition of pro-Palestinian supporters who planned to protest the Israeli blockade of Gaza by attempting to sail from Greece to Gaza. Although the effort was not successful, the incident is characteristic of Alice Walker. She remains uncompromising in her articulation of and willingness to act in support of what she believes is right. Like Celie, her long-lived and controversial protagonist, Walker remains, most assuredly, "here."

Works Cited

"Alice Walker Goes Home to Eatonton, Georgia for 'Color Purple' Premiere." *Jet Magazine* 10 Feb. 1986: 28–30.

Arrighi, Bob. *Staughton and Alice Lynd Collection*. University Libraries, Kent State University, 10 Jan. 2012. Web. 28 Feb. 2011.

Bates, Gerri. *Alice Walker: A Critical Companion*. Westport, CT: Greenwood, 2005.

Driscoll, Margarette. "The Day Feminist Icon Alice Walker Resigned as My Mother: *The Color Purple* Brought Alice Walker Global Fame, but Her Strident Views Led to an Irreconcilable Rift, Her Daughter Tells." *Sunday Times* 4 May 2008.

Guy-Sheftall, Beverly. "Black Women and Higher Education: Spelman and Bennett Colleges Revisited." *Journal of Negro Education* 51.3 (1982): 278–87.

Howard Zinn: You Can't Be Neutral on a Moving Train. Dir. Deb Ellis and Dennis Mueller. Perf. Howard Zinn, Matt Damon, Alice Walker, First Run, 2005. Film.

Kershner, Isabel. "Israel Rescinds Its Warning to Gaza-Bound Journalists. *The New York Times*. NY Times Co., 27 June 2011. Web. 10 July 2011.

Lauret, Maria. *Alice Walker*. New York: Macmillan, 2000.

Lefever, Harry G. *Undaunted by the Fight: Spelman College and the Civil Rights Movement, 1957–1967*. Macon, GA: Mercer UP, 2005.

Logan, Rayford. *What the Negro Wants*. Chapel Hill: U of North Carolina P, 1944.

Lynd, Robert S., and Helen Merrell Lynd. *Middletown: A Study in Contemporary American Culture*. New York: Harcourt, 1929.

_____. *Middletown in Transition: A Study in Cultural Conflicts*. New York: Harcourt, 1937.

Morejon, Nancy; Alice Walker, ed. *Letters of Love and Hope: The Story of the Cuban Five*. Melbourne, Austral: Ocean, 2005.

Read, Florence M. *The Story of Spelman College*. Princeton, NJ: Princeton UP, 1961.

Rosenbloom, Stephanie. "Evolution of a Feminist Daughter." *New York Times*. NY Times Co., 17 Mar. 2007. Web. 28 Feb. 2011

Saxe, Robert Frances. *Settling Down: World War II Veteran's Challenge to the Postwar Consensus*. New York: Palgrave, 2007.

The Color Purple. Dir. Steven Spielberg. Perf. Whoopi Goldberg, Oprah Winfrey, Danny Glover. Warner Bros., 1985. Film.

Walker, Alice. *Absolute Trust in the Goodness of the Earth: New Poems*. New York: Random, 2003.

_____. *Alice Walker: Banned*. San Francisco: Aunt Lute, 1996.

_____. *Anything We Love Can Be Saved: A Writer's Activism*. New York: Random, 1997.

_____. *By the Light My Father's Smile*. New York: Random, 1998.

_____. *The Chicken Chronicles*. New York: New Press, 2011.

_____. *The Color Purple: A Novel*. New York: Pocket, 1982.

_____. *The Complete Stories*. London: Phoenix, 2005.

_____. *Finding the Green Stone*. Illus. by Catherine Deeter. New York: Harcourt, 1991.

_____. *Five Poems*. Highland Park, MI: Broadside, 1972.

_____. *Good Night, Willie Lee, I'll See You in the Morning*. New York: Harcourt, 1979.

_____. *Hard Times Require Furious Dancing*. Novato, California: New World Lib., 2010.

_____. *Her Blue Body Everything We Know: Earthling Poems 1965–1990 Complete*. New York: Harvest Poems, 1991.

_____. *Horses Make a Landscape Look More Beautiful*. New York: Harcourt, 1984.

_____. *In Love and Trouble: Stories of Black Women*. New York: Harcourt, 1973.

_____. *In Search of Our Mothers' Gardens: A Womanist Prose*. New York: Harcourt, 1983.

_____. *Langston Hughes: American Poet*. Illustrated by Don Miller. New York: Amistad, 2002.

_____. *Living by the Word: Selected Writings, 1973–1987*. San Diego: Harcourt, 1988.

_____. *Meridian*. New York: Pocket, 1976.

_____. *Now Is the Time to Open Your Heart*. New York: Random, 2004.

_____. *Once: Poems*. New York: Harcourt, 1968.

_____. *Overcoming Speechlessness: A Poet Encounters the Horror in Rwanda, Eastern Congo, and Palestine/Israel*. New York: Open Media, 2010.

_____. *A Poem Traveled Down My Arm: Poems and Drawings*. New York: Random, 2003.

_____. *Possessing the Secret of Joy*. New York: Washington Sq., 1992.

_____. *Revolutionary Petunias and Other Poems*. New York: Harcourt, 1973.

_____. *The Same River Twice: Honoring the Difficult, Meditations on Life Spirit, Art, and the Making of* The Color Purple. New York: Scribner, 1996.

_____. "Saying Goodbye to My Friend Howard Zinn." *Boston Globe*. NY Times Co., 31 Jan. 2010. Web. 16 July 2011.

_____. *Sent by Earth: A Message from the Grandmother Spirit After the Bombing of the World Trade Center and the Pentagon.* New York: Open, 2001.

_____. *The Temple of My Familiar.* New York: Washington Sq., 1989.

_____. *There Is a Flower at the Tip of My Nose Smelling Me.* Illustrated by Stefano Vitale. New York: Harper, 2006.

_____. *The Third Life of Grange Copeland.* New York: Pocket, 1970.

_____. *To Hell with Dying.* Illustrated by Catherine Deeter New York: Voyager, 1988.

_____. *The Way Forward Is with a Broken Heart.* New York: Ballantine, 2000.

_____. *We Are the One We Have Been Waiting For: Inner Light in a Time of Darkness.* New York: New Press, 2006.

_____. *The World Has Changed: Conversations with Alice Walker.* Ed. Rudolph P. Byrd. New York: New Press, 2010.

_____. *You Can't Keep a Good Woman Down.* New York: Harcourt, 1981.

Walker, Alice, ed. *I Love Myself When I Am Laughing . . . and Then Again When I Am Looking Mean and Impressive: A Zora Neale Hurston Reader.* Old Westbury, NY: Feminist, 1979.

Walker, Alice, and Isabel Allende. *Giving Birth: Finding Form.* Boulder, CO: Sounds True, 1993. Audiocassette.

Walker, Alice, and Pema Chödrön. *Pema Chödrön and Alice Walker in Conversation on the Meaning of Suffering and the Mystery of Joy.* Sounds True, 2005. CD.

Walker, Alice, and Pratibha Parmar. *Warrior Marks: Female Genital Mutilation and the Sexual Blinding of Women.* New York: Harcourt, 1996.

Walker, Alice, and Michael Toms. *Gardening the Soul.* Carlsbad, CA: Hay, 2000. Audiocassette.

Walker, Rebecca. *Baby Love: Choosing Motherhood after a Lifetime of Ambivalence.* Riverhead, 2007.

_____. *Black, White, and Jewish: Autobiography of a Shifting Self.* New York: Riverhead, 2001.

_____. *Rebecca Walker.* Rebecca Walker, n. d. Web. 28 Feb. 2009.

White, Evelyn C. *Alice Walker: A Life.* New York: Norton, 2004.

Zinn, Howard. *A People's History of the United States: 1492–Present.* 1980. New York, Harper, 2003.

Pushing Gender Scripts and Color Lines in Alice Walker's *The Color Purple* and Sapphire's *Push*_____

Ciara Miller

Both Alice Walker and Sapphire trace the historical roots of race and gender oppression in the characters of their novels *The Color Purple* and *Push*. Their protagonists, Celie and Precious, illustrate an urge to repossess their voices through writing and witnessing other women exercise agency. In the former novel, the narrator's sister (Nettie), her daughter-in-law (Sofia), and love interest (Shug Avery), inspire her to liberate herself by being, respectively, educated, nonmuzzled, and sexually self-gratifying. In the latter novel, Precious discovers her voice through the assistance of GED instructor, Ms. Blue Rain, who encourages her to document her life tribulations. Although the novel depicts a time in the 1980s (unlike the former novel, which captures the late twentieth century), Sapphire's Precious is a near carbon copy of Celie. Both authors demonstrate the cyclical damage of slavery and the effect it has on the mind and body of their characters. However, *The Color Purple* grants its heroine the ability to rebuild a kinship with her sister and children, while *Push* illustrates the irrevocable consequences of blacks reenacting slave master and slave relationships.

Celie is raped by her father and husband; Precious is molested by both mother and father. In the former novel, Mr. _____ behaves much like the white slave master who can have his pick of any slave girl. Precious's mother is abusive partially due to her inability to see herself as meeting the white standard of beauty. Both antagonists commit crimes against the bodies of these women due to an urge to *possess* like the master. Celie and Precious seek sisterhood outside their bloodline to understand a love that can be shared amongst women. According to critic Linda Abbandonato's "A View from 'Elsewhere'" both novels can be categorized as "womanist" texts. Walker gives several definitions for the term: "A black feminist or feminist of color . . . Usually referring to outrageous, audacious, courageous, or willful behavior

---

. . . A woman who loves other women, sexually and/or nonsexually" (1107).

I examine the recurring theme of black Americans using the tactics of white oppressors to gain a sense of self-worth, even at the cost of abusing their own children, and examine in *The Color Purple* Celie's relationships with other characters including Pa, Nettie, Mr. _____, Sofia, and Shug Avery to demonstrate how she is directly affected by and accepts their concepts of race and gender. In *Push*, history influences Precious's self-perception, and her interactions with her father, mother, Ms. Rain, Ms. Weiss, and classmates. Both Celie and Precious push gender scripts and color lines in order to grow as individuals who reimagine history and work toward building a better future.

In *The Color Purple*, Celie's agency is compressed by racist, heterosexist, and linguistic oppressions. She has no possession of self or of her sexuality. She has been raped by Pa (the man she believes is her father) and impregnated twice. Both times he disposes of her children. Reflecting on his perception of her and his criminal acts, she writes: "He act like he can't stand me no more. Say I'm evil an always up to no good" (3). Celie is not allowed to possess her children. Like a slave master, Pa usurps her authority as mother by removing her children. He also defines what is good and bad without turning the gaze toward his own atrocities similar to the way many white slave masters equated the blackness of their slaves with evil. Celie's acceptance of Pa's ability to define power obstructs her assessment of self.

In the very beginning of the novel, Pa says to Celie: "You better not tell nobody but God" (1). According to critic Cheung King-Kok, in Celie's subconscious mind, the almighty God merges with the all-powerful earthly father" (Cheung 166). Although she writes to God, she does so with restraint because she views the higher power as masculine and many of the men she knows have persecuted her. Later in the novel, when she envisions God as a woman, she is able to write to her sister Nettie. She unfetters her thoughts and writes with the belief that she will be heard.

Pa removes Celie from school after her first pregnancy while Nettie is allowed to continue her schooling and teaches Celie how to read (16). Pa later separates the sisters by giving Celie to Mr. _____, along with a cow, stating: "She good with children . . . Never heard her say a hard word to nary one of them. Just give 'em everything they ast for, is the only problem" (11). Pa obviously believes she can have an alternative response to the children's commands and subconsciously wants her to repossess her voice and say "no." However, Mr. _____ establishes the same authoritarian rule over Celie as her father; she is beaten and forced to provide domestic care to him and his children. His lack of a last name implies that he is entitled to respect solely because of his gender and not because of any respectability that is traditionally indicated by a family's last name.

Celie seems to build a relationship with Mr. _____'s oldest son, Harpo, who has a romantic interest in Sofia. Sofia does not fit the general script of standardized white beauty despite having "bright skin," an asset often admired by African Americans due to its presumed proximity to whiteness. Sofia is a heavy-set woman, who, unlike Celie has a mind of her own and isn't afraid to express it. When Harpo asks his father how to make her "mind," Mr. _____ says: "Well how you spect to make her mind? Wives is like children. You have to let 'em know who got the upper hand. Nothing can do that better than a good sound beating" (35).

After taking his father's advice, his face is "a mess of bruises" (36). Sofia fought him back and later explained to Celie:

All my life I had to fight. I had to fight my daddy. I had to fight my brothers. I had to fight my cousins and my uncles. A girl child ain't safe in a
family of men. But I never thought I'd have to fight in my own house. . . .
I loves Harpo . . . God knows I do. But I'll kill him dead before I let him
beat me. Now if you want a dead son-in-law you just keep on advising him
like you doing (40).

The reader can clearly distinguish Sofia from Celie. When Sofia defends herself, Celie observes her virility. Celie's fascination with self-governing women is furthered by Shug Avery, "a sexy and snappy blues singer" (Cheung 167). She is aware of Mr. _____'s lust for Shug upon first entering his home. Celie stares at Shug's photo and views her as someone who can guide her toward freedom. After Shug comes to stay with the family, she converses with Celie about Mr. _____: "He weak . . . Can't make up his mind what he want. And from what you tell me he a bully" (77). She has not experienced the same brutality he has inflicted upon Celie because she takes ownership of herself. She encourages Celie to explore her sexuality when discussing her sexual experiences with Mr. _____. "I have to confess, I just *love* it. Don't you?" (77) Celie responds that he "just do his business, get off, go to sleep" (77). Shug then asks Celie to look at herself "down there" and to examine her breasts to see the parts of her body that can lead to sexual satisfaction. According to Abbandonato:

> for Celie, the discovery of the clitoris (and of the possibility of sexual fulfillment with a woman) is accompanied by a whole range of other discoveries that relegate man to the margins of a world he has always dominated (1112).

Historically, the slave's job never included doing self-fulfilling work. Celie's body has always been used for the pleasure of another rather than her own. She is penetrated by both father and husband but never excited by the act. She only considers her breasts pleasing the tongues of her babies that have never been in her care. Celie's love and admiration for Shug allows her to construct a new identity.

Celie's turn from docility to womanist unfolds alongside her sister's narrative. Nettie runs away from a life of servitude and escapes to Africa as a missionary. Coincidentally, she works alongside Celie's children and their adopted parents, Samuel and Corrine. Nettie writes to her sister about her adventures throughout the years, but Mr. _____

hides her letters in attempts to keep Celie ignorant. Like a slave master, he wants to prevent her from seeking freedom. Together, Shug and Celie discover a heap of hidden letters in his trunk (126). In one letter, Nettie writes about how literacy has been Celie's savior: "I remember one time you said your life made you feel so ashamed you couldn't even talk about it to God, you had to write it, bad as you thought your writing was" (130).

At the very beginning of the novel, Celie writes about the cruelties inflicted upon her because she does not believe God will listen with compassion to her voice. All of the men in her life have acted as dictators. Through writing letters to Nettie, she reenvisions a God as a woman, which permits her to recognize her own power.

Nettie discloses the bias of certain orthodox religious teachings and confirms what Celie has learned from Sofia and Shug: it is okay to establish a sense of self that deviates from societal norms. Nettie writes to Celie that in the Olinkas' version of the biblical creation myth, Adam was not the first man but the "first man that was white" and that Adam and Eve were driven out not by God but by blacks (Cheung 167). Despite being abused by black men and living in an oppressed black environment, Celie is able to recognize the power of blacks.

During this time, Sofia, who has never accepted subservience, is imprisoned for refusing to work as a maid for the mayor's wife. She becomes a servant for the mayor's family while Harpo dates Squeak who is more silent and compliant with his demands (198). Instead of Celie being discouraged by what appears to be patriarchy's defeat of women's agency, she uses the strength she gathered from Sofia and other women characters to finally free herself of Mr. _____'s dictatorship. Shug asks Celie to travel with her as she pursues her singing career. Mr. _____ is intolerant of Celie leaving, which causes her to explode:

> You a lowdown dog is what's wrong . . . It's time to leave you and enter into the Creation. And your dead body just the welcome mat I need. . . . You took my sister Nettie away from me. . . . And she was the only person

love me in the world. . . . But Nettie and my children coming home soon. And when she do, all us together gon whup your ass. . . . I got children . . . being brought up in Africa. Good school, lots of fresh air and exercise. Turning out a heap better than the fools you didn't even try to raise (200).

Harpo attempts to interject, but Celie gives him a piece of her mind: "if you hadn't tried to rule over Sofia the white folks never would have caught her . . . you was all rotten children, I say. You made my life a hell on earth. And your daddy ain't dead horse's shit" (200).

Mr. _____ reaches across the table to slap Celie; she picks up a knife and jabs it into his hand. He calls her a bitch, a derogatory title to assert his masculine power over her, but his tyrannical tactics to keep her under his control are no longer effective. She has discovered her voice and has every intention to continue using it.

After traveling with Shug, Celie realizes her creative talent for making pants. "I got pants now in every color and size under the sun. Since us started making pants down home, I ain't been able to stop. I change the cloth, I change the print, I change the waist, I change the pocket. I change the hem, I change the fullness of the leg" (211). Shug helps Celie expand her own business by posting advertisements and suggesting that she get women workers to help sew and cut the fabric—this is revolutionary for many women in the early 1900s (213). Many were confined to domestic duties and dependent on the man's income. The various pants she makes are symbolic of the different personas she can take on while still taking ownership of herself or "wearing the pants."

Shug later falls in love with a younger man while still claiming to be in love with Celie: "all I ast is six months. Just six months to have my last fling. I got to have it Celie. I'm too weak a woman not to. But if you give me six months, Celie, I will try to make our life together like it was" (250). Despite being Celie's source of inspiration to speak out against Mr. _____, Shug now appears to be incapable of detaching herself from men. Celie, grounded in her new sense of self, responds: "I love you. . . . But I can't stay here" (251). She finally understands her need for loyalty and is willing to walk away from a relationship if it is not achieved, unlike when she first lived with Mr. _____ and did not mind Shug sleeping with him.

Ironically, one of the only people who Celie believes understands her heartbreak is Mr. _____, who now illustrates a sense of maturity and understanding since she has left. They speak to one another like old friends, instead of enemies. When reflecting on Shug, Mr. _____ says, "Shug act more manly than most men. I mean she upright, honest. Speak her mind and the devil take the hindmost. You know Shug will fight. Just like Sofia. She bound to live her life and be herself no matter what" (269).

Within his statement is the assumption that only men are unafraid to speak their minds. Celie refutes: "Harpo not like this. You not like this. What Shug got is womanly . . . Specially since she and Sofia the ones got it" (269). Mr. _____ understands Shug to be a woman who does not subscribe to gender roles. He then goes on to confess his awareness of Celie's suffering throughout the years: "if a mule could tell folks how it's treated, it would. But you know some womens would have just love to hear they man say he beat his wife cause she wasn't them" (271). He does not yet understand what many of the women characters in the text have come to understand and that is their need to support one another because all are suffering from the same oppressive patriarchal system that would render them voiceless.

Celie shares her knowledge of Africa with Mr. _____, explaining to him that the way gender is constructed in the United States is different from how it is fashioned there: "Men and women both preshate a nice dress . . . and men sew in Africa, too" (271). With his matured sense of self, he confesses: "When I was growing up, I use to try to sew along with mama cause that's what she was always doing. But everybody laughed at me. But you know, I liked it" (271). Mr. _____ is no longer concerned about proving his manhood. He recognizes that he can no longer possess Celie, who does not support heteronormative values, and who has a clear sense of self. Instead of using oppressive tactics to degrade him, Celie comforts him: "Well, nobody gon laugh at you now . . . Here, help me stitch in these pockets" (271).

The cyclical effects of slavery are evident in Sapphire's *Push*. The novel is written more than a decade after *The Color Purple* and depicts a time at least six decades later, but the protagonist Precious bears several similarities to Celie. Both protagonists use the epistolary format to express their mistreatment despite not having a full grasp of the English language. Historically, African Americans were denied the right to literacy; it was a strategy to keep them from rebelling against their slave masters. Precious is a link in the chain of African Americans affected by literacy discrepancy due to race and socioeconomic status. Precious claims to have an interest in math class because she can protect the teacher from other students who try to take advantage of the instructor. However, she behaves volatilely toward her teacher when asked to turn to a particular page and read because she is illiterate. She explodes, " 'I say, I ain' going nowhere mutherfucker till the bell ring. I came here to learn maff and you gon' teach me.' . . . I didn't want to hurt him or embarrass him like that you know. But I couldn't let him, anybody, know, page 122 look like page 152, 22, 3, 6, 5—all the pages look alike to me" (Sapphire 5).

Precious, unlike Celie, has a brazenness attached to her language but does not fully possess herself or her words. Her speech is given to her from her mother who speaks "ugly" because she does not feel beautiful by white societal standards. Precious is kicked out of school because she is sixteen years old and pregnant for the second time, and presumably violent by nature; however, the reader can see that she tries to defend herself against people who she believes attack first. When Mrs. Lichenstein, a white woman who is Precious's social worker, inquires about her pregnancies, like Miss Beasley does regarding Celie, and discovers the children are from her father, which Miss Beasley does not discover, Precious understands that the social worker regards her as animalistic and sexually deviant. Precious reverses these images and calls Mrs. Lichenstein a cunt bucket: "That's what my muver call women she don't like, cunt buckets. I kinda get it and I kinda don't get it, but I like the way it sounds so I say it too" (7). Without full knowledge of what some of the words mean, she uses them as weapons because they have been used to dehumanize her. At home, Precious does not "wanna stand here 'n hear Mama call [her] slut" (9), but she propagates such language because it is familiar. The unloving, raging words used by her mother and the distance between herself and women like Mrs. Lichenstein leave her in a state of isolated repression. Precious cannot see Mrs. Lichenstein as an ally because she mainly sees their dissimilarities.

African American women have historically been viewed as over-sexualized and as incapable of being raped because their bodies invite violation. Precious's mother accepts this assertion by sexually assault-ing her daughter. She is incapable of empathizing with Precious's op-pression because she doesn't see herself as beautiful or deserving of something better than welfare. She wants the traditional nuclear fam-ily in which the household contains a mother and father; her desire for this perceived happiness comes from what she sees on television. Her daughter is excluded from the vision and she dismisses the cir-cumstances that prevent her dream from becoming reality, that is, her own ignorance, unemployability, and lack of self-awareness. When Mrs. Lichenstein rings their doorbell to discuss school opportunities, Precious's mother says: "Press LISTEN stupid!" Precious does not re-spond out loud to her mother's verbal abuse: "I wanna say I ain't stupid but I know I am so I don't say nothin', 'cause also I don't want her to go hit me" (15). Negative perceptions of self are fostered within her household. She does not yet possess the language to define a brighter future for herself. She accepts the master's definition of her, and in this case the master is female as opposed to male. Laurie Stapleton, author of *A New Learning System*, advocates for a Freirean "pedagogy [for] the oppressed." She writes: "Precious's suspension illustrates that "she has been oppressed and rejected by traditional educational institutions.

Precious's discontent with this decision reflects some level of desire—although unwitting—to liberate herself" (Stapleton 214).

The standard of white beauty is ubiquitous for Precious. She is constantly reminded that she does not fit the norm and therefore, her first child, born with Down syndrome, must also be ugly and/or disgraceful. Her father, very similar to the white slave master, Pa, and Mr. _____ from *The Color Purple*, assumes that she enjoys sex with him: "See, you LIKE it! You jus' like your mama—you die for it!" (24). He does not realize that the daughter and mother are dying to fit the white, hegemonic standard of beauty and womanhood. He is a product of the cyclical damage of slavery and wears the mask of the slave master. He acts not as the protector of his family, but as a predator; he feels he can have sex with any woman within his household.

Mrs. Lichenstein finally convinces Precious to attend GED classes where Ms. Rain will be her teacher. Ms. Rain exercises a mutually beneficial student-teacher relationship which allows students room to become critical thinkers (Stapleton 213). Precious reflects on her new experience reading *The Color Purple* while in school: "I cry cry cry you hear me, it sound in a way so much like myself" (Sapphire 81). Clearly Sapphire gives recognition to Alice Walker by naming *The Color Purple* in her own text.

Ms. Rain encourages Precious to develop her own ideas and nurtures her as she matures. Precious attaches standardized ideas of beauty upon each of her classmates before getting to know their stories. In observing Rhonda, she says: she has light-skin but "got big lips, pig nose, she fat fat" (43). Rhonda willingly volunteers information about why she is in the GED program, but Precious is unable to see the beauty in her openness because she has features similar to her own. She describes another classmate, Consuelo Montenegro, as being "a pretty Spanish girl, coffee-cream color wit long ol' good hair" (45). Precious regards her as more beautiful because of her physical attributes despite her being more profane and withdrawn from the class.

Precious appreciates the novel *The Color Purple* but proclaims: "I ain' no butch like Celie" (81). She is inspired by the speeches of black activist Louis Farrakhan, who encourages homophobia, but Ms. Rain, who identifies herself as a lesbian, argues that if Precious does not like homosexuals, then she doesn't like her (81). She reexamines her beliefs considering Ms. Rain has proven to be more loving toward her than her own mother. "Ms Rain say homos not who rape me, not homos who let me sit up not learn for sixteen years, not homos who sell crack fuck Harlem. It's true. Ms Rain the one who put the chalk in my hand, make me queen of the ABCs" (81).

Precious also draw parallels between Farrakhan's speeches about slavery and her relationship with her mother and father: "I think what my fahver do is what Farrakhan said the white man did to the black woman. Oh it was terrible and he dood it in front of the black man; that's really terrible." Farrakhan speaks of black men being hurt by witnessing slave masters having sex with black women slaves (Sapphire 68). Precious's mother is desensitized to Carl's rape of their daughter. The mother can be likened to the black man during slavery; she has parental power that cannot be fully accessed due to her oppressions. Precious's mom later tells her that her father died of the AIDS virus (85). Unlike *The Color Purple,* which ends with Celie being reunited with Nettie and her children, Precious knows her ending will be an early death.

Precious finds it difficult to discuss her personal life with her new social worker Ms. Weiss because she is white. Instead, Precious chooses to write in her journal like Celie, who also finds solace in writing. Ms. Weiss invites Precious's mother to discuss the domestic violence issues written about in her daughter's journals. Her mother confesses her desire to be loved at the risk of endangering her daughter.

So he on me. Then he reach over to Precious! Start wif his finger between her legs. I say Carl what you doing! He say shut your big ass up! This is good for her. Then he git off me, take off her Pampers and try to stick his thing in Precious. . . . I say stop Carl stop! I want him on *me*! I never wanted him to hurt her. I didn't want him doing *anything* to her. I wanted my man for myself. Sex me up, not my chile. So you cain't blame all that shit happen to Precious on *me*. I love Carl, I love him. He her daddy, but he was my man!" (135–6)

During this moment one can view the mother as pitifully human or blatantly profane. Her willingness to subject her daughter to the husband's abuse stems from feeling undesirable; however her narcissistic feelings are no excuse for aiding and abetting her own daughter's destruction. Precious's innocence is denied to her before she could ever vocalize an objection. Her mother fails to see that sex does not guarantee love, commitment, or an unburdened life.

The institution of family coupled with the silence and shame of incest and sexual abuse create the spiritual destitution of the female protagonists in *The Color Purple* and in *Push*. Both Celie and Precious desperately need to define themselves. For Precious, the failures of the educational system as well as media propaganda shape her self-perception. Celie's lack of formal education puts her in a vulnerable position, and the time in which she lived forced her to learn to comply with male authority in order to survive.

Both protagonists are unable to use "proper" English, but their versions of black English, one Southern folk speech and the other urban ghetto talk, enable them to assert selfhood. Celie thinks to herself: "Look like to me only a fool would want to you to talk in a way that feel peculiar to your mind" (216). Both Celie and Precious speak a language that is self-created and practical. Prior to seeking self-possession, many of the ideas they had of themselves were handed down to them and did not fit their personal truths. Abbandonato states eloquently: "if women are constituted as subjects in a man-made language, then it is only through the cracks in language, and in the places where ideology fails, that they can begin to reconstruct themselves" (1108).

In an interview with Kelvin Christopher James, Sapphire has said that "one of the myths we've been taught is that oppression creates moral superiority. I'm here to tell you that the more oppressed a person is, the more oppressive they will be" (45). She later retracts a bit by listing the choices people have in dealing with oppression: "even when in slavery, in our most deprived state, we had choices. . . . We can say that Precious' mother and father, and many of the people in the culture, find themselves in a steel box. That's how bad the oppression is. You can sit there in that steel box, you can kill yourself in that box, or you can turn on your young and kill yourself that way. Even when the choices are limited, you still have choices" (*BOMB* 42). One can choose to do none of the aforementioned as Walker's text illustrates. The affirmation of the human spirit to rise from any circumstance and strive for a better life is what makes *The Color Purple* a classic in a way that *Push: A Novel* might never be.

When examining Celie and Precious, one may assert that the more oppressed a person is, the more likely he or she is to acquiesce to systemic oppression, but despite the propagation of violence being a possibility for the protagonists, both illustrate the ability to break away from a chain of abuse. They find themselves in steel boxes, their home environments, where they refuse to kill themselves or their young. Instead, they realize other women are in the same box but face a different side: domestic violence, homophobia, drug addiction, etc. Recognizing that others, who are seemingly different, battle similar repressions allows for the protagonists to necessitate reimagining and reinventing themselves. But unlike Celie, Precious faces a doomed future resulting from her exposure to the AIDS virus. Unlike Mr. _____ in *The Color Purple*, there are no transformations of the villainous characters in Sapphire's book. This is not to say that oppression does not sometimes decimate the human spirit, for any check of facts demonstrates that abuse can appear to destroy all that is human. However, the point that Walker makes is that it does not have to. The myth "oppression creates moral superiority" is not necessarily a myth, for if it does not kill you, it might indeed lay the foundation for moral excellence.

Works Cited

Abbandonato, Linda. "'A View from "Elsewhere': Subversive Sexuality and the Rewriting of the Heroine's Story in *The Color Purple*." *PMLA* 106.5 (1991): 1106–115. *JSTOR*. Web. 9 Mar. 2012.

Cheung, King-Kok. "'Don't Tell': Imposed Silences in *The Color Purple* and *The Woman Warrior*." PMLA 103.2 (1988): 162–74. *JSTOR*. Web. 9 Mar. 2012.

Sapphire. *Push: A Novel*. New York: Vintage, 1997.

_____. "Sapphire." Interview by Kelvin Christopher James. *BOMB* 57 (1996): 42–45. *JSTOR*. Web. 9 Mar. 2012.

Stapleton, Laurie. "New Learning System: A Freirean Reading of Sapphire's Push." *Women's Studies Quarterly* 32.1/2 (2004): 213–33. *JSTOR*. Web. 9 Mar. 2012

Walker, Alice. *The Color Purple: A Novel*. New York: Harcourt, 1982.

CRITICAL READINGS

"But Where Was the *Man* in Me?" Alice Walker's *The Third Life of Grange Copeland*

Rudolph P. Byrd

The Third Life of Grange Copeland, Alice Walker's debut novel, is the first in a series of major works of fiction—*In Love and Trouble: Stories of Black Women*, *Meridian*, and *The Color Purple*—which take place in her native Georgia. *The Third Life of Grange Copeland* is a historical novel spanning the period from 1920 to 1960. "The most disturbing incident in the novel," writes Walker in her afterword to the novel, "the brutal murder of a woman and mother by her husband and the father of her children, is unfortunately based on a real case. In my small hometown of Eatonton, Georgia, there was when I was growing up, and there still is now, an incredible amount of violence" (342). Most incredibly, as Walker tells us, the woman, shot in the face by her husband, was also named Walker. Walker became familiar with the tragic case of Mrs. Walker through the late Ruth Walker, one of her elder sisters, who for a period of time was a cosmetologist, and who applied her "magic tricks arsenal of assorted powders and paints" to both the living and the dead (343). Ruth invited her younger sister to the black funeral home, which was located next door to the black beauty shop, to witness her efforts to prepare Mrs. Walker for her funeral.

Walker gazed upon the corpse of Mrs. Walker, "the victim around whose demise [the novel] is built," and even then she was practicing the cold-eyed objectivity so essential to the artist. "I describe her in the novel exactly as she appeared to me then," recalls Walker. "Writing about it years later was the only way I could be free of such a powerful and despairing image. Still, I see it; not so much the shattered face— time has helped to erase the vividness of that sight—but always and always the one calloused foot, the worn, run-over shoe with a ragged hole, covered with newspaper, in its bottom" (343). In contemplating the ravaged body of Mrs. Walker, Walker experienced an expansion of consciousness for she realized that Mrs. Walker's experiences were emblematic of the experiences of black women in her family, and women beyond her family. Another result, among many, of Walker's fateful encounter with a victim of domestic violence was the creation of the character Mem, the dignified, brave but doomed wife of Brownfield Copeland, her husband and murderer. "Seeing the dead body of Mrs. Walker there on the enamel table, I realized that indeed, she might have been my own mother and that perhaps in relation to men she was also symbolic of all women, not only including my husband's grandmother and mother, who were as different from my own, I had thought, as possible, but also of me. That is why she is named Mem, in the novel, after the French *la même*, meaning 'the same'" (344).

The vivid and spare language whose function is to produce clear images, to enable us to see, in this case, the destruction of Mem, is one of the strengths of Walker's novel, and a hallmark of her fiction. Occurring in December 1944 just before Christmas, Mem's death comes at the end of yet another long day as a domestic, a job that is an outcome of the carefully planned "come down" by her husband Brownfield. She is going home to rest, she hopes, in preparation for another day of service to a white family, but Brownfield, in his role as murderer, gives her eternal rest: "Mem looked up at the porch and called a greeting. It was a cheerful greeting, although she sounded very tired, tired and out of breath. Brownfield began to curse and came and stood on the steps until Mem got within the circle of the light. Then he aimed the gun with drunken accuracy right into her face and fired" (172). Daphne, Ornette, and Ruth, the children of Mem and Brownfield, are traumatized by their mother's death. It is Ruth, the youngest who, as a toddler, has the courage to call her father a "sonnabit"(153) and who notices the miserable state of her mother's shoes: "And she noticed for the first time, that even though it was the middle of winter, there were large frayed holes in the bottom of her mother's shoes. On Mem's right foot the shoe lay almost off and a flat packet of newspaper stuck halfway out" (172). In the details of Mem's terrible death, Walker honors

Mrs. Walker who, as cadaver, gave Walker the strange gift of her own brutally extinguished life, a life Walker has elevated to the level of art.

In contemplating the death of Mem, we are challenged to identify and explain the several factors that produced this tragedy. Chief among them is the performance of a species of black masculinity that is stained by patriarchy, which the scholar and feminist bell hooks defines as "a system of domination" (hooks 7). Beneath this plane of human experience there is another whose shaping power emerges from a dysfunctional relationship between a father and his son. Of course, these factors are interrelated, and together they produce a toxic synergy that frames and then extinguishes Mem's life. The dynamics between a father and son and the construction of black masculinity, along with Walker's unblinking examination of domestic violence, are the defining elements within the novel.

In taking up the question of father and son relationships, that is, the highly charged and violent relationship between Grange Copeland and his only son Brownfield, I turn first to an examination of a leitmotif within the novel: the search of the son for the father. After the suicide of his mother Margaret and infanticide of his half-brother Star, Brownfield sets outs, at the age of fifteen, to find his absent father who, unbeknown to his young son, is living a haphazard existence in the fabled North. Wishing to escape the neo-slavery of the sharecropping system that Shipley, a white landowner and the father of Star, would impose upon him, Brownfield is filled with "the urge to sample his new freedom . . . He would be his own boss. . . . As he left the clearing a thousand birds began wildly singing good luck" (33).

As Brownfield traverses the landscape of Green County, Georgia, he remarks to the black woman who is kind enough to feed him, "Mizes Mamie Lou Banks," and to that "family of women" who also tender him a generous hospitality "that he was 'kinda' looking for his daddy." It is these black women, "whose various husbands and boy friends were off hunting," who provide Brownfield with a bath, "pressed his new shirt and yellow satin tie, and gave him a shoe box for his things, which they said would be easier to carry than the trunklike box he had." When Brownfield describes Grange to this "family of women," "they looked at one another and smiled and smiled; but they would not say if they had seen him" (44). These knowledgeable women choose not to reveal all that they know, but instead "insisted that Brownfield take a certain road, and no other, which ran a certain way, and which would bring him by dusk to a certain peaceful town" (44). As he will soon discover, the women provide Brownfield with directions to the Dew Drop Inn and its owner, Fat Josie: Grange's safe harbor in his own strange and compelling odyssey.

Electing to embed the leitmotif of the search of the son for his father, Walker links her novel to one of the oldest works in the canon of Western literature—Homer's *The Odyssey*. The young Brownfield shares in the melancholy condition of "princely Telemachus. For he was sitting with the suitors, sad at heart, picturing in mind his noble father,—how he might come from somewhere, make a scattering of the suitors, take to himself his honors, and be master of his own" (Homer 3–4). The son of a king and the son of a sharecropper are burdened with deeply existential questions: how shall I make my way in the world? And what shall be the role of my father in this effort? Both young men yearn for the love and guidance of their absent fathers for Grange, like his mythic counterpart Odysseus, "also was a rover among men" (5). With the assistance of "clear-eyed Athene," Telemachus is reunited with his father Odysseus. Before they set sail together to return to Ithaca and purge the palace of the suitors who have presumed to court the much beleaguered Queen Penelope in Odysseus' absence, "the long-tried royal Odysseus" makes this observation to his young prince: "Now shall you learn, Telemachus, by taking part yourself while men are battling where the best are proved, how not to bring disgrace upon your line of sires; for they from ancient times were famed for strength and bravery through all the land" (305).

By contrast, in Brownfield's "quest of [his] long-absent father," he does not find Grange, but rather they discover one another through their attachment to the sly, manipulative, Janus-faced Fat Josie who regards Brownfield, in the domain of sex, as a serviceable substitute for his father. Oddly, Brownfield continues his search for Grange through the "incredible softness" and "experienced warmth" of Josie. "What she had said about the much bigger man with the same name didn't begin to haunt [Brownfield] until it was too late" (50). At first, Brownfield is perplexed by the fact that Grange and Josie were lovers. Later, he is not at all concerned about this chapter in his father's biography, and failing to read it, as it were, he is instead guided by only his own pleasure: "Besides, what did he care if he now plowed a furrow his father had laid? Josie's old field had never lain fallow" (65).

In constructing this dimension of the novel, Walker skillfully invokes and then dispels the taboo of incest for in copulating with Josie, Brownfield is, in one sense, also copulating with his father Grange. Through an unconscious process of redirection that Sigmund Freud termed "displacement," a process that involves the displacement of aggressive and sexual impulses from an object perceived as dangerous to one perceived as safe, Brownfield seeks in Josie's "experienced warmth" the warmth, the physical contact, which Grange had denied him all of his life (Gay 647–49). In order to substantiate this claim, we recall a poignant encounter from Brownfield's childhood that functions, tragically, as the expanding floor of his violent and unfulfilled relationship with his father.

> Brownfield pretended to be asleep. . . . He saw Grange bend over him to inspect his head and face. He saw him reach down to touch him. He saw his hand stop. . . . Brownfield was crying silently and wanted his father to touch the tears. He moved towards his father's hand, as if moving unconsciously in his sleep. He saw his father's hand draw back without touching him . . . . Even in private and in the dark and with Brownfield presumably asleep, Grange could not bear to touch his son with his hand. (28)

When Grange, "graying, bushy-haired, and lean as a wolf," descends upon Baker County after a ten-year sojourn in the North, he finds Brownfield established in the bedroom he had shared with Josie through all of his years of marriage to Margaret, his first wife. Predictably, Brownfield assumes the unfortunate role of a suitor whom Grange must expel from the Dew Drop Inn before he can marry Josie, who in this reading recalls but is very far from Penelope in station and temperament, among other things. In this primordial scene, the long-nurtured hatred of the son for his father is on full display:

> Curses erupted from Brownfield. His first impulse was to knock his father down. But he realized immediately, and it made him sob, that he was still afraid of him. He might still have been a child from the fear he felt. So instead of fighting his father, Brownfield cursed him and cried and left one of his socks near Josie's bed. Grange stood against the wall near the door gazing from Brownfield to Josie and finally resting his eyes on Josie. (92–93)

Although defeated, Brownfield makes a feeble, pathetic, and unsuccessful effort to reestablish his claims over Josie: "Brownfield put his arms around Josie's neck. His tears dripped onto her bosom. But Josie looked beyond him, over his shoulder; for the final time she pushed him away" (93). Grange and Josie ignore Brownfield and subsequently marry each other two weeks after this scene.

Brownfield's search for his father ends dramatically in the Dew Drop Inn. In contrast to the reunion between Telemachus and Odysseus, the reunion between Grange and Brownfield is not defined by love but instead by curses. They do not plan together the rescue of a queen, but instead Brownfield, now in his mid-twenties, declares war upon his father. In most of the remaining years that they have together Grange, like Odysseus in relation to his son Telemachus, seeks to teach Brownfield "how not to bring disgrace upon your line of sires." Grange seeks to teach his wounded, unforgiving son what it means to be a man, and thus avoid bringing further disgrace upon himself, his family, and the Copeland line.

In *Gender Trouble: Feminism and the Subversion of Identity* (1990), the scholar Judith Butler has theorized gender in illuminating and radical ways that reveal the fluid and contingent nature of gender identities. Butler argues that gender should be considered "as *a corporeal style*, an 'act,' as it were, which is both intentional and performative, where '*performative*' suggests a dramatic and contingent construction of meaning" (177). She remarks upon the ways in which we punish those who fail to perform their gender in obedience to the "law of heterosexual coherence" (175) and in the process once again reminds us that gender is a performance: "Hence, as a strategy of survival within compulsory systems, gender is a performance with clearly punitive consequences. Discrete genders are part of what 'humanizes' individuals within contemporary culture; indeed, we regularly punish those who fail to do their gender right" (178). Butler insists that gender "ought not to be construed as a stable identity or locus of agency from which various acts follow; rather, gender is an identity tenuously constituted in time, instituted in an exterior space through a *stylized repetition of acts*. The effect of gender," she writes, "is produced through the stylization of the body and, hence, must be understood as the mundane way in which bodily gestures, movements, and styles of various kinds constitute the illusion of an abiding gendered self"(179). Butler provides us with an understanding of gender as performance or a "*stylized repetition of acts*" rather than as an expression that would suggest an essence or preexisting gender identity. Between the shadow and the act, as it were, there is the possibility of change, of gender transformation. "The possibilities of gender transformation are to be found precisely in the arbitrary relation between such acts, in the possibility of a failure to repeat, a de-formity, or parodic repetition that exposes the phantasmatic effect of abiding identity as a politically tenuous construction" (179).

By way of conclusion, Butler leaves us with this warning regarding what a failure to apprehend gender as a performance obscures along with the unwelcomed political and social effects that an obeisance to a "regulatory fiction," as she at one point aptly terms this self-blinding, produces: "That gender reality is created through sustained social performances means that the very notions of an essential sex and a true or abiding masculinity or femininity are also constituted as part of the strategy that conceals gender's performative character and the performative possibilities for proliferating gender configurations outside the restricting frames of masculinist domination and compulsory heterosexuality" (180).

The "compulsory system" most relevant to our analysis of the performance of black masculinity is the sharecropping system which during Grange's first life largely sapped his energy and will. From the time that Brownfield weds the innocent Mem, it is also the system which defines completely his life and his conception of himself as man, husband, father, and human being. Only during that brief period when he is a handyman at the Dew Drop Inn and later when he lives in the "City House" with Mem and his daughters is Brownfield able to earn an income through a means other than sharecropping. In his first life Grange's existence is defined by the sharecropping system, and thus his performance of black masculinity is stained by the operations of a system which prized the labor of black people, and sought their complete subordination regardless of the costs. As we examine more closely Grange as a sharecropper, we discover other dimensions that fill out the riveting portrait of the first life.

Within the dehumanizing framework of the sharecropping system of the 1920s, conjugal life between Grange and Margaret is ordered by a rhythm largely determined by Grange's moods. Walker tells us "by Thursday Grange's gloominess reached its peak and he grimaced respectfully, with veiled eyes, at the jokes told by the man who drove truck." Toil-blasted, "by Friday Grange was so stupefied with the work and the sun he wanted nothing but rest the next two days before it started all over again." After an evening with Fat Josie at the Dew Drop Inn on Saturday night, "Grange would come home lurching drunk, threatening to kill his wife and Brownfield, stumbling and shooting off his shotgun. He threatened Margaret and she ran and hid in the woods with Brownfield huddled at her feet" (15). In the weekly rhythm of family life, we observe the morose and violent nature of Grange's performance of masculinity. This is a performance shaped in deep and powerful ways by the limitations imposed upon his life by the sharecropping system, and, equally as important, his inability to direct the violence outward and away from his family towards Shipley and other oppressors.

Walker, with insight and empathy, sketches for us the race rituals that define Grange's relationship to Shipley. We note how the man who would have a brief affair with Margaret, the outcome of which would be Star, does not deign to touch Brownfield, a child worker, with his hand but rather the handle of his cane. The forbidding presence of Shipley, which is an unmixable mix of savagery—"the smooth brownish hair of an animal"—and sweetness—"a smell of mint on his breath"—has a profoundly dehumanizing effect upon Grange. As Grange fears Shipley, Brownfield also learns to fear him, and other white men. Grange's performance of masculinity reflects the obedient posture he must assume before Shipley and other white men. For Grange to step outside this highly choreographed race ritual, in other words "to fail to do his gender right," is to invite death for himself and potentially for other members of his family.

In Grange's first life the chief objective is to survive, in some manner, the dehumanizing effects of the sharecropping system. Unable to direct his rage towards his oppressors, he instead directs it towards his wife and son with, as we have seen, devastating and tragic results. Grange's second life occurs in New York City. Spanning the years 1926 to 1936, he acquires a perspective on his life in Georgia that sets in motion certain profound changes, all of which alter his worldview and his performance of masculinity. By the middle of the summer of 1926, Grange "had worked, begged, stolen his way North, to New York. Among the frozen faces and immobile buildings," writes Walker "he had been just another hungry nobody headed for Harlem" (205–6). As Walker makes clear, Grange is a part of that historic migration of African Americans from the south to the north that spanned the 1890s to the 1920s.

Approximately three years after his arrival in New York, Grange's turning point occurs when he witnesses a tryst between a white heterosexual couple in Central Park. The young man is dressed in a military uniform, and the young woman is hugely pregnant. Observing the white couple, Grange witnesses the dissolution of their relationship. It appears that the young solider already had a wife, and he has come to the park to share this devastating fact with the pregnant woman. The pregnant woman rejects the ring offered to her by her potential husband (or bigamist) as well as the money, $700.00. The solider then leaves the mother-to-be in the park where she seemed to be trying to "cry herself . . . to a long forgetful sleep." Grange is deeply moved by what he has witnessed: "It was the first honestly human episode he had witnessed between white folks, when they were not putting on airs to misinform the help" (210).

Mistakenly believing that misery "leveled all beings," Grange approaches the pregnant woman after he has divided the money. He intends to "give her three hundred, he would keep four hundred. She could also have the ring" (213). Very respectfully—he even removes his hat—Grange approaches the pregnant woman and offers her the ring and three hundred dollars, notwithstanding her promise to scream and her denials that she has any connection to either. After counting the money, she contemptuously remarks to Grange: "'This ain't all of it . . . . I want all of it! You ain't going to have any of it; before I let *you* sneak off with it I'll throw it into the pond! . . . . Look at the big burly-head,' she said, and laughed again." Grange is stunned by her response. The situation deteriorates dramatically. While demanding all of the money, the pregnant woman calls Grange "nigger," kicks him in the shin, and again calls him "nigger." Although vulnerable, she is not afraid of Grange who is caught in the web of his plantation training, rooted in his place in the park out of fear that she might scream. "Misjudging the distance and the weight of her heavy body," Walker writes, "she fell through the ice into the pond." As a human being, Grange's first impulse is to attempt to save the life of the drowning pregnant woman. "He stretched out his arm and nearly touched her," writes Walker. "She reached up and out with a small white hand that grabbed his hand but let go when she felt it was *his* hand. Grange drew back his dirty brown hand and looked at it. . . . Finally she sank. She called him 'nigger' with her last disgusted breath" (217).

While the death of the pregnant woman was "simple murder," it also "liberated" Grange. Purged of fear for the first time in his life, Grange's performance of his masculinity assumes a new power, a new rebelliousness, a new aggressiveness, even a certain grandeur. "He was like a tamed lion who at last tasted blood," Walker writes. "There was no longer any reason not to rebel against people who were not gods. His aggressiveness, which he had vented only on his wife, and his child, and his closest friends, now asserted itself in the real hostile world. For weeks after the incident at the pond he fought more Italians, Poles, Jews . . . and in this fighting too he tasted the sweet surge of blood rightfully directed in its wrath that proclaimed his freedom, his manhood. Every white face he cracked," observes Walker, "he cracked in his sweet wife's name" (220–21).

Grange soon realizes that he cannot fight every white person he meets. And since he cannot defeat them, he decides that "he would withdraw completely from them, find a sanctuary, make a life that need not acknowledge them, and be always prepared, with his life, to defend it, to protect it, to keep it from whites, inviolate" (221). Grange decides to return to Baker County, Georgia. He persuades Fat Josie to sell her cherished Dew Drop Inn, and with the money from the sale of her business combined with that which he has saved, he purchases his farm: "the rock of his refuge." During his second life, Grange acquires a vital perspective on his first life as a sharecropper. Chief among the many lessons learned is that he must direct his anger towards those who oppress him, not those who love him.

In his third life, Grange commits himself to repairing his much damaged relationship with Brownfield. Illustrative of this focus is a difficult
dialogue that Grange has with Brownfield which takes place on the day
of Ruth's birth. Grange reconstructs the impact of work as a sharecropper upon himself and members of his family: "Like I been trying to tell
you, ever since I come back, there's a lot I *done* I didn't *agree* with. It
was the times, I reckon. You could work so *hard,* for nothing. And as
tight as times was they started tightenin' up some more. I was worked
so hard, I tell you the truth, my days had done all run together. There
wa'n't no beginning nor no end" (101). Brownfield is indifferent to his
father's perspective on his first life, to his effort at dialogue. He bitterly
reminds Grange of his abandonment of Margaret, and implicitly its
impact upon him: "Margaret's days all run together *too,* after *you* left"
(101). Brownfield's condemnation of Grange does not initially influence his efforts at reconciliation. Contemplating Mem's greatly altered
physical appearance, irrefutable evidence of eight years of domestic
abuse, Grange "felt, among all the other reasons for her being laid so
low, his own guilt," writes Walker. "That was why he spent so much
time with her and his grandchildren, and bought them meat and vegetables, and gave them money on the sly, and reaped in the full anger of
his wife and the unflagging bitterness of his son" (104).

The other project that endows Grange's third life with purpose and
direction is his devotion to his third granddaughter Ruth, who comes
to live with him and Fat Josie on their farm after Brownfield is imprisoned for the murder of Mem. As Ruth matures, Grange comes to realize what he must do for her, regardless of the costs. Grange assumes
the difficult but loving task of protecting and preserving her innocence
by teaching her to protect herself (he teaches her how to shoot, for
example), and by providing her with the security and autonomy that
inheriting the farm would bring her. Given Brownfield's unforgiving
and bitter stance, it is Grange's devotion to Ruth that becomes the focal
point of his third life.

As Grange both prepares Ruth to enter the world, and yet also protects her from that world, he performs a black masculinity that is illustrative of the change that he now embodies as a man reborn. As we have seen, Grange's performance of black masculinity is marked by introspection, generosity, an acceptance of responsibility for past wrongs, and a deep awareness of time, for he knows that his third life constitutes his last opportunity to prepare the ground for Ruth to "survive whole," (272) notwithstanding all of the challenges that attend that loving and idealistic vision. Equally as important, Grange's performance of black masculinity is also marked by his capacity to change, to consciously carry the lessons of one life into the next, and to apply those lessons in a manner that has a radical and positive impact upon his life and the lives of those he loves.

By contrast, Brownfield is the embodiment of an evil stasis. The concepts of change are completely alien to him except as they relate to the achievement of greater states of evil. As to the high calling that Odysseus challenges his princely son Telemachus to meet—that is, the imperative "of not to bring disgrace upon your line of sires"— Brownfield is indifferent to such conceptions of honor. He performs a species of black masculinity that meets the low, racist, expectations of the white supremacists who control his existence. For example, after Brownfield provides Captain Davis with yet another assurance that he will be moving with Mem and his daughters to "Mr. J.L's place," Captain Davis, feeling the weight of the white man's burden, observes to himself: "Pity how you got to look after 'em, he thought, as he wrapped his good hand round his stub" (113).

In a powerful instance of teaching and self-interrogation, Grange, to his own chorus of "but where was the *man* in me," reflects upon his abandonment of family and his exploitation of Fat Josie, and finally delivers to his son a sermon on the relationship between manhood and personal responsibility. Grange delivers a truth that steadies him before a younger, disrespectful, and relentless Brownfield:

"But my answering for everything had to be to her, don't you understand yet how it go? Nobody give a damn for me but your ma, and I messed her up trying to be a big man! . . . All I am saying, Brownfield," said Grange, his voice sinking to a whisper, "is that one day I had to look back on my own life and see where I went wrong, and when I did look back I found out your ma'd be alive today if I hadn't just as good as shot her to death, same as you done your wife. We *guilty*, Brownfield, and neither one of us is going to move a step in the right direction until we admit it." (290)

Angrily, Brownfield dismisses Grange's sermon as so much bluster from an old man. Undaunted, Grange delivers the core message of his sermon: "I am talking to *you*, Brownfield . . . and most of what I am saying is *you got to hold tight a place in you where they can't come* . . . . We keep killing ourselves for people that don't even mean nothing *to* us" (290–91). Uttering a truth for the ages, Grange realizes that no amount of reasoning and exalted, principled talk will make a difference in Brownfield's ruined life, a life for which Grange, as he fully acknowledges, is responsible.

Works Cited

Butler, Judith. *Gender Trouble: Feminism and the Subversion of Identity*. 1990. New York: Routledge, 1999.

Gay, Peter, Ed. *The Freud Reader*. New York: Norton, 1989.

Homer. *The Odyssey*. Trans. George Herbert Palmer. New York: Barnes, 2003.

hooks, bell. *Feminism Is for Everybody: Passionate Politics*. Cambridge, MA: South End, 2000.

Walker, Alice. *The Third Life of Grange Copeland*. 1970. New York: Pocket, 1988.

Meridian and *We Are the Ones We Have Been Waiting For:* Alice Walker's Evolving Vision of the Spiritual Warrior

Shirley Toland-Dix

In the Introduction to *The World Has Changed: Conversations with Alice Walker,* Rudolph Byrd usefully divides Walker's "enormous complex body of work" into two primary phases. The first phase is made up of the writings she produced between 1968 and 1983 in which Walker pays particular attention to the "impact of region [the American South] and social change upon the individual" (25). The second phase encompasses the work she has produced from 1984 to the present. While acknowledging important "points of convergence," Byrd clearly delineates the distinctiveness of the writings produced during this second phase. Most significant for my purposes is his balanced recognition that, although a deeper concern "with questions related to spirituality and the need for a spiritual practice" is characteristic of her later work, a belief in the importance of activism connects all of her writing (26–27).

As one who came of age in the crucible of the civil rights movement, Alice Walker experienced the 1960s and 1970s as "an era marked by deep sea-changes and transitions" (Broken Heart xiv). *Meridian* (1976) is set in the immediate aftermath of the civil rights movement. In this her second novel, Walker raises critical questions that grew out of her intense involvement in the movement, questions that she continues to engage in her most recent writing. Walker's encompassing, syncretic spirituality is already evident in her characterization of Meridian Hill, a young black woman who grows up in a small Georgia town in the 1950s. Even as a child, Meridian is uncomfortable with the narrow, patriarchal, repressive Christianity that contains her mother but is drawn to the Amerindian spirituality that engrosses her father. As a college student her room is decorated with "photographs of trees and rocks and tall hills and floating clouds, which she claimed she *knew*" (27), fore-shadowing the "pagan" spirituality Walker later embraces.

We Are the Ones We Have Been Waiting For: Inner Light in a Time of Darkness—Meditations (2006) is primarily a collection of talks, ranging from a commencement address at Agnes Scott College to a dharma talk at the African American Buddhist Conference Retreat. Speaking as an elder, Walker insists that this "is a time when all of us will need the most faithful, self-generated enthusiasm (enthusiasm: to be filled with god) in order to survive in human fashion." She does not proselytize. Instead she suggests that we each contemplate what spiritual practice(s) we are drawn to: "Whether we reach this inner state of recognized divinity through prayer, meditation, dancing . . . feeding the hungry or enriching the impoverished is immaterial. We will be doubly bereft without some form of practice that connects us, in a caring way, to what begins to feel like a dissolving world." Walker concludes urgently that "now is the time" to choose a spiritual practice and "to put it to use" (109–10).

In a 2000 interview with Scott Winn, Walker identifies herself as a "pagan Buddhist who was brought up as a Christian" (qtd. in Simcikova 20). In the books written during her second phase, Walker has explored different aspects of her encompassing spirituality. In *We Are the Ones We Have Been Waiting For*, she focuses on Buddhist philosophy, explaining that, although she is "not a Buddhist" (94): "I have found a support in the teachings of the Buddha that is beyond measure, as I have found comfort and support also in those teachings I have received from Ancient Africans and Indigenous people of my native continent" (105). She maintains that "just as Jesus Christ was not a Christian," Buddha was not a Buddhist; however, both were enlightened beings. The challenge she has accepted is "not to be a follower of something but to embody it" (94).

Walker also reaffirms her commitment to spiritually grounded and historically aware political activism. In one of her talks, she observes that yoga and meditation have been essential spiritual practices in her own efforts to attain spiritual "warriorship." She asserts that "(k)now-ing what happened to our ancestors' lives is the only way we can begin deconstruction of the dysfunction in our own" (238). Yet how do we deal with these "harrowing tales" from the past and how do we man-age the kind of "psychic assault" that African Americans and Native Americans are still subject to: "What do we do with the shock? What do we do with the anger? The rage? What do we do with the pain?" (89). Walker contends that we must cultivate a warriorship typically assigned to "heroic leaders: Mandela, Che, King, Tubman, Truth, Mal-colm X." Walker maintains that this warriorship is something we can all attain; by warriorship she means "holding protective *chi,* or life force, that enables one's self and the community to heal" (238).

Walker began developing her still evolving concept of the spiritual warrior in *Meridian.* The philosophy of nonviolent resistance taught by Martin Luther King Jr. is the foundation of Walker's vision of con-scious political activism as an important component of what it means to be a spiritual warrior. Over the years, Walker has expressed her core belief that "the ground or root of wakefulness and sanity . . . exists as a potential within every human being" (Trungpa 27). Her conviction that all of us can and must contribute to healing the earth and improving the quality of life for all is not utopian; it is pragmatic and organic, based on her own spiritual evolution. In the introduction to *Anything We Love Can Be Saved: A Writer's Activism* (1997), Walker maintains that she has "been an activist" all of her adult life, and that her activism—"cultural, political, spiritual"—is rooted quite simply in her "love of nature" and her "delight in human beings":

> I believe people exist to be enjoyed, much as a restful or engaging view might be. As the ocean or drifting clouds might be. Or as if they were the human equivalent of melons, mangoes, or any other kind of attractive, seductive fruit. When I am in the presence of other human beings I want to revel in their creative and intellectual fullness, their uninhibited social warmth. I want their precious human radiance to wrap me in light. I do

not want fear of war or starvation or bodily mutilation to steal both my pleasure in them and their own birthright (xxii).

When she lived in Mississippi from 1967 to 1974, Walker observed that those who were "most directly confrontational . . . often ended up severely beaten, in prison, or dead. Shot down in front of their children, blown up in cars or in church, run over by racist drunks, raped and thrown in the river" (*Anything We Love* xxii). She acknowledges that in this context, she and many others were "plagued by the notion that, given the magnitude of the task before us—the dismantling of American apartheid—our individual acts were puny." However, Walker notes that she came to understand how each person's seemingly small act of commitment and courage can contribute to "the building of an edifice of hope." In a society in which "the daily news of disaster" can be a "numbing assault" to the spirit, "one's own activism, however modest . . . provides at least the possibility of generating a different kind of 'news.' A 'news' that empowers rather than defeats" (*Anything We Love* xxii). Both the cultivation of awareness and the commitment to making a conscious contribution to the greater good are required of Walker's spiritual warriors.

The central dilemma in *Meridian* is introduced with the elegiac epigraph from *Black Elk Speaks* (1932) that opens the novel. What does one do after the initial fervor of social movements that promise freedom and change and deliver some of it, but always also disappoint? How does one move through the pain and disappointment, the backlash and unexpected aftermath, and maintain integrity and commitment in the face of repressive forces that seem overwhelming? The particular question that confronts Meridian is: "Will you kill for the Revolution?" (14). The question initiates a spiritual quest for Meridian, described as a reserved, somewhat aloof person who possessed an inner life that was valuable and intriguing. Although a decade later, the would-be rebel women who answered the question glibly have actually done nothing revolutionary, it is a question that Walker and her protagonist take very seriously. Another characteristic of Walker's spiritual warriors is a belief in the sacredness of life. Who will we become if we simply kill those we deem deserving of death? On what basis do we make that determination? Meridian is involved with "a group of students, of intellectuals" who had come to believe in violence "only after witnessing the extreme violence against black dissidents, of the federal government and police. Would they rob a bank? Bomb a landmark? Blow up a police station? Would they ever be face to face with the enemy, guns drawn? Perhaps. Perhaps not. . . . The point was, she could not think lightly of shedding blood. And the question of killing did not impress her as rhetorical at all" (15). Meridian is described as "*held* by something in the past"—her memories of ordinary black people who possess a dignity, a depth of spirituality, an innocence that she values. Meridian particularly remembers "the sight of young girls singing in a country choir, their hair shining with brushings and grease, their voices the voices of angels." When she has been spiritually "transformed in church it was always by the purity of the singers' souls, which she could actually *hear.*" Poetically, Meridian wonders, "if they committed murder—and to her even revolutionary murder was murder—*what would the music be like?*" (15).

These questions still reverberate in Walker's writing. When is it acceptable for the spiritual warrior to use violence? What are the costs? Reflecting the ambivalence she depicts in her character Meridian, Walker's answers to these questions vary. In a scene in *Now Is the Time to Open Your Heart* (2004), an indigenous medicine woman known as Grandmother declares that even Buddha "*would not mock those who take up arms against their own enslavement. Sometimes there is no way, except through violence, to freedom.*" According to Grandmother, Buddha also teaches that "*living in violence is not the best use of life, however. . . .What needs killing is not the person; what needs killing is his or her idea that torturing another person will create happiness*" (196–97).

Meridian's epigraph is taken from the conclusion of *Black Elk Speaks* (1932), the testimonial of an Oglala Sioux medicine man. Now an old man, Black Elk looks back and reveals what happened to his people after the US Army massacred close to three hundred Lakota women and children at Wounded Knee, South Dakota, on the morning of December 29, 1890:

> I did not know how much was ended. When I look back now . . . I can still see the butchered women and children lying heaped and scattered all along the crooked gulch as plain as when I saw them with eyes still young. And I can see that something else died there in the bloody mud, and was buried in the blizzard. A people's dream died there. It was a beautiful dream . . . the nation's hoop is broken and scattered. There is no center any longer, and the sacred tree is dead.

Walker frequently depicts Native Americans and African Americans as "irrevocably linked" through shared suffering (*We Are the Ones* 238). In *Meridian,* she queries whether the aftermath of the civil rights movement would replicate the tragic aftermath of the Ghost Dance movement. Patricia Riley comments that "[l]ike the Ghost Dance movement, the civil rights movement was visionary . . . and rooted in the principle of nonviolence. And, as with the Ghost Dance movement, that nonviolence was too often plagued by a violent response on the part of a fearful Euro-America that misinterpreted and misunderstood what the movement was all about or . . . understood all too well and moved to prevent its success" (243).

Walker has observed that Native Americans and African Americans who have retained knowledge of their ancient heritage are also linked by "the belief that everything is inhabited by spirit. This belief encourages knowledge perceived intuitively" (*Mothers' Gardens* 252). The five-hundred-yard Sacred Serpent was a Native American burial mound located on Meridian's father's sixty acres of farm land; it was said to be thousands of years old. Riley observes that a kind of "shamanistic tradition" runs through Meridian's family. It entails "descending into the well of the coiled serpent's tail and experiencing an altered state of consciousness that carries the individual past the boundaries of this world and into contact with the infinite" (246). Meridian has been told that her great-grandmother Feather Mae had had an extraordinary experience when she entered the "center of the Serpent's coiled tail": Feather Mae "felt as if she had stepped into another world, into a different kind of air. . . . She felt renewed, as from some strange spiritual intoxication" (49–50). Meridian has actually seen her father enter "the deep well of the Serpent's coiled tail and return to his cornfield with his whole frame radiating brightness like the space around a flame" (50). Intrigued, Meridian enters the Sacred Serpent and has her own ecstatic experience:

> it was as if the walls of earth that enclosed her rushed outward, leveling themselves at a dizzying rate, and then spinning wildly, lifting her out of her body and giving her the feeling of flying. And in this movement she saw the faces of her family, the branches of trees, the wings of birds, the corners of houses, blades of grass and petals of flowers rush toward a central point high above her and she was drawn with them, as whirling, as bright, as free, as they (50).

Meridian and her father tell no one else of their visionary experiences, but they discuss them. Mr. Hill believes that he has experienced what dying feels like, when "the body seemed to drop away" and the spirit was "set free in the world." Meridian describes her experience as capturing the intensity of life, as "a way the living sought to expand the consciousness of being alive" (51).

Though each experience is personal, Meridian, her father, and great-grandmother experience a deep sense of oneness with all that exists. Walker celebrates their shared capacity for wonder. In *We Are the Ones We Have Been Waiting For*, she affirms: "I have experienced many difficulties and hardships in my life and yet despair is a state in which I rarely remain for long. This is largely because despair cannot share the same space as wonder, and it is wonder that I have had from childhood, and in abundance" (36). Feather Mae had ultimately "renounced all religion that was not based on the experience of physical ecstasy" (50). In the same way, Meridian seeks to recapture her ecstatic experience. When the county seizes her father's farm and turns the Sacred Serpent into a debased theme park, it is a tragic loss for all.

Walker wrote *Meridian* while she was living in Mississippi, "being part of the Movement for black liberation and also relentlessly observing it" (*We Are the Ones* 166). She specifically depicts women's commitment to the movement as well as the blatant sexism they often encountered. Barbara Christian observes that for Walker, the "deepening of self-knowledge and self-love . . . seems to have much to do with her contrariness, her willingness at all turns to challenge the fashionable belief of the day, to reexamine it in the light of her own experiences and of dearly won principles which she has previously challenged and absorbed." Walker consistently engages "the 'forbidden' . . . as a possible route to truth. At the core of this contrariness is an unwavering honesty about what she sees" (40).

Meridian is introduced to the civil rights movement when a group of black and white young people come to her town to initiate a voter registration drive. At seventeen, she is married, a high school dropout, and the mother of a baby boy. Meridian has been in a trance-like state, drifting disconnected through her life, and contemplating suicide. Joining the civil rights movement is her awakening, providing her with a sense of purpose and the beginnings of self-awareness. Exposed to possibilities she has never imagined, Meridian makes some life-altering decisions. She divorces her husband, gives her son up for adoption, and wins a scholarship to Saxon College, a school in Atlanta for young black women. However, at Saxon, Meridian encounters the same colonizing, puritanical attitudes toward black women's sexuality that she had experienced in her small town. The narrator explains that at Saxon, the emphasis was "on form, and the preferred 'form' was that of the finishing school girl whose goal, wherever she would later find herself in the world, was to be *accepted* as an equal because she knew and practiced all the proper social rules" (91). Although Meridian rebels against these strictures intellectually, she has internalized them. On the one hand she is proud of the independence and determination it had taken for her to get into Saxon; on the other hand she is torn by guilt because she chose to give up her child. In a pattern that continues for more than a decade, Meridian's inner turmoil manifests as physical illness: "She began to have headaches that were so severe they caused her to stutter when she spoke. She dreamed of such horrible things she would wake up shaking" (90). Her growing participation in the Atlanta Movement is not only an escape from her inner turmoil, it also provides Meridian with the feeling, which she craved, of connectedness to something larger than her small self.

Throughout the novel, Truman Held's development is parallel to that of Meridian for he is by turns comrade, adversary, lover, and initiate. With this character, Walker depicts some of the ways in which the selfhood of black women was overlooked within a supposedly liberatory movement. The ideal black woman was either a nurturant or sexualized body. Meridian discovers that intelligence and individuality were at best inconvenient. Images imposed by nationalist black men vied with those imposed by white supremacist society. In both instances, the representations had little to do with the women but revealed much about the vested interests of those who created them. Despite his glib praise of her warm brown beauty, Truman is displaying an apparent preference for white women. Meridian is bewildered by the preference. Proud of the courage and initiative she had summoned to join the movement and come to Saxon College, Meridian likes to think of herself as "an adventurer. It thrilled her to think she belonged to the people who produced Harriet Tubman, the only American woman who'd led troops in battle." However, she has come to realize that "Truman, alas, did not want a general beside him." He was not looking for a woman "who tried, however encumbered by guilts and fears and remorse, to claim her own life. She knew Truman would have liked her better as she had been as Eddie's wife . . . an attractive woman, but asleep" (107).

Spiritual warriors must come to terms with and transcend societal images imposed upon them. One of Meridian's biggest challenges is overcoming the intense self-hatred she has developed. Meridian feels that in giving away her child, she has desecrated the sacred institution of black motherhood. Even though Meridian knows that she did what was best for her child and herself, on a "deeper level than she had anticipated or had even been aware of, she felt condemned, consigned to penitence, for life" (87). She is particularly haunted by the legacy of enslaved women who had gone through unimaginable hardships in their efforts to keep the children they had borne who would have belonged legally to the "white person who 'owned' them all." Meridian knew that "the daughters of these enslaved women had thought their greatest blessing from 'Freedom' was that it meant they could keep their children. And what had Meridian Hill done with *her* precious child? She had given him away" (87).

Throughout the novel, however, Walker reveals the complexity of black women's actual response to motherhood. Although Meridian idealizes her mother, we see that Mrs. Hill resents her children for "stealing" her "serenity for shattering her . . . emerging self" (41). Walker also includes several vignettes of black women who responded to motherhood by committing suicide or infanticide. She focuses on women's lack of knowledge about their bodies and their lack of choice about motherhood. She depicts women who feel that their bodies have betrayed them. They have been made pregnant with little awareness of how it happened and no awareness of what motherhood entails. Meridian is deeply fearful of her sexuality because it has only brought her shame and pain. The one time that she allows herself to have sex with Truman, she becomes pregnant. By the time she discovers the pregnancy, Truman has become involved with one of the white exchange students. Walker's depiction of the consequences for Meridian is searing:

Later, as the doctor tore into her body without giving her anesthesia (and while he lectured her on her morals) and she saw stars because of the pain. . . . It enraged her that she could be made to endure such pain, and that he was oblivious to it. She was also disgusted with the fecundity of her body that got pregnant on less screwing than anybody's she had ever heard of. It seemed doubly unfair that after all her sexual "experience" and after one baby and one abortion she had not once been completely fulfilled by sex. (112)

While Walker describes the 1960s as a "glorious decade of black awakening" (*We Are the Ones* 230–31), she also discusses the physical, psychological, spiritual cost. In an essay addressed to her former husband twenty-five years after their divorce, Walker recalls the depression she had suffered when they lived as an interracial couple in Mississippi. Of the therapist who "casually prescribed Valium," Walker comments: "She did not care enough to suggest perhaps we were simply trying to do too much. That we were throwing our young lives against a system that had crushed lovers and idealists for centuries" (*Broken Heart* 29). In *Meridian,* Walker reveals the cost to her characters of participation in the movement. Meridian is haunted by images of incidents she had "witnessed in the Atlanta streets": "black children, with short, flashing black legs, being chased by grown white men brandishing ax handles. . . . old women dragged out of stores and beaten on the sidewalk. . . . young black men of great spiritual beauty changed overnight into men who valued nothing" (92). Meridian's personal turmoil, her "battle fatigue," and her desire to experience transcendent spiritual states lead to her embrace of martyrdom and the denial of the body that follows. Madhu Dubey notes Meridian's desire to "scourge her body of some vague, unspecified sense of personal guilt" (Dubey 143). In particular, we note Meridian's response when she and other demonstrators are attacked by police, for she welcomes the confrontations other demonstrators dread. The narrator describes Meridian as experiencing "an inner gaiety, a sense of freedom, as she saw the clubs slashing down on her." On one occasion, when she was beaten into unconsciousness, "it was not the damage done to her body that she remembered when she woke up, but her feeling of yearning, of heartsick longing for forgiveness . . . and her feeling of hope as the harsh light of consciousness began to fade" (*Meridian* 93). Dubey criticizes this scene for shifting focus away from the police brutality inflicted on the marchers, but that is frequently decried. Instead, Walker explores the complexity of Meridian's motivation, for her political commitment is combined with a debilitating sense of shame and unworthiness. In part this is what her boldness springs from, but it is a disregard of self that Meridian must eventually heal.

Meridian is characterized throughout by her questions and by what the narrator calls her "profound ambivalence." Others find her insistence on looking at issues in all of their complexity exasperating and disturbing. When she is ousted from the group of would-be revolutionaries, Meridian returns to the South to reconnect with the people who had originally inspired her participation. Killing for the revolution cannot be abstract for her. She is cast out of the group because of her insistence on trusting her inner knowing rather than acceding to the demands of the group.

Learning to trust one's inner knowing is vital for the spiritual warrior. In her analysis of Walker as a "spiritual thinker," Karla Simcikova points out that a recurring theme in Walker's work is the need for people to achieve self-love which "is closely related to . . . acceptance of ourselves the way we are, in our unique, sometimes deviant-from-the-norm, ways" (44). Simcikova observes that while Walker agrees that "knowing who we are racially and/or culturally, and acknowledging our heritage give us a sense of communal belonging and of being grounded," she warns us that we must challenge cultural traditions that are "detrimental to our health, growth, and freedom" even if this makes us "outcasts or outsiders within our own groups." According to Simcikova, Walker sees "positive value" in being an outsider for it provides the distance we need to "achieve a fresh perspective." Away from the constrictions of "societal or familial prejudice," we are free to discover our own "unique point of view" (48).

Meridian's decade-long sojourn in a series of small Southern towns is a spiritual retreat. Rather than rushing to act, Meridian embarks on what Walker later describes in "All Praises to the Pause; The Universal Moment of Reflection," as "the pause" (*We Are the Ones* 48).Walker explains that all of us experience times when "it is all simply too much. We've heard enough. We've seen too much. It is hard to bear our own human thickness. Our laziness and stupidity. . . . Our ways of thinking and behaving. Life hears our weariness. And into it begins to pour moments of the pause. We slow down. We can't think. Our hair attracts lint. Our socks don't match. It isn't easy to see that this is a good time" (64). Walker acknowledges that our culture makes it difficult for us to claim the pause that wisdom demands. However, if we refuse, "the Universe will likely give it to us. In the form of illness . . . in the form of our car breaking down, our roof starting to leak, our garden starting to dry up. Our government collapsing. And we find ourselves required to stop, to sit down, to reflect. This is the time of 'the pause,' the universal place of stopping. The universal moment of reflection" (*We Are the Ones* 49).The pause allows Meridian to heal, to learn self-acceptance and self-love. It also allows her to come to terms with loss.

The second chapter of the novel opens with a list of some of those murdered during the 1960s, from Martin Luther King to Che Guevara to Denise McNair to Robert Kennedy. This is followed by the declaration that "*It was a decade marked by death. Violent and inevitable. Funerals became engraved on the brain, intensifying the ephemeral nature of life*" (21). We are then shown the stark image of a young, grieving Meridian Hill watching the "first televised Kennedy funeral" with other Saxon College students. In her writing about the civil rights movement and its aftermath, Walker laments the fact that they never allowed themselves to mourn. In a passage that echoes the novel's *Black Elk Speaks* epigraph, Walker acknowledges that "we never took the time . . . to properly grieve what we lost," neither the personal loss nor the deaths "by assassination and terrorism of so many people in public life whom we admired and loved, because to do so would have simply overwhelmed us" (*Broken Heart* 50).

Buddhist teacher Chogyam Trungpa describes warriorship as a spiritual tradition of bravery and fearlessness that has existed throughout history, in many cultures. In teachings that Walker affirms, Trungpa asserts that the "key to warriorship . . . is not being afraid of who you are" and knowing that in the midst of life's many challenges "we can be heroic and kind at the same time" (Trungpa 28). Although "everyone has a responsibility to the larger world, we can create additional chaos if we try to impose our ideas or our help upon others." Instead, we must begin by examining "our own experience to see what it contains that is of value in helping ourselves and others to uplift their existence" (29). *Meridian* is a framed narrative that opens with Truman finding Meridian in a small town and joining her spiritual retreat. As a result of the pause, Meridian has gained self-knowledge and is learning self-acceptance. She begins to achieve clarity about what kind of revolutionary she will be.

As the novel concludes, Meridian and Truman revisit the question that dominates the novel: "Will you kill for the Revolution?" Meridian voices her discomfort with the "othering" killing requires, arguing that "revolutionary killing is systematic. You line people up who have abused you, as a group, and you simply eradicate them, like you would eradicate a disease" (191). Drawing on her own experience of being ostracized because she questioned, Meridian maintains that she doesn't "trust revolutionaries enough to let them choose who should be killed. I would probably end up on the wrong side of the firing squad, myself" (192). She believes that revolution should begin not with murder, "but with teaching" (192). Meridian imagines revolution as "a circle of earnest people sitting down to ask each other meaningful questions. I don't see it as a handing down of answers" (192).

Not surprisingly, Walker is not done with this question. Meridian's most important realizations take place in a black church that has been transformed by the movement. On this Sunday, the congregation is celebrating the life of a young man who had, with the "gentleness at the heart of the warrior" (201), chosen to join the movement. He had been murdered. As Meridian observes the self-love and commitment to community that this church embodies, as she hears the tributes to the young man and the care offered to his father, she decides that there might be some concrete instances when she would have the capacity to kill, but she carefully establishes conditions: "even the contemplation of murder required incredible delicacy as it required incredible spiritual work. . . . Only in a church surrounded by the righteous guardians of the people's memories could she even approach the concept of retaliatory murder. Only among the pious could this idea both comfort and uplift" (205).

Writing in 1997, Walker declares that more and more people in the world are "attempting to decolonize their spirits"; this is a "crucial act of empowerment" (*Anything We Love* 4). During the service, Meridian experiences a transformative epiphany when she finally understands that her first responsibility is to treat herself with gentleness, respect, and loving care: "the respect she owed her life was to continue, against whatever obstacles, to live it, and not to give up any particle of it without a fight to the death" (204). Thus Meridian releases the culture of martyrdom and embraces the expansive consciousness of life she had experienced in the Sacred Serpent. As part of her process of healing, Meridian has become Truman's spiritual teacher. At the end of the novel, when her pause ends, she leaves the small house they have shared, and returns "to the world cleansed of sickness" (227). Truman is now also on the path to become a spiritual warrior. He now surrenders to the necessary space of introspection, realizing that the challenge of "bearing the conflict in her soul" which Meridian had "imposed on herself —and lived through—must be borne in terror by all the rest of them" (228).

Meridian does not resolve the issue of sexuality and the body that Walker works through in her later discussions of sacred sexuality. In later works, she explores in detail the issue of how black women can transcend outwardly imposed images that can cause them to be self-destructive and to seek, as Meridian did, to harshly discipline bodies and selves seen as unruly. She teaches a deeply spiritual embrace of the sacred Feminine. Part of what Truman must learn is a respect for women and an awareness of their equal humanity. This is evident in the change in his relationship with Meridian. In later works Walker celebrates the ways in which feminism and feminist scholarship have contributed to the awareness and embrace of the sacred Feminine.

The essays in *We Are the Ones We Have Been Waiting For* are in the tradition of Walker's calls to action and greater awareness. They are characterized by her ongoing honesty and refusal to romanticize. She speaks with absolute clarity about the obstacles we face; nevertheless she remains committed to a global revolution based on an exciting and deeply spiritual sense of the possible. "There is much work to be done, sister and brother Earthlings. But we have, if we work earnestly enough, all of eternity to do it" (23). We must begin by embracing all that we are and treating ourselves with unfailing tenderness. In the poem "A Blessing" she encourages us to do as best we can what we are called to do and then "*Let it alone, don't try so hard. / This is God, too*" (52).

Walker continues to emphasize evolution and continual process. She is deeply distrustful of utopias and the violence people are willing to perpetrate to attain their own visions of reality. A critical attribute of the spiritual warrior is the ability to accept and work with what is. This necessarily includes the ability "to accept the fact that we risk disappointment, disillusionment, even despair, every time we act" (*Anything We Love* xxiv), and to act anyway. Ultimately, the spiritual warrior is sustained by a deep faith in the goodness of the Universe. Through her own commitment, Walker has seen and experienced this belief as truth. She continues to offer us her testimony that the path of the spiritual warrior, though challenging, is open to all.

The essence of the spiritual warrior is our trust "that the Universe will respond to our fidelity to our true nature by teaching us ways of being that will help us carry our unique burden—our deep, inevitable, irrevocable caring about people and the world— which is, at the same time, our most magnificent flower" (*We Are the Ones* 240).

Works Cited

Byrd, Rudolph. P. Introduction. *The World Has Changed: Conversations with Alice Walker*. Ed. Rudolph P. Byrd. New York: New Press, 2010. 1–35.

Christian, Barbara. "The Black Woman Artist as Wayward." *Alice Walker*. Ed. Harold Bloom. New York: Chelsea, 1989. 39–58.

Dubey, Madhu. *Black Women Novelists and the Nationalist Aesthetic*. Bloomington: Indiana UP, 1994.

Riley, Patricia. "Wrapped in the Serpent's Tail: Alice Walker's African–Native American Sensibility." *When Brer Rabbit Meets Coyote: African–Native American Literature*. Ed. Jonathan Brennan. Urbana: U of Illinois P, 2003. 241–256.

Simcikova, Karla. *To Live Fully, Here and Now: The Healing Vision in the Works of Alice Walker*. New York: Lexington, 2007.

Trungpa, Chogyam. *Shambala: The Sacred Path of the Warrior*. Boston: Shambala, 1988.

Walker, Alice. *Anything We Love Can Be Saved: A Writer's Activism*. New York: Random, 1997.

_____. *In Search of Our Mothers' Gardens: Womanist Prose*. New York: Harcourt, 1983.

_____. *Meridian*. New York: Harcourt, 1976.

_____. *The Way Forward Is with a Broken Heart*. New York: Random: 2000.

_____. *We Are the Ones We Have Been Waiting For: Inner Light in a Time of Darkness—Meditations*. New York: New Press, 2006.

Looking for God: Alice Walker's *The Color Purple* and Gloria Naylor's *Mama Day*_____

Paula C. Barnes

Much has been written on the relationship between Alice Walker's *The Color Purple* (1982) and Zora Neale Hurston's *Their Eyes Were Watching God* (1937), undoubtedly due to Walker's acknowledgment of Hurston as her literary foremother. Based upon the citations in the Modern Language Association (MLA) Bibliography, there are approximately fifty critical articles and dissertations that explore Walker's novel in light of Hurston's. The number remains almost the same for essays that discuss *The Color Purple* in conjunction with other texts, yet only 25 percent of them examine the novel in relation to works by subsequent African American women writers, many of whom had the benefit not only of studying creative writing in the academy but also of having access to the works of their cultural literary foremothers. Among this cadre of African American women writers is Gloria Naylor. Much has been written about her indebtedness to literary works in the traditional Western canon—Dante's *Inferno*, Shakespeare's *The Tempest*, *Hamlet*, and *King Lear*. In addition, Naylor's novels have been discussed in conjunction with those by African American women writers, such as Ann Petry's *The Street*; Toni Morrison's *Song of Solomon*, *Beloved*, and *Tar Baby*; Paule Marshall's *Praisesong for the Widow*; and Walker's *Possessing the Secret of Joy*—but notably absent from the list is *The Color Purple*. Yet *The Color Purple* is a pivotal text in the African American female literary tradition as suggested by the volume of criticism (over two hundred articles in the MLA Bibliography alone) dedicated to it, the awards, including the Pulitzer Prize and National Book Award, that Walker has received for it and its adaptation into a film with eleven Grammy award nominations and a Broadway musical that earned eleven Tony awards (Whitted "*The Color Purple*"). *The Color Purple* has proven to be a "text that 'talks' with and to other texts"; among such texts within the African American women's literary tradition is Gloria Naylor's *Mama Day* (1989) (Storhoff). Not only does *Mama Day* "talk with" *The Color Purple*; it revises certain aspects of the novel and exists in a "corrective relationship" for others (Smith-Wright 20); these features suggest that *The Color Purple* is a literary antecedent of *Mama Day*.

There are a number of similarities to suggest the influence of *The Color Purple* on *Mama Day*: both novels are set in the South; both privilege orality over the written text by utilizing a rhetorical strategy identified by Henry Louis Gates Jr. as "the speakerly text," where language patterns produce the "illusion of oral narration" (181); and both use the narrative technique of "free indirect discourse" (Gates 248; Storhoff). These similarities are also applicable when *Mama Day* is compared to *Their Eyes*, Walker's "pre-text"; however, there are many other parallels that are unique to *Mama Day* and *The Color Purple* (C. Wall 141). These novels not only attempt to replicate the protagonists' language patterns but also intentionally involve the reader as their audience. According to Mary Jane Lupton, "the reader is . . . included by implication" in *The Color Purple* in the salutation of Celie's final letter: "Dear God. Dear stars, dear trees, dear sky, dear peoples" (416). In the introductory chapter of *Mama Day,* the reader is directly addressed not only by the imperative to "listen. Really listen" but also by the phrase "the only voice [you hear] is your own" (Naylor 10). The only voice the readers hear in *The Color Purple* is also their own, for the novel is composed entirely of letters.

Both novels are centered on a female community that includes three principal characters: Celie, Shug, and Nettie in *The Color Purple* and Sapphira Wade, Miranda (Mama) Day, and Ophelia (Cocoa) Day in *Mama Day,* yet it is with their respective protagonists, Celie and Cocoa, that the similarities become most apparent. Both women are orphaned; they are emotionally damaged by the perceptions of others—Celie is labeled black, "pore," and ugly (Walker 206) while Cocoa is called a leper because she is near-white in a community that treasures brown-skinned women; they are "saved" by another who provides a "life-giving intimacy"—Celie by Shug and Cocoa by her husband, George (Byrd 375). Finally, letters are crucially important to them: Celie communicates by letters—fifty-six to God, and fourteen to her sister, Nettie. Cocoa communicates by letter with her grandmother Abigail and great-aunt Mama Day while she resides in New York; according to Betina Entzminger, Cocoa has written seventy-seven letters home (60).

The motif of hearing/listening is significant to *The Color Purple* and *Mama Day*. Because Celie has been ordered by her (step)father "to tell nobody but God" of the incest that leads to her birthing two children, she writes to God and continues to do so even after she learns that her husband (whom she identifies only as Mr. _____) has been keeping Nettie's letters from her (Walker 1). It is when Nettie informs her that the man they believe to be their father is actually their stepfather that Celie ceases to write to God. When Shug asks what happened to her letters to God, Celie says, He's "trifling, forgitful and lowdown." When Shug cautions that God might *hear* her, Celie responds: "Let 'im *hear* me. . . . If he ever *listened* to poor colored women the world would be a different place" (Walker 192, my emphasis). Visualizing God as sitting in heaven and "glorying in being deef" [i.e. deaf], Celie is angry because He seems not to listen to her prayers (Walker 193, 195). In *Mama Day*, hearing/listening is crucial, thus, the instruction to "listen. Really listen" (Naylor 10). Listening with Mama Day, readers hear about the beginning of the Days as a woman "humming a lost and ancient song" heads "toward the east bluff over the ocean," and they hear the coming storm (Naylor 118, 226–27). With Cocoa, readers hear the silent whispers in the west woods telling her she is going to break George's heart, and they eventually realize that they are listening to George as he speaks from the grave (Naylor 223, 224). Walker and Naylor use the hearing/listening motif to prepare readers to move from the realm of the natural to the realm of the spiritual: because Celie thinks her God, whom she views as a white man, does not listen to her, she becomes receptive to Shug's notion of God as neither he nor she, but "It," and as readers learn to listen in *Mama Day*, they are presented the choice, like George, to move beyond the rational with its verifiable facts to that which cannot be verified by facts but must be accepted through belief (Walker 195).

Perhaps the most subtle of the similarities in these novels is the incorporation of the color purple itself. The passage in *The Color Purple*, where Shug discusses the nature of God to Celie, has been often quoted:

> God love everything you love—and a mess of stuff you don't. But more than anything else, God love admiration.
>
> You saying God vain? I ast.
>
> Naw, she say. Not vain, just wanting to share a good thing. I think it pisses God off if you walk by the color purple in a field somewhere and don't notice it. (Walker 196)

The reference to purple in *Mama Day* is also from a passage about God:

> It seems like God reached way down into his box of paints, found the purest reds, the deepest purples, and a dab of midnight blue, then just kinda trailed his fingers along the curve of the horizon and let 'em all bleed down. And when them streaks of color hit the hush-a-by green of the marsh grass with the blue of the Sound behind 'em, you ain't never had to set foot in a church to know you looking at a living prayer. (Naylor 78)

In this passage, purple appears not only with mention of the color itself but also through its composite colors, blue and red; consequently, its significance is underscored by the repetition. In both novels, purple becomes significant because of its association with God.

Noting the dearth of early critical attention on the spiritual aspect of *The Color Purple*, Alice Walker states that it is "a theological work"

(Thyreen 49). Discussing its theological nature, scholar Jeannine Thyreen asserts that the novel seeks to answer the question "What is God?" (50). Gloria Naylor is also interested in the spiritual enterprise; consequently, *Mama Day* is organized around "tropes of spiritual power and Biblical revision" (Naylor and Ashford). Therefore, it is within the context of their explorations of God that *Mama Day* becomes a literary descendant of *The Color Purple*. As they undertake such an examination in their novels, Walker and Naylor begin "in the beginning"—with the biblical story of creation.

The Biblical Creation Story

The biblical story of God and His original encounter with humans is revealed in Genesis 1 and 2, which scholars generally agree are comprised of two narratives—one that relates the creation of the world, the other that recounts the creation of mankind (Tsumura 27–29). These two narratives appear, with some variations and revisions, in *The Color Purple* and *Mama Day*.

The creation story in *The Color Purple* is from the Olinkas, the African tribe to whom Samuel, Corinne, and Celie's sister Nettie are missionaries. Joseph, their African translator/guide, tells them that the white missionaries had shared the story of Adam and Eve's being tricked by the serpent and expelled from the Garden of Eden. When the Olinkas heard the part of the biblical narrative where Adam and Eve became aware of their nakedness, they laughed. Explaining that the Olinka word for *naked* is *white*, the Olinkas informed the missionaries that "it was they who put Adam and Eve out of the village" because of the couple's nakedness (Walker 273). In the Olinka version of the biblical creation story, Adam was not the first man, but the first *white* man (Walker 272, my emphasis). Thus, as Wendy Wall explains, the Olinka displaced "the Christian myth of origin. . . . Instead of the creation myth explaining the fall, the Olinkas read it as an explanation of white prejudice."

The second Olinka story reveals the tribe's conception of God. The translator/guide also relates the story of the roofleaf to the black missionaries during the village's welcoming ceremony. The leaf of a certain plant that grew in abundance was used by the Olinka for the roofs of their huts. After the chief began to cultivate the land with other crops to trade with whites on the coast, a powerful storm arose that destroyed the roofs of Olinka huts. Joseph describes the storm:

> For six months the heavens and the winds abused the people of Olinka. Rain came down in spears, stabbing away the mud of their walls. The wind was so fierce it blew rocks out of the walls. . . . Then cold rocks, shaped like millet balls, fell from the sky, striking everyone . . . . By the end of the rainy season, half the village was gone.
>
> The people prayed to their gods and waited impatiently for the seasons to change. (Walker 153)

When the storm season finally ceased, the Olinka discovered that only a few dozen roofleaf beds remained. They recultivated the crop, and when it returned, they repaired their roofs, celebrated with song and dance, and from that time on worshipped the roofleaf. Turning to the missionaries, Joseph explains, "We know a roofleaf is not Jesus Christ, but in its own humble way, is it not God? (Walker 154). Because the Olinka received no answer during the storm, they changed the focus and locus of their worship—from "their gods" to "a place without walls but with a leaf roof" (Walker 152). The relocation of worship from "their gods" to the roofleaf was intracultural; however, it also influenced the Olinkas' perspective of the Christian God. Implied in the comparison of the roofleaf to God—"its own humble way, is it not God?"—is the premise that the roofleaf is equal to God. The corollary then is that God is the roofleaf. For the Olinkas, the Christian God is supplanted by the roofleaf.

The first of the two accounts that relate to the biblical creation story in *Mama Day* appears as one of the novel's three "introductory texts"

(Page 172). A genealogical chart tracing the lineage of the Day family beginning with its ancestor, Sapphira Wade, is located between a map of the island of Willow Springs and a copy of Sapphira's slave bill of sale. The chart outlines six generations of the Day family, including two consecutive generations of seven males followed by generations of females. In the first generation is an echo of the biblical creation narrative: Sapphira gives birth to seven sons each carrying the name of an Old Testament prophet. Only the seventh son carries the surname Day, which is accompanied by an asterisk. Below the names of the two females of the sixth generation is the notation for the asterisk—two sentences: "'God rested on the seventh day and so would she.' Hence the family name" (Naylor 1). Shirley A. Stave summarizes the import of elements of the genealogical chart. She writes,

> given that the two generations [of males] replicate the chronology of the Bible, one would assume one male progenitor to head the family tree. On this family tree, however, the line of descent begins not with a man but with a woman. . . . No male counterpart is cited on the document; hence, the original forebear, the one who was in the beginning and set into motion the prophets and apostles, . . . cannot be read as God the Father" (98).

Unlike the Olinka creation myth, which displaces the biblical story of human origin, the genealogical chart in *Mama Day* invokes it; its revision is that the "original forebear" is a woman. The import of this revision is underscored in the repetition of the genealogical chart—in prose form—later in the novel.

The second creation myth in *Mama Day* addresses the origin of the island of Willow Springs:

> The island got spit out from the mouth of God, and when it fell to earth it brought along an army of stars. He tried to reach down and scoop them back up, and found Himself shaking hands with the greatest conjure woman on

earth. 'Leave 'em here, Lord,' she said. 'I ain't got nothing but these poor black hands to guide my people, but I can lead on with light. (Naylor 110)

The God who creates Willow Springs appears in this version of the Genesis creation story. However, when He reaches down to retrieve the stars, He meets a woman who asks Him to leave them so she can "lead on with light." The phrase is an important one, for it is linked to Candle Walk, the annual Willow Springs celebration held December 22 that supplants Christmas. The original purpose of the celebration—and the light—has altered with time, but the omniscient narrator, able to trace it back two generations, explains: when Miranda was a child, people would walk to the ocean bluff beyond the east woods, raise their candles and say, "Lead on with light, Great Mother. Lead on with light"; the people of Miranda's father's generation worshipped his African-born grandmother, "a slave woman who *took* her freedom," and the candles were to light her way (Naylor 111). The two explanations of Candle Walk reinforce the two versions of the novel's creation story and their singular argument of God as woman. However, just as the Olinka story of the roofleaf does not displace the Christian God, God is not displaced in the creation myths in *Mama Day*. In Naylor's variants of the creation story, God is "the first creator," yet there is a "powerful female partner" (Levy 219).

Within the two biblical creation stories in *The Color Purple* and *Mama Day* are three thematic strands—the nature of God, the creation of the world, and the Adam and Eve story. Each of these strands is developed in the novels: what is not addressed in the myths themselves is presented through textual references to creation. When Shug tells Albert (Celie's Mr. _____) that she is taking Celie to Memphis, he replies, "Over my dead body," to which Celie responds, "It's time to leave you and enter into the Creation. And your dead body just the welcome mat I need" (Walker 199). The image of Celie entering Creation by walking over the "dead body" of Mr. _____ evokes the image of the biblical Eve standing over an awakened Adam; therefore, it is a subtle revision of the creation of woman. But, more importantly, the image is also one of Celie's rebirth. Celie enters into a new world as a new person; thus, in this passage of *The Color Purple* is the thematic strand of the biblical creation of the world. In *Mama Day,* it is the Adam and Eve story that is recounted when Cocoa takes George through the west woods to the other place. Seeing the flowering trees with "bursts of color among all the dark greens and browns: magnolia, yellow jasmine and wisteria" as a "wild garden," a "paradise," George suggests that they play "Adam and Eve" (Naylor 217, 222). George's perspective of Willow Springs is that of the Garden of Eden before the Fall and the fig leaves. Having grown up there, Cocoa knows that Willow Springs is Eden after the Fall and Adam's biting into the forbidden fruit; therefore, she informs George that the consequence of his becoming naked in the west woods of Willow Springs is being bitten by the red ants (Naylor 222). In these references to the biblical creation story in each novel is an allusion to death. In *The Color Purple* the reference is explicit: Celie eventually verbalizes her cloaked desire to kill Mr. _____ because he has withheld Nettie's letters. In *Mama Day*, the allusion is oblique: Cocoa gets George to acknowledge the realities of life in paradise after the Fall by mentioning the immediate consequences in the Adam and Eve story. What she does not mention—and does not want to acknowledge even to herself—is the long-range consequences: a knowledge of good and evil, and with it, the inevitability of death. Cocoa does not share with George her knowledge that the other place is linked to death.

Walker and Naylor's revisions of the biblical creation story are significant. Both authors revise the biblical narrative in terms of gender, but Walker also revises it in terms of race. The Bible is displaced in *The Color Purple*; it is signified upon in *Mama Day*. The Olinka myths in *The Color Purple* further Walker's pantheistic vision; the creation myths in *Mama Day* expand the Biblical creation story to include the aspect of the feminine. However, incorporation of the biblical creation stories in both novels becomes part of a larger enterprise—questioning the concept of God.

Depictions of God in *The Color Purple* and *Mama Day*

If *The Color Purple* is a spiritual descendant of *Their Eyes Were Watching God* as Jane Davis argues, then *Mama Day* is a spiritual descendant of *The Color Purple*. Walker's novel is a conscious effort to revise the patriarchal image of God that appears in *Their Eyes*, and Naylor's novel is a conscious effort to revise the depictions of God in *The Color Purple*.

The depiction of God as a white man appears in *Their Eyes* when Janie and her husband Tea Cake, who are among those who do not leave before the hurricane arrives, become silent during the raging winds, thunder, and lightning—the evidence that "Ole Massa is doin' *His* work" (Hurston 150). The implication that "Ole Massa" (a synonym since slavery for the white man) is God not only is suggested by the capitalization of "His" but also made explicit in a subsequent line that serves as the novel's title: "their eyes were watching *God*" (Hurston 151, my emphasis). The image is revised in *The Color Purple*, but first it is repeated. In the passage where Shug asks Celie why she no longer writes to God, Celie describes God at Shug's request:

He big and old and tall and graybearded and white. He wear white robes and go barefooted.

Blue eyes? [Shug] ast.

Sort of bluish-gray. Cool. Big though. White lashes. I say.

She laugh . . . .

Then she tell me this old white man is the same God she used to see when she prayed. (Walker 194)

Walker begins the conversation with *Their Eyes* by repeating the white male God image; Naylor begins by rejecting it. Therefore, *Mama Day* enters into dialogue with *The Color Purple* through what is identified as a "corrective relationship" (Smith-Wright 20); the novel modifies the question on the nature of God from "What is God?" in *The Color Purple* to "Who is God?"

Mama Day begins its revision of the nature of God by switching "the gender of the deity" (Stave 99): God is depicted as a woman. This substitution is implied in the introductory genealogical chart, for Sapphira Wade is presented as the sole creator of the Days/days (i.e., time). Sapphira is depicted as having other characteristics of the divine: like the biblical YHWH, her name is "too sacred to be spoken aloud" (Ohlsen 16:f2); folks in Willow Springs "only whisper the name Sapphira" (Naylor 151). While awaiting the coming storm, the natural event that shapes the novel, the people of Willow Springs send up "prayers . . . to be spared from what could only be the workings of Woman. And She has no name" (Naylor 251). The residents of Willow Springs worship the Woman with no name; the capitalization suggests that she is God. Even the rationally minded George acknowledges that God is a woman; sitting quietly and helplessly during the storm, he recognizes that "the winds coming around the corners of that house was God" (Naylor 251).

Naylor's revision of Walker's depiction of God does not end with a regendering; she complicates the issue by depicting God as both male and female. The female God, Sapphira Wade, is present in the genealogical chart, but so is a male God. Both are there in the beginning: he "rested on the seventh day and so would she" (Naylor 1). The two deities also appear together in the Willow Springs creation myth: when God reaches down to gather up the stars, He shakes hands with Sapphira, who requests that He leave them so that she can lead with light. God complies with her request; a handshake binds their agreement, and the two enter into an equal partnership. James Robert Saunders provides a third example; he writes, "there is the suggestion . . . that God is a woman. Mama Day . . . 'prays to the Father and Son as she'd been taught. But she falls asleep murmuring the names of women'" (60). Naylor's intent is not to displace the traditional Christian God; instead, she seeks to expand the concept of God. As Stave so aptly explains it, "*Mama Day* can be read as Naylor's exploration of what a theology of [the] feminine counterpart [to the male Jahweh] might entail" (98).

Finally, and perhaps most importantly, *Mama Day* provides a counterpoint to Walker's notion of pantheism: the elements of nature are not God; they are controlled by God—more specifically, the female God. When Shug instructs Celie to "git man off [her] eyeball" by "conjur[ing] up flowers, wind, water," Celie responds, "He been there so long, he don't want to budge. He threaten lightening, floods, earthquakes" (Walker 197). *Mama Day* counters this by clearly indicating that conjuring is the domain of women as seen through Sapphira, Mama Day, and her nemesis Ruby. Moreover, the natural elements in Shug's list—flowers, wind, and water—are specifically linked to Sapphira. At the beginning of the Days/days, Sapphira places flowers in the garden *she* designed—zinnias, morning glories, the deeper-colored [i.e., purple] wisteria—as well as flowering bushes (224, 226, 243; my emphasis). She leaves the island by wind in 1823, but returns in 1985, bringing wind and water together to form a hurricane:

> far off and low the real winds come in. It starts on the shores of Africa, a simple breeze among the palms and cassavas, before it's carried off . . . on a strong wave heading due west. A world of water . . . weeks of water, and all them breezes die but one. . . . [I]t starts to spin counterclockwise against the march of time. . . . A center grows within the fury of the spinning winds. . . . Calm. . . . A buried calm with the awesome power of its face turned to Willow Springs. It hits the southeast corner of the bluff, raising a fist of water into them high rocks. (Naylor 249–50)

Naylor makes it clear that the God who "threaten[s] lightening, floods, earthquakes" is a woman.

In *Mama Day*, time is Sapphira's domain. The genealogical chart makes it clear that Sapphira *creates*—and names—the Days/days (the oral nature of the text is important here: by listening, the reader hears the wordplay); the Days/days, thus time, do not exist until she names them. In addition, as Valerie Lee notes, in producing seven sons in one thousand days, "Sapphira is not fixed by time," she manipulates it (130).

Sapphira also controls nature and land:

> She could walk through a lightning storm without being touched; grab a
> bolt of lightning in the palm of her hand. . . . She turned the moon into
> salve, the stars into a swaddling cloth, and healed the wounds of every
> creature walking up on two or down on four. (Naylor 3)

Willow Springs becomes hers because, according to George, she "talked a man out of a whole island (Naylor 219). All acts of nature, including the island's major storms of 1823, 1920, and 1985, are manifestations of her power over nature. Shug's belief that "God is everything" is corrected in *Mama Day*, whose premise is that God is the *Creator* of everything (Walker 195).

Naylor further advances the premise that nature is not God but rather "the realm of God" through an extended counterargument using tree imagery, addressed in both novels within the context of spirituality (Harris 96). The first significant reference to a tree in *The Color Purple* is in Celie's explanation of her coping strategy when being beaten by Mr. _____: "It all I can do not to cry. I make myself wood. I say to myself, Celie, you a tree" (Walker 22). Shug later affirms Celie's notion of becoming one with the tree when she explains the steps in her evolutionary process from traditional Christianity to pantheism. Shug's "first step from the white man [is] trees"; then, believing that God was in everything, she acknowledges that if [she] cut a tree, [her] arm would bleed" (Walker 195, 196). After experiencing a life-saving transformation under Shug's tutelage, Celie, like Shug, views nature as God. In response to Mr. _____'s insolence when he is told that she is going to Memphis with Shug, Celie pronounces a curse on him and then predicts that everything he dreams of will fail. Explaining her source for this newfound act of courage, which occurs after Celie has abandoned her communication with God, Celie says, "it seem to come to me from the trees" (Walker 206). Celie's total acceptance of Shug's philosophy of pantheism is expressed in her final letter in *The Color Purple*; she writes, "Dear God. Dear stars, dear trees, dear sky, dear peoples. Dear everything. Dear God" (Walker 283). Like Shug, Celie comes to view God as/in everything; consequently, a number of the elements of nature, including trees, are listed in the salutation.

To underscore Shug and Celie's spiritual journeys to nature in America, Walker provides a parallel in Africa. Shug's worship of trees corresponds to the Olinkas' worship of the roofleaf, which takes on the properties of a tree as its leaves provide shelter and protection. The mass destruction of the roofleaf, first by the village chief and then by the white men from the coast, indicates that as a God, it is as powerless as the missionaries' Christian God (Walker 227). The equivalent, then, to the Olinkas' abandonment of the worship of the roofleaf God is Celie's abandonment of the Christian God, for both discover that their God is powerless to help them.

Perhaps because the tree becomes God in *The Color Purple*, it is an important image in *Mama Day*. Setting figures prominently here: the island's name, Willow Springs, is part tree (even though there are no willow trees there). Also, there are three sets of woods on the island; consequently, trees of all kinds are in abundance. Although Sapphira had planted peach and pecan trees in her original garden, she is primarily connected to wind and water. It is her twentieth-century counterpart, Mama Day, who is more closely aligned with trees. Just as Sapphira "could walk through a lightning storm without being touched," the young Miranda, or Little Mama, could "walk through a dry winter without snapping a single twig" or "disappear into the shadow of a summer cottonwood"; as a result, "folks started believing [that] John-Paul's little girl became a spirit in the woods" (Naylor 3, 79). Unlike Celie, the young girl does not become wood (i.e., tree); rather, she becomes a spirit *in the woods*. Reaching adulthood, Mama Day retains her connection with trees. The evening she takes a stroll in Ambush Duvall's woods, the narrator reveals that "she can still stand so quiet she becomes part of a tree" (Naylor 81). The emphasis in this sentence is on Mama Day's ability to be so quiet that she *appears* to become part of a tree. As Cheryl Wall explains, Mama Day's quiet standing is a model for the kind of listening that is required in Willow Springs—a stillness that allows one to hear the sounds of nature (178). Finally, at the other place after the hurricane, Mama Day

> runs her fingers in the ridges of the tree trunk. . . . Under the grayish light her skin seems to dissolve into the fallen tree, her palm spreading out wide as the trunk, her fingers twisting out in a dozen directions, branching off into green and rippling fingernails. She tries to pull her hand away, only to send the huge fingers and nails rippling and moving in the air. She cries out startled, pulling so fiercely she scrapes her knuckles before realizing her thumb is stuck under a branch. (Naylor 255)

Mama Day does not merge with the tree; in fact, it seems to be antagonistic. Nonetheless, the tree communicates with Mama Day. Licking her bloody knuckles, she tastes death and the pain Bernice Duvall feels because her son has died. In contrast to Celie, Mama Day remains separate from the tree; like Sapphira, she works in conjunction with nature; thus, the message is clear: the tree is not God.

The corrective relationship between *The Color Purple* and *Mama Day* concerning the nature of God is threefold. The traditional God of Christianity is not displaced as in *The Color Purple*; instead, God is explored in the feminine. Moreover, God is not "gender-neutral" (Andujo 73); on the contrary, God becomes inclusive, incorporating both the masculine *and* the feminine, as revealed in a passage in the Genesis creation story that has been ignored: "[s]o God created man in His own image, in the image of God created he him; *male and female* He created them" (*Genesis* 1:27, my emphasis). Thus, Naylor restores the image of God to the biblical original. Finally, in response to the pantheism in *The Color Purple*, *Mama Day* proposes that God is not in nature; God is God *of* nature. Walker's theological question "What is God?" is replaced with the question "Who is God?"

As *Mama Day* enters into the theological debate with *The Color Purple*, it becomes to *The Color Purple* what Jane Davis argues *The Color Purple* is to *Their Eyes Were Watching God*—a spiritual descendant. Another literary work is added to those claimed to have influenced *Mama Day*, but, just as importantly, because of the dialogue between *The Color Purple* and *Mama Day*, Alice Walker not only has a literary foremother, she is a literary foremother.

Works Cited

Andujo, Patricia. "Rendering the African-American Woman's God through *The Color Purple*." *Alice Walker's The Color Purple*. Eds. Kheven LaGrone and Michael J. Meyer. Amsterdam, Netherlands: Rodopi, 2009. 61–76.

Byrd, Rudolph P. "Spirituality in the Novels of Alice Walker: Models, Healing, and Transformation, Or When the Spirit Moves So Do We." *Wild Women in the Whirlwind: Afra–American Culture and the Contemporary Literary Renaissance*. Eds. Joanne M. Braxton and Andrée Nicola McLaughlin. New Brunswick, NJ: Rutgers UP, 1990. 363–78.

"*The Color Purple*." *Theatrical Rights Worldwide*, Theatrical Rights Worldwide, 2010. Web. 8 July 2011.

Davis, Jane. "*The Color Purple*: A Spiritual Descendant of Hurston's *Their Eyes Were Watching God*." *Griot: Official Journal of the Southern Conference on Afro-American Studies* 6.2 (1987): 79–86.

Entzminger, Betina. "The Legacy of Sapphira Wade: European and African Cultural References in Gloria Naylor's *Mama Day*." *Griot: Official Journal of the Southern Conference on Afro-American Studies* 24:1 (2005): 57–68.

Gates, Henry Louis, Jr. *The Signifying Monkey: A Theory of African-American Literary Criticism*. New York: Oxford UP, 1989.

Genesis. *The Holy Bible*. King James Version. Camden, NJ: Nelson, 1970.

Harris, Trudier. "The Eye as Voice and Ear: African Southern Orality and Folklore in Gloria Naylor's *Mama Day*." *The Power of the Porch: The Storyteller's Craft in Zora Neale Hurston, Gloria Naylor, and Randall Kenan*. Athens: U of Georgia P, 1996. 53–104.

Hurston, Zora Neale. *Their Eyes Were Watching God*. New York: Harper, 1990.

Lee, Valerie. *Granny Midwives and Black Women Writers: Double-Dutched Readings*. New York: Routledge 1996.

Levy, Helen. *Fiction of the Home Place: Jewett, Cather, Glasgow, Porter, Welty, and Naylor.* Jackson: UP of Mississippi, 1992: 198–222.

Lupton, Mary Jane. "Clothes and Closure in Three Novels by Black Women." *Black American Literature Forum* 20.4 (1986): 409–21.

Naylor, Gloria. *Mama Day.* New York: Random, 1989.

Naylor, Gloria, and Tomeiko R. Ashford. "Gloria Naylor on Black Spirituality: An Interview." *MELUS* 30.4 (2005): 73–87.

Ohlsen, Leslie. *Perspectives on Old Testament Literature.* New York: Harcourt, 1978.

Page, Philip. *Reclaiming Community in Contemporary African American Fiction.* Jackson: UP of Mississippi, 1999. 157–90.

Saunders, James Robert. "From the Hypocrisy of the Reverend Woods to Mama Day's Faith in the Spirit." *The Critical Response to Gloria Naylor.* Eds. Sharon Felton and Michelle C. Loris. Westport, CT: Greenwood, 1997. 48–61.

Smith-Wright, Geraldine. "Revision as Collaboration: Zora Neale Hurston's *Their Eyes Were Watching God* as Source for Alice Walker's *The Color Purple.*" *SAGE: A Scholarly Journal on Black Women* 4.2 (1987): 20–25.

Stave, Shirley A. *Gloria Naylor: Strategy and Technique, Magic and Myth.* Newark: U of Delaware P, 2001.

Storhoff, Gary. "'The Only Voice Is Your Own': Gloria Naylor's Revision of *The Tempest.*" *African American Review* 29.1 (1995): 35–45. *Academic Search Premier.* Web. 25 June 2006.

Thyreen, Jeannine. "Alice Walker's *The Color Purple*: Redefining God and (Re)Claiming the Spirit Within." *Christianity and Literature* 49.1 (1999): 49–66.

Tsumura, David T. "Genesis and Ancient Near Eastern Stories of Creation and the Flood: An Introduction." *I Studied Inscriptions From Before the Flood: Ancient Near Eastern, Literary and Linguistic Approaches to Genesis 1–11.* Eds. Richard S. Hess and David T. Tsumura. Winona Lake, IN: Eisenbrauns, 1994. 27–57. *Google Books.* 20 Sept. 2011.

Walker, Alice. *The Color Purple.* Orlando: Harcourt, 1982.

Wall, Cheryl. "Writing Beyond the Blues: *The Color Purple.*" *Worrying the Line: Black Women Writers, Lineage, and Literary Tradition.* Chapel Hill: U of North Carolina P, 2005: 140–61.

Wall, Wendy. "Lettered Bodies and Corporeal Texts in *The Color Purple.*" *Studies in American Fiction* 16.1 (1988): 83–97.

Whitted, Qiana. "*The Color Purple.*" *The New Georgia Encyclopedia.* 13 Aug. 2001. Web. 8 July 2011.

Walker's Womanist Agenda

In Search of Our Mothers' Gardens: Womanist Prose (*Gardens*) is a compilation of Walker's articles, reviews, and essays written between 1968 and 1983. The very structure of this text can be envisioned as a garden because, like the many varieties of flowers one would expect to find in a well-tended garden (shape, color, size, balance), each written piece represents a distinct aesthetic and intellectual event. The essays are specimens of Walker's lively curiosity, political discernment, idealism, and fearless engagement with the world of ideas.

In many of her essays, Walker encourages personal growth and social change, addresses the necessity of acknowledging one's ancestors and history, and stresses the need for individual and collective healing and wholeness as they influence the quality of life on the planet. Finally, in a departure from the mainstream ideology that predominated during the time in which the essays were written—an ideology she saw as narrow and exclusive—Walker originated an alternative ideology that sought to correct the rift of exclusion due to one's gender, race, or culture, that supports her humanistic stance, and allows her to be black-woman-focused. She designated this ideology as "womanism."

In 1981, Alice Walker introduced the term "womanist" in a book review about the life of Rebecca Cox Jackson, an itinerant black female minister who spent the later years of her life with a spiritual sister and companion, who was also named Rebecca. Walker objected to the use of the word "lesbian" by the nonblack editor of Jackson's writings, who was attempting to describe the nature of the exclusive relationship these two women shared. According to Walker, Jackson's writings expressed nothing overtly that indicated the relationship was a sexual one. Indeed, she felt that the relationship was one of mutual love of God and all things spiritual. Therefore, she questioned the label of "lesbian." In her mind, black women had been woman-bonding and loving each other nonsexually for centuries, which is an aspect of African culture. Walker found this editor culturally incompetent to define the relationship between Jackson and her companion. In this particular circumstance—where the nature of the relationship between these two black women was not specified in Jackson's own words— she decided that certainly "lesbian" was not a suitable term for black women and their relationships:

> I can imagine black women who love women (sexually or not) . . . refer-
> ring to themselves as "whole" women, from "wholly" or "holy." Or as
> "round" women—women who love other women, yes, but women who
> also have a concern, in a culture that oppresses all black people . . . for
> their fathers, brothers, and sons, no matter how they feel about them as
> males. My own term for such women would be "womanist" (81).

The use of "womanist" by black women to define themselves would not limit itself to simply woman-bonding, but it:

> would have to be both spiritual and concrete, and it would have to be or-
> ganic, characteristic, not simply applied. A word that said more than that
> they choose women over men. . . . [T]o be consistent with black cultural
> values . . . it would have to be a word that affirmed connectedness to the
> entire community and the world, rather than separation, *regardless* of who
> worked and slept with whom (81).

There is a strong spiritual core for the term "womanist"; however, when Walker first defined the term as it is found in the opening pages of *Gardens*, it was in a racial/cultural context: "A black feminist or feminist of color." Walker was intent on emphasizing the fact that black women did not share a common history or tradition with white women. For Walker, even the term "feminist" later became inadequate because it was a term used by elite, privileged white women who have historically ignored the complex realities of black women and other women of color. Walker found dissatisfaction in the narrow and exclusive stance of the feminist movement of the 1970s—a social movement that had as its major objective the abolishment of the sexual, political, and economic oppression of women, a movement that tended to subsume the intricate realities of non-Anglo women within it, thus rendering them invisible. This led her to search for a more inclusive ideology. She saw that white women and black men, preoccupied with their own agendas for power and influence in American society, shared the same inability to empathize with the marginalization of black women, this in spite of the fact that feminists claimed a commitment to relieving the oppression of *all* women. Some black men selfishly claimed the political debate for black liberation as their own preserve and discouraged black women's political involvement.[1] As Walker says, "white women feminists revealed themselves as incapable as black men of comprehending blackness and feminism in the same body" (374). Another shortcoming of the feminist movement at the time was some American feminists did not consider the global or universal oppression of women. Walker says, "when [I] thought of women moving, [I] automatically thought of women all over the world. . . . [I] had traveled and had every reason to understand that women's freedom was an idea whose time had come, and that it was sweeping the world" (378). Furthermore, during her early career as an educator, the exclusion of black women's written work from the scholarly and literary pursuits of white feminist academicians, as well as the neglect of black women's artistic works in feminist art exhibits, disheartened Walker.

Walker discovered that some mainstream feminists did not see her as a woman, but as simply black. To wit, "white 'feminists' are very often indistinguishable in their behavior from any other white persons in America" (388); which is to say that in America, black people are sometimes not seen by many whites as anything more than an extension of their race—gender does not enter the discussion. As a result, Walker seeks to avoid classification as a "black" feminist because the very term is incongruous to her. Perhaps she wondered why the adjective "black" needing placement before the noun "feminist," and why her support of the feminist movement justified the necessity of using the term "black feminist." Perhaps she questioned whether a black feminist was any more visible than was a white feminist. Consequently, Walker was interested in finding a term that did not exclude black women, yet did not make them visible simply *because* they were black. In a 1989 interview Walker said, "As a poet, I really object to these words where you have to hang on some color or other thing to make it visible. I wanted a word that was visible in itself because it came out of my own culture" (DeVeaux, 122).

Walker introduced the word *womanist* because it does not ground itself in sexual or class politics, does not disparage males, has a spiritual orientation, and seeks to be a unifying force. While some strongly argue that Walker's fictional depiction of black men is negative, one could argue that she is not castigating black men per se, but rather their brutal behavior towards black women, who are ultimately their counterparts in racial oppression. Womanism expands and contracts to embrace the broader perspective as well as the intricate networks that connect all life, animate and inanimate, within the composition of the whole universe. In this sense, as members of the human race we share a common experience—the gift of life, a gift that has been bestowed upon us by the Spirit which we must all nourish as well as cherish. Above all, Walker wanted a word that did not necessarily connote sexual preference. "You could be a womanist, period. That's why the foundation of it is not about your sexual preference, but about your self-love. *You* are the center of your world" (122).

In the years since Walker originated the term *womanist*, sexual preference is no longer the central issue; however, the focus on womanhood and spirituality remains. In 1993, the word *womanism,* as defined by Walker, was added to *The American Heritage Dictionary* (Nnaemeka). According to Obioma Nnaemeka, womanism as a concept "has had a profound influence in the formulation of theories and analytical frameworks in women/gender studies, religious studies, black studies, and literary studies. Because of the linking of black women and spirituality in Walker's project, many African American female theologians have incorporated womanist perspectives in their work" (Nnaemeka). We find the term used in a variety of ways: acknowledging one's fore-mothers, a way of reading black women's literature, a way of emphasizing spirituality in black religion from a female perspective.[2]

Womanism has shape and dimension. In Walker's own words, womanism is "'round' . . . spiritual and concrete . . . organic, characteristic . . . affirm[s] connectedness to the entire community and the world" (81). Womanism can contract to confine itself to the experience of the Self, or it can expand to encompass the Universe. From a mystical standpoint, one could interpret womanism as a way of attaining an understanding of the relationship of the Self to the totality of life. The attainment of this understanding signals closure of the final breach between the Self and completely being.

In many of her essays, Alice Walker pays homage to those who have come before her and who have been ignored. In "From an Interview," she names several female and male writers that span literary history, race, and cultures who have had an impact on her. However, to develop her craft as a black woman writer, black female and male literary ancestors provided the standard she needed to develop a voice that was consistent with and characteristic of her culture. The integration of European, international, as well as white and black American influences in her writing is a direct result of her search for models and exemplified in the development of her womanism as a configuration of inclusion (251, 257–60, and 262). In "Saving the Life That Is Your Own: The Importance of Models in the Artist's Life," the opening essay of *Gardens*, she states that a writer must have models in order to depict the world. In the context of this essay, Walker's use of the term "models" seems to take into consideration not only a predecessor or the product of an individual's creative outpourings, but the act of creating an image or an idea where it did not before exist, or the fulfillment of a specific need for the benefit of oneself and others. As she says of her craft, "to write the books one wants to read is both to point the direction of vision and, at the same time, to follow it" (8). For Walker, models provide the writer with an example that allows her to conceptualize and evolve her own vision. However, there are times when there is an "absolute lack of models" (4) that force the writer to create and be the model at the same time. At times, the work can be restricted because it is not representative of lived experience.

Lived experience is not solely one's confrontation with a specific event or events spanning someone's lifetime, but the conception, formulation, and enactment of something that is definitive and that exists by virtue of its own creation. *Restricted* refers to the acceptance the work may not get from society because of its singularity or because society ridicules or ignores work it does not yet understand, and in its disdain, seeks to force the artist to conform to a standard that it *does* understand. This can limit the artist and society because there is no provision for advancement or change in the artistic rendering of existence. Therefore, for the writer (and society), the absence of models can be "an occupational hazard for the artist simply because models in art, in behavior, in growth of spirit and intellect—even if rejected—enrich and enlarge one's view of existence" (4).

Upon the writer's exposure to models, there is an opportunity to expand and substantiate one's work; however, the writer's representation or depiction of being cannot be narrow if it is to have any impact on society at all. The writer's presentation of her perception of the world should be broad in scope and universal as her definition of womanism proclaims. Her definition also speaks to the importance of wholeness.

At the crux of "Saving the Life That Is Your Own" is Walker's explanation as to why she "felt such a desperate need to know and assimilate the experiences of earlier black women writers" and the "need to study them and teach them" (9). The formal education she received while at college was bereft of black female literary models. Thus, when Walker began to write about black women, she realized that neither her formal education nor family lore had prepared her for the task. Well-meaning educators had "directed [her] instead toward a plethora of books by mainly white male writers who thought most women worthless if they didn't enjoy bullfighting or hadn't volunteered for the trenches in World War I" (6). As such, these educators could provide her with no relevant models from which to develop as a writer.

A search for a model to emulate in order to write a fictional treatment of a racial incident from her mother's past ultimately led Walker to Zora Neale Hurston. Walker's discovery of this anthropologist, folklorist, and creative writer kindled her interest in black female writers. The example that Hurston set, with her deep love for and pride in black rural folkways, spurred Walker on to experiment with various aspects of Hurston's technique, namely, the use of black rural dialect, the function of imagery to establish a sense of place, the art of storytelling, and fully realized black female protagonists (the prototype being Janie Crawford from *Their Eyes Were Watching God*). Hurston as model served to improve and fortify her own writing style, which is especially evident in her third novel, *The Color Purple*.[3]

With respect to a model of the lived experience of a black female literary ancestor, Walker's essay, "Zora Neale Hurston: A Cautionary Tale and a Partisan View," pays homage and addresses itself to the limitations Hurston faced as a black female writer. More importantly, this essay forthrightly voices the fears and uncertainties Walker experienced as an aspiring writer after reading what others had to say about Hurston ("From an Interview," 260–61). Walker was stunned to find that the derogatory things said about Hurston had little to do with the quality of her work, but were instead directed at Hurston's lifestyle. This castigation coupled with Hurston's financial and creative struggles served as a cautionary tale for Walker. Her decision to fight back was twofold: to bring Hurston back into the black literary mainstream, and to have the right to be her own writer. Even though Walker grappled with fears about her success as a writer, she chose to follow Hurston's example by being true to her own vision. She determined not to allow critics to silence and render her invisible by attacking her lifestyle as had been Hurston's fate. For example, many of her detractors thought her interracial marriage was incompatible with her love of black people, and used it to devalue her work (See "In the Closet of the Soul," *Living by the Word* 92).

Walker's original definition of womanism acknowledges the connectedness of one to the entire community (with respect to time and place), brings past literary ancestors into the here and now, and ensures their presence in the future. In relation to spirituality, the contraction and expansion of the womanist concept is profoundly evident in the sense that as an individual, Walker saved Hurston's life in the spirit of caring and love, and in a fulfillment of the need to keep Hurston's groundbreaking work alive for the benefit of others. On a cumulative scale, Walker seeks to introduce to other aspiring black writers the importance of passing on the cultural legacy that black literary ancestors have to impart, which can never occur if we do not save their lives.

The exploration of the interior lives of black women by black women writers is an effort to break the restrictions on the freedom to name one's own experience. Walker and some other black female writers have been the target of harsh criticism by black male critics because they dared to utter the forbidden, and because of their refusal to continue to ignore the cruel treatment that some black women have experienced within the black community and by extension within the wider society.[4] Walker is quick to point out to her critics, however, that her literary vision is a representation of how *she* sees the world. As a writer, she is unwilling to allow some aspects of the black experience to remain hidden, particularly from the members of the very community of which she writes (*Living by the Word* 78–92). To do so would be to submit to an enforced restriction on self-determination or to the circumscribed view sanctioned by an elite, white male perspective (and perpetuated by some black intellectuals), which she feels does a disservice to black literature. Further, not to tell the truth about the whole reality of the black woman's experience would hinder the potential for healing, personal transformation, and social change that resides within the literature.

Walker's perspective on social change was shaped by her keen political and social awareness, a by-product of her coming of age during the civil rights movement of the 1960s. She arrived at Spelman College at the height of the student nonviolent movement and participated in marches, sit-ins, and demonstrations ("From an Interview" 253–55). Clearly, Walker believes that politics and art cannot be separate pursuits for the black writer. When she wrote "The Unglamorous but Worthwhile Duties of the Black Revolutionary Artist, Or of the Artist Who Simply Works and Writes" in 1970, Walker had spent time in Mississippi working as an activist and educator. She was exposed to black men and women—young and old—who had no faith in their worth either as human beings or Americans. Most importantly, they had no concept of their history as a people; in short, they had no heroes to emulate. She saw that her education had not prepared her for compensating for the lack of individual and collective wholeness from which her people suffered. She concluded that black people needed their own models from which to learn: "For where my duty as a black poet, writer, and teacher would take me, people would have little need of Keats and Byron or even Robert Frost, but much need of Hughes, Bontemps, Gwendolyn Brooks and Margaret Walker" (132). This is not to say that Walker is discounting the relevance of Keats, Byron, or Robert Frost to the lives of black people. *She* knew who those writers were, but that is because she had the privilege of a liberal arts education. Many of the black people she knew and later met were either uneducated or miseducated. The black revolutionary artist, in the capacity of educator must ask: How are blacks to recognize themselves in the works of these poets? Where is the frame of reference, or the basis for comparison? Where is the language of the folk? How does one empower black people without concrete examples set by those who came before them in social and literary history? If these examples are not easily accessible, where are black people to turn to find them? For Walker, answers to these questions require an engagement with the works of writers like Gwendolyn Brooks, Langston Hughes,

Arna Bontemps, Margaret Walker, W. E. B. Du Bois, and Booker T. Washington, writers who spoke about the American experience from their perspectives as black people.

To this end, the black writer brings about revolution in the form of personal and collective change. This means combining the reality of the black experience as it stands in the present with the documented reality of the past. It is the duty of the artist to present the whole story, as it is and as it was. If the black artist is to be truly revolutionary, she must understand that she is at once the "voice of the people" and "The People" (138). However, not only does Walker want the "voice of the people" to be heard, she wants the voices of black women to be heard. Through the media of fiction, poetry, and essays, Walker explores the material realities of black women in society. For Walker and her contemporaries, it is necessary work to empower black women to be at the forefront of collective social change. What she also recognizes is that black women must be encouraged to reclaim this power through collaborative work with her sisters.

Within the configuration of womanism, the points of origin and departure (i.e., expansion and contraction) are the Self. When seeking to empower others with a belief and a pride of one's heritage, it is necessary to turn inward for models within one's own experience. To this end, "In Search of Our Mothers' Gardens," written in 1974 and still germane today, can be regarded as more than a feminist tribute to the uncelebrated artistic struggles of our foremothers. The essay is Walker's exhortation to her readers to look at the organic creative spirit that is possessed within the Self, and to realize the important implications it has for the improvement of the qualities of one's life and one's community. Walker cites examples of this artistry, such as the use of familiar or discarded materials for quilting, or the creative use of the spoken word in storytelling, or gardening and cooking.

Walker provides black women an opportunity for self-reflection to value women's history, and reiterates the importance of restoring our female ancestors to their rightful place in the collective consciousness.

Walker is concerned with the lack of "wholeness" of her people and ultimately of all people. The essay also addresses the lack of awareness that black foremothers had about their genius due to the fact that they led lives of fulfilling other people's needs before meeting their own. Walker describes these women as "exquisite butterflies trapped in an evil honey, toiling away their lives in an era, a century, that did not acknowledge them, except as 'the *mule* of the world'" (232). Most importantly, by writing about African American foremothers and the effects of not fulfilling their need for artistic expression, Walker speaks to the absolute necessity of sustaining one's spirituality because it is the very foundation of one's creativity:

> For these grandmothers and mothers of ours were not Saints,
> but Artists; driven to a numb and bleeding madness by the springs
> of creativity in them for which there was no release. They were
> Creators, who lived lives of spiritual waste, because they were so
> rich in spirituality—which is the basis of Art. (233)

Walker also defines a womanist as someone who "loves herself. *Regardless*" (xii). In the volume's final essay "Beauty: When the Other Dancer Is the Self," Walker exemplifies womanist self-love and addresses the removal of restriction that one places on the Self. The injury of Walker's eye when she was eight years old shattered her sense of wholeness. At age 27, Walker made peace with her handicap because of an observation her daughter made one day when she noticed that one eye was bluer than the other one. Focusing on the blind right eye, the child said, "Mommy, there's a world in your eye. . . . Mommy, where did you get that world in your eye?" (370). From Rebecca's astute association of the blue in her mother's eye with the opening of a children's television program (*Big Blue Marble*), Walker experienced healing, release, and joy. In this moment of epiphany she realized, "There *was* a world in my eye. And I saw that it was possible to love it: that in fact, for all it had taught me of shame and anger and inner vision, I *did* love it" (370). Walker comes to understand that the injury—an event that turned her world *outside in*—also exposed her to experiences she may never have had if the accident had not occurred. The loss of the eye was actually a gain, one that placed her on a different path that would take her out of poverty, to Spelman College, to Sarah Lawrence, throughout the United States, and to countries like Africa, Cuba, China, and Bali. Out of her struggle with her wounded eye emerges a woman who can face the world with her head high, her gaze unwavering. Out of this struggle emerges a womanist with a commitment to sharing her vision with others through the written word and influencing society in a positive way. That Walker chose to place this essay at the end of *Gardens* signaled a self-acceptance and provided a sense of closure to an unhappy phase in her life. One also feels Walker's readiness to undertake larger issues that affect her and the lives of her readers—her womanist agenda. Hence the poignant dedication of the book: "To my daughter Rebecca / Who saw in me / What I considered / a scar / And redefined it / As a world" (x).

Walker's womanist vision posits, "We are indeed the world. Only if we have reason to fear what is in our own hearts need we fear for the planet. Teach yourself peace. Pass it on" (*Living by the Word*, 193). Alice Walker compels us to look inside and beyond ourselves, and reminds us that if we fight for each other instead of against each other, there is a strong chance that we as a life force will advance and endure.

Notes

1. For discussions about the historical exclusion of black women by white feminists, see bell hooks, *Ain't I A Woman: Black Women and Feminism* (Boston: South End, 1981) and *Feminist Theory: From Margin to Center* (Boston: South End, 1984); Angela Davis, *Women, Race, and Class* (New York: Vintage, 1983), and for a philosophical approach see Elizabeth V. Spelman, *Inessential Woman: Problems of Exclusion in Feminist Thought* (Boston: Beacon, 1988).

2. Chikwenye Okonjo Ogunyemi writes about "Womanism: The Dynamics of the Contemporary Black Female Novel in English," in *Signs: Journal of Women and Culture in Society* 11.1 (1985): 63–80; theologian Katie G. Cannon has

published *Womanist Ethics* (Atlanta: Scholars, 1988); and Renita J. Weems, *Just A Sister Away: A Womanist Vision of Women's Relationships in the Bible* (San Diego, CA: LuraMedia, 1988). Others include: Toni King, *Black Womanist Leadership: Tracing the Motherline* (New York: SUNY P, 2011); Maria del Guadalupe, *Convergences: Black Feminism and Continental Philosophy* (New York: SUNY P, 2010); Stephanie Sears, *Imagining Black Womanhood: The Negotiation of Power and Identity Within the Girls Empowerment Project* (New York: SUNY P, 2010); Laura Gillman, *Unassimilable Feminisms: Reappraising Feminist, Womanist, and Mestiza Identity Politics* (New York: Routledge, 2010); Kalenda Eaton *Womanism, Literature, and the Transformation of the Black Community, 1965–1980* (New York: Routledge, 2008); and Layli Phillips, *The Womanist Reader* (New York: Routledge, 2006).

3. For a penetrating discussion of Walker's use of black rural dialect in *The Color Purple*, see Henry Louis Gates Jr., *The Signifying Monkey: A Theory of African American Literary Criticism* (New York: Oxford UP, 1988), 239–58.

4. See Calvin Herndon, "Who's Afraid of Alice Walker," *The Sexual Mountain and Black Women Writers* (New York: Doubleday, 1987), 1–36; Barbara Christian, "The Contrary Women of Alice Walker: A Study of Female Protagonists in *Love and Trouble*," *Black Feminist Criticism* (New York: Pergamon, 1988), 31–46; and Walker's essay, "In the Closet of the Soul," *Living by the Word*, 78–92.

Works Cited

Armstrong, Toni, Jr. "Spirit Helper for Modern Times: Alice Walker." *Hot Wire: The Journal of Women's Music and Culture* 7.1 (1991): 5.

Chigwedere, Yuleth. "The African Womanist Vision in Vera's Works." *Journal of Literary Studies* 26.1 (2010): 20–44.

DeVeaux, Alexis. "Alice Walker." *Essence* 20.5 (1989).

Floyd-Thomas, Stacey. *Deeper Shades of Purple: Womanism in Religion and Society.* New York: New York UP, 2006.

Nnaemeka, Obioma. "Womanism—Bibliography." *Science.jrank.org.* Net Industries and Its Licensors, 2012. Web. 31 Mar. 2012.

Phillips, Layli, Kerri Reddick-Morgan, and Dionne Stephens. "Oppositional Consciousness within an Oppositional Realm: The Case of Feminism and Womanism in Rap and Hip Hop, 1976–2004." *Journal of African American History* 90.3 (2005):253–77.

Sesanti, Simphiwe. "Reclaiming Space: African Women's Use of the Media as a Platform to Contest Patriarchal Representations of African Culture—Womanists' Perspectives." *Critical Arts: A South-North Journal of Culture & Media Studies* 23.2 (2009): 209–23.

Spelman, Elizabeth V. *Inessential Woman: Problems of Exclusion in Feminist Thought.* Boston: Beacon, 1988.

Walker, Alice. *In Search of Our Mothers' Gardens: Womanist Prose*. New York: Harcourt, 1983.

_____. *Living by the Word*. New York: Harcourt, 1989.

Spiritual Colonialism

Deborah Plant

"What is happening in the world more and more," writes author-activist Alice Walker, "is that people are attempting to decolonize their spirits. A crucial act of empowerment, one that might return reverence to the Earth, thereby saving it, in this fearful-of-Nature, spiritually colonized age" (*Anything We Love* 4). In the context of Walker's writings, a colonized spirit is a spirit that is dominated by forces external to itself. In one respect, spiritual colonization is a consequence of centuries of empire building by imperial governments. Such governments sought to expand their empires directly, through outright acquisition of lands— whether uninhabited or inhabited by other peoples or governments— or indirectly, through political or economic influence or dominance. As the purpose of imperialism is the geographical, political, and economic growth and predominance of an empire, colonies are established to control and exploit acquired lands, and to dominate and subjugate the peoples or nations that inhabit such lands. Given that freedom and independence are innate aspects of the human spirit, the conquest, subjugation, and "pacification" of a people, that is, the forced suppression or elimination of a targeted population, typically follow in the aftermath of physical violence, material destruction, psychological confusion, and mayhem. The effect of colonization is separation: the separation of humankind from nature; the separation of indigenous peoples from their lands; the separation of the fruits of labor from those who labor; the separation of people from their culture; the separation of the individual from her or his own intuitive spirit.

In her political activism and literary works, Alice Walker documents and explores the impact of historical and contemporary colonization, particularly as it reflects Western and/or European imperialist practices of domination and exploitation. Domination is domination regardless of form; thus she documents and explores other oppressive systems as well—such as patriarchy, sexism, and racism. Walker's analysis of the politics and impact of colonization and domination extends to planet Earth—its waters, mountains, trees, skies—and all creatures that inhabit it. As human populations have been colonized, so has Earth itself, with the end result being a host of demoralized and disempowered people, disappeared human beings, extinct cultures and nations, and a planet in peril. Just as hundreds of plant and animal species have become endangered, Walker warns that in undermining the essence of humanity—Spirit—humanity, too, is endangered. In the epigraph of her work, *Sent by Earth: A Message from the Grandmother Spirit after the Attacks on the World Trade Center and the Pentagon* (2001), Walker excerpts a passage from a letter written by author Richard Wright to existentialist philosopher Jean-Paul Sartre: "The Great danger in the world today is that the very feeling and conception of what is a human being might well be lost" (9).

From antiquity to modern times, colonization has been a tool of human society. Colonization and systemic discrimination based on class, ethnicity, gender, sexual orientation, religion, ideology, and other social markers have diminished the human spirit. The force of colonialism is the force of domination, exploitation—greed and endless consumption—violence, death, and destruction. Humankind has internalized this adverse force to its own detriment and that of planet Earth.

Where W. E. B. Du Bois stated that the problem of the twentieth century is the problem of the color line, Walker exclaims that the problem of the twenty-first century is the survival of our individual and collective humanity, which requires a reclamation of Spirit. This has been Walker's preoccupation: "the spiritual survival, survival *whole* of my people," and in particular, exploration of "the oppressions, the insanities, the loyalties and the triumphs of black women." As she continues in her author-activist career, her effort is "to be of assistance to the world in its dire hour of need." "We've turned a scary corner, as humans," Walker remarks. "We may have ruined our nest. . . . We will need to know many different kinds of things to survive as a species worth surviving" (*The World Has Changed* 317–18). Among those things humankind needs to know is how to grow the spirit: Soul growth or what Walker describes as "ensoulment"—bringing the body and soul together—as the possibility of transforming the world (*We Are the Ones* 240; *Sent by Earth* 57). As Spirit is ever-present, what is essential is the ability to see what obscures it. Thus Alice Walker's life-work has been about seeing and telling the truth, and facing, resisting, and dismantling those systems and forces that undermine and diminish Spirit, the life-force of all that exists.

Walker's work is grounded in and inspired by her own family history, which is intertwined with America's colonial past. Her political activism took form in the midst of the civil rights movement. Compelled by television footage of a calm and dignified Reverend Martin Luther King Jr. being shoved into the back of a police van, Walker intuited her calling. She, too, would stand for justice (*In Search* 144). Born in Eatonton, Georgia, in 1944, she would know, firsthand, the impact of systems of domination. As a black child, she would know the experience of racial apartheid in the American South, or what has been described historically as Jim Crow. A social and political structure designed to keep white people separate from black people (and other peoples of color) and to exclude blacks from equal participation in American social and political life, the Jim Crow system was sanctioned by the United States Supreme Court's 1896 *Plessy v. Ferguson* decision. This Court decision upheld racial segregation under the separate-but-equal doctrine. Cultural anthropologist and author Zora Neale Hurston gives a candid description and analysis of Jim Crow in her essay "Crazy for This Democracy":

> These Jim Crow laws have been put on the books for a purpose, and that purpose is psychological. It has two edges to the thing. By physical evidence, back seats in trains, back-doors of houses, exclusion from certain places and activities, to promote in the mind of the smallest white child the conviction of First by Birth, eternal and irrevocable. . . .

No one of darker skin can ever be considered an equal. Seeing the daily humiliations of the darker people confirms the child in its superiority, so that it comes to feel it the arrangement of God. By the same means, the smallest dark child is to be convinced of its inferiority, so that it is to be convinced that competition is out of the question and against all nature and God.

All physical and emotional things flow from this premise. It perpetuates itself. The unnatural exaltation of one ego, and the equally unnatural grinding down of the other. (*I Love Myself* 167–68)

Rather than accepting the status quo, however, Alice Walker, like her parents and community members, resisted this unnatural order of things. Rather than submit, Walker committed herself to the dismantling of structures that supported social and economic injustices and inequities in her hometown of Eatonton, Georgia; the American South, in particular; and the United States in general. She would go on to stand for justice all over the world.

After graduating from a segregated high school in Eatonton, Walker boarded a segregated Greyhound bus to Atlanta, Georgia, to continue her education at Spelman College. There in Atlanta, she joined civil rights movement marches and protests. Walker attributes her activism, first, to her great-great-great-great-grandmother May Poole. Sold on a Virginia auction block in the early 1800s, May Poole "walked to Eatonton with a baby straddled on each hip" (*Anything We Love* vi). Eatonton is a city in Putnam County, Georgia, and Walker's ancestral home. Georgia was established as a British colony in 1732. In 1751, proslavery advocates in the British Parliament and the Georgia Province elected to utilize forced African labor to establish their economy and increase their material wealth. Thus, they officially introduced chattel slavery into the colony (Spalding and Jackson 30, 67, 77). Among those Africans sold into slavery in Georgia were Walker's ancestors. May Poole literally and symbolically connects Walker to a colonial legacy of slavery—a legacy of pain, suffering, and dehumanization. At the same time, May Poole represents dignity, resilience, and triumph. She lived to be 125 years of age. Though she lived her entire life enslaved, and was even given to a white woman as a wedding gift, she had an indomitable spirit. In the one photograph she has of May Poole, Walker discerns her strength: "I can still see the attitude and courage that made it possible for her to attend the funerals of almost everyone who ever owned her" (*Anything We Love* xiii). This strength, too, is Walker's legacy. Walker would tap her spiritual legacy to defy Georgia's colonial legacy. For even though slavery was abolished in 1865, the belief in domination, subjugation, and exploitation that gave the institution of slavery in America the descriptive "peculiar," its force persisted in other guises. In tandem with the Jim Crow system were the systems of sharecropping and tenant farming. As the predominant function of Jim Crow was to control social interaction between races, the predominant function of sharecropping and tenant farming was to control the acquisition and distribution of material wealth.

On America's frontlines and in her writings, the great-great-great-great granddaughter of May Poole would actively resist, investigate, and expose social and economic injustices as an expression of her commitment to the spiritual survival, whole, of her people. In her collection of essays, *Sent by Earth: A Message from the Grandmother Spirit after the Attacks on the World Trade Center and Pentagon* (2001), Walker speaks to the "challenge of remaining human under the horrific conditions of American Apartheid in the Southern United States during [her] parents and grandparents' time" (9). Walker's parents, Willie Lee and Minnie (Lou) Tallulah Grant Walker were heroic in their efforts to provide and care for their eight children with pride and dignity. In spite of their brave and valiant spirits, they, like their forebears lived diminished and deprived lives:

They and their children faced massively destructive psychological and physical violence from landowners who used every conceivable weapon to keep the sharecropping/slave labor system intact. It was a system in which a relatively few ruling class white people had the possibility of having as much food, land, space and cheap energy to run their enterprises as they wanted, while most people of color and many poor white people had barely enough of anything to keep themselves alive. (*Sent by Earth* 9–10)

The life of black sharecroppers in the rural South is one of the stories that have been silenced in the historical record. It is the story of Walker's parents and great-grandparents. It is the story of Walker and her five brothers and two sisters. It is the story of generations of black folk who eked out a living in an inimical environment. It is an American story. "Looking back on my parents' and grandparents' lives," Walker writes, "I have often felt overwhelmed, helpless, as I've examined history and society, and especially religion, with them in mind, and have seen how they were manipulated away from a belief in their own judgment and faith in themselves" (*Anything We Love* 4). This tragedy—of the separation of an individual from his own good opinion of himself—is poignantly depicted in the life of Brownfield Copeland, son of Grange and Margaret Copeland, characters who people Walker's first novel, *The Third Life of Grange Copeland*. Brownfield watched the disintegration of the lives of his parents, as each lost sight of the other, of him, and their hopes and dreams. His father labored as a sharecropper in Green County, Georgia, and his mother "pulled bait." Between the two of them, they never earned enough to live a life beyond bare subsistence. Sharecropping was an economic system comparable to peonage, except that no matter how hard or how long blacks worked within the system, they remained in perpetual debt, thus in perpetual economic bondage. This was Grange's future.

Grange Copeland could not afford to send his son to school, as he needed his hands in the cotton fields. He couldn't give his wife a new dress, just as he couldn't prevent Shipley, "the bossman," from being sexually involved with his wife and perhaps fathering her second child. In his despair, Grange abandoned his wife and son and fled north to New York. Unable to cope with the despair of her abandonment,

Margaret poisoned herself and her odd-colored baby, Star. Left to his own devices, Brownfield assumes the sharecropper's life from which his father escaped: lack, deprivation, impoverishment, and endless debt to landowners, slavery of another kind. The bloom of his marriage to Mem faded in the wake of dead dreams. Brownfield's marriage, like that of his parents, became a "harmony of despair" (59). Treated as brutes, they came to live brutal lives. Their lives weren't their own, but conveniences for the privileged white ruling class and the means by which the ruling class accrued their wealth. He and his family were traded off from one white landowner to another, as though they were "a string of workhorses" (79). Mem protested:

> Being forced to move from one sharecropper's cabin to another was something she hated. She hated the arrogance of the white men who put them out, for one reason or another, without warning or explanation. She hated leaving a home she'd already made and fixed up with her own hands. She hated leaving her flowers, which she always planted whenever she got her hands on flower seeds. Each time she stepped into a new place, with its new, and usually bigger rat holes, she wept. Each time she had to clean cow manure out of a room to make it habitable for her children, she looked as if she had been dealt a death blow. . . . She slogged along, ploddingly, like a cow herself, for the sake of the children. Her mildness became stupor; then her stupor became horror, desolation and, at last, hatred. (59)

For as much as Brownfield resented how he and his family were treated, he felt himself powerless to do anything about it. He hated the Captain Davises and Mr. J. L.s of the world, but felt too "small and black and bug-like" to stand up to them for fear of being squashed (79). He could not resist and fight against them, so he fought his wife and mistreated and abused his children. Brownfield rationalized his behavior to his wife, "You know how hard it is to be a black man down here . . . You knows I never wanted to be nothing but a man! Mem, baby, the white folks just don't let nobody *feel* like doing right" (95). Brownfield was stupefied by the lack of control he had over his own life. "No matter which way he wanted to go, he said, some unseen force pushed him in the opposite direction" (165). Over the course of his life, Brownfield became bereft of any sense of responsibility for the condition of his life and bereft of any feeling but hate. He eventually destroys his family and murders his wife.

Where Brownfield was caught in his rigid "belief in misery" (227), his father began to believe in the possibility of and need for his own personal transformation. Grange Copeland's experiences "up North" had him realize that hatred was not the answer, neither was absolving oneself of any and all responsibility for one's character and quality of relatedness to others. Through his love for his granddaughter Ruth and his determination to create a more promising future for her, Grange redeems his spirit. "I know the danger of putting all the blame on somebody else for the mess you make out of your life," he says. "I fell into the trap myself!" Grange realizes his agency, his personal power. He acknowledges his errors in judgment and action and assumes responsibility for the desertion of his family and the consequences that ensued. In sharing his regretful story with Brownfield, he encourages Brownfield to move past blame to self-responsibility. "Nobody's as powerful as we make them out to be," he tells him, and asks: "We got our own souls don't we?" (207). Grange reaches out to his son, but Brownfield rebuffs him.

As the world's population continues to struggle with colonial legacies and contemporary systems of oppression, we are challenged to remain present to our humanity and to the well-being of the planet. Increasingly in her fiction, Walker creates characters who "explore what it would feel like not to be imprisoned by the hatred of women, the love of violence, and the destructiveness of greed taught to human beings as the 'religion' by which they must guide their lives (*Anything We Love* 4). In *The Color Purple*, Walker critiques the system of patriarchal domination in America and brings a critical eye to European colonialism in Africa. The voice we hear in this epistolary novel is that of the rural black female in the American South, a silenced voice to which Walker gives expression. As her life was seen to have little value, her story had never been told. Through the protagonist Celie, Walker portrays her life through letters written first to God, then to Celie's sister Nettie. Through Celie's letters, the reader grasps the quality of her existence within a patriarchal structure where domestic violence is a key component. The first page of the novel is a snapshot of patriarchal domination. Alfonso rapes fourteen-year-old Celie, his stepdaughter (who at the outset of the novel believes him to be her biological father). When she cries out in pain, he chokes her into silence. Then he demands her submission, "You better shut up and git used to it" (1). His wife is "half dead" from frequent childbearing, and he has impregnated Celie. She is confused, afraid, and isolated in her misery as Alfonso threatens her, "You better not never tell nobody but God. It'll kill your mammy" (1).

Having been violated at home, Celie doesn't think twice about the abuse inflicted on her by her husband Albert, whom she refers to as Mr. _____. Albert believes being a man and a husband grants him privileges and entitlements, one of which is beating his wife. "Wives is like children," he teaches his son Harpo. "You have to let 'em know who got the upper hand. Nothing can do that better than a good sound beating" (35). Though her sister Nettie and others in her community of women encourage her to stand up for herself, Celie is too cowed; "But I don't know how to fight," she responds, "All I know how to do is stay alive" (17). Believing Nettie to be dead, Celie believes fighting to be futile. She resigns herself to a submissive state: "What good it do? I don't fight, I stay where I'm told. But I'm alive" (21). To escape the fate of her mother and sister, Nettie leaves the family homestead. She finds work with Reverend Samuel and his wife Corrine, caring for their children (her niece and nephew). They all later travel to Africa to carry out missionary work. Nettie writes her sister as she promises, but Albert, as he promises, withholds Nettie's letters from Celie, leaving Celie with the impression that her sister is dead. In keeping Nettie's letters, Albert not only dominates Celie physically, but psychologically and spiritually as well. Celie remains in a state of confusion because logic tells her that her sister is dead since Nettie declared that "nothing but death can keep me from [writing]" (18). Yet in her heart she is not so sure. Thus Celie experiences an endless grieving. Having, in any case, lost the one person who loved her, she is dispirited, listless, lifeless.

In Shug Avery's presence Celie begins to transform. The two women bond as Celie cares for Shug through her illness. Initially Albert's lover, Shug becomes Celie's lover and protector. Shug Avery symbolizes the feminine principle that is systematically repressed in patriarchal societies. An expression of the Divine Feminine, Shug is maternal, loving, and protective, and stands strong in her care for the weak and vulnerable. When Celie confides that Albert beats her, "For being me and not you," Shug promises to stay. "I won't leave, she says, until I know Albert won't ever think about beating you" (75). In the warmth of Shug's love and protection, Celie is inspired. She is enlivened. When she later learns that her sister Nettie is alive, she even "begin to strut a little bit" (148).

In her discovery and recovery of Nettie's letters, Shug is instrumental in reconnecting Celie with her family roots and her cultural roots in Africa. Celie not only learns that her sister is alive, but also that her two children are with her. Further, Nettie's letters restructure her family tree: "My daddy lynch. My mama crazy. All my little half-brothers and sisters no kin to me. My children not my sister and brother. Pa not pa" (177). As Celie is enlightened about her family heritage and history, she is simultaneously enlightened about her cultural heritage and history. Nettie's letters convey the geographical beauty of Africa and the physical beauty and cultural complexity of the Olinka people in particular, among whom she lived. As Nettie observes the beauty there, she also observes the traditions among the Olinka in relation to females and she observes the impact of European colonialism in relation to the Olinka. Although she, Samuel, and Corrine are allowed to teach the boys, they are not allowed to teach the girls: "The Olinka do not believe girls should be educated. When I asked a mother why she thought this, she said: A girl is nothing to herself; only to her husband can she become something." Unless a woman becomes the mother of a man's children, she is "not much" (155). Nettie commented further that the communication between Olinka women and men was similar to that between women and men at home in Georgia:

> There is a way that the men speak that reminds me too much of Pa. They listen just long enough to issue instructions. They don't even look at women when women are speaking. They look at the ground and bend their heads toward the ground. The women also do not 'look in a man's face' as they say. To 'look in a man's face' is a brazen thing to do. They look instead at his feet or his knees. And what can I say to this? Again, it is our own behavior around Pa (162).

As females were conceived of as "not much" among the Olinka, African peoples were conceived of as not much among the Europeans. During the end of their stay in Africa, Nettie and Samuel bear witness to how the Olinka people were dispossessed of their village and land. After paving a road up to the village of the Olinka, British colonials then destroyed their homes and crops. "The white builders wanted the village site as headquarters for their rubber plantation. It is the only spot for miles that has a steady supply of fresh water," Nettie conveyed (226). The Olinka were relocated "on a barren stretch of land that has no water at all for six months of the year" (226). When they had to build dwellings topped with corrugated tin roofs that they had to buy from the British, they felt defeated (227). What happened to the Olinka was prevalent on the continent. As erstwhile British expatriate Doris Baines explained it, "First there's a road built to where you keep your goods. Then your trees are hauled off to make ships and captain's furniture. Then your land is planted with something you can't eat. Then you're forced to work it. That's happening all over Africa, she said. Burma too, I expect" (228–29).

Through Celie and Nettie's letters, Walker compares and contrasts various systems of domination, whether in the guise of official political or social structures or cultural traditions. The effect is consistent across systems and continents: separation, exploitation, and a diminishment of the human spirit. In many ways, *The Color Purple* is Walker's answer to the question posed by Grange in *The Third Life of Grange Copeland*: "We got our own *souls*, don't we?" Grange emphasizes the word "soul," as he believes it to be essential to one's humanity. His love for his granddaughter Ruth proved to be his soul's salvation. "The white folks hated me," he told Ruth, "and I hated myself until I started hating them in return and loving myself. Then I tried just loving me, and then you, and *ignoring* them much as I could. You're special to me because you're a part of me; a part of me I didn't even used to want" (196). As Grange learned to let go of his hatred of whites, Celie learned to let go of her fear of men—beginning with the "big and old and tall and graybearded and white" God in her head who also closely resembled the town's mayor in the attention he paid to colored women (*Color Purple* 194, 195). She learned from Shug that God was neither a *he* nor a *she*, but an It: "It ain't something you can look at apart from anything else, including yourself. I believe God is everything," Shug tells Celie. "Everything that is or ever was or ever will be. And when you can feel that, and be happy to feel that, you've found it" (195).

In Shug's pantheistic vision, she saw all life as connected and she experienced "that feeling of being part of everything, not separate at all." She goes on to say, "I knew that if I cut a tree, my arm would bleed" (*Color Purple* 195–96). Shug's love of Celie proved to be Celie's soul's salvation and that of Albert's as well. The emptiness and numbness Celie felt and her desire to kill Albert for keeping Nettie's letters, thus Nettie, from her for over thirty years dissolved in Shug's warm embrace and soft counsel. And when Celie could then see Albert as "a natural man," not a god, she found the courage within to stand up to Albert herself. With an empowering concept of God, Celie not only loses her fear of Albert, she could look past his meanness: "Now that my eyes opening, I feels like a fool. Next to any little scrub of a bush in my yard, Mr. _____'s evil sort of shrink" (197). In his turn, Albert learns to open his heart again and even becomes a comfort to Celie.

In *Sent by Earth*, Walker shares Clarissa Pinkola Estes's understanding that "while it is true that the soul can never be destroyed, it can certainly leave us and take up residence elsewhere" (37). Thus an individual becomes empty, numb, vacant, out of touch with their feelings, disconnected from self, others, and one's environment. In *The Temple of My Familiar*, Miss Lissie, a timeless elder who moves through dimensions in different forms—both human and animal—expounds on the need to remember and be mindful of one's spirit, one's soul. Miss Lissie has a dream wherein she mistreats, then imprisons her familiar, which then grows wings and flies away. In the absence of her familiar, she is alone, isolated, and estranged in a life devoid of meaning. She comes to realize that the familiar was her own spirit. Its temple was freedom. She could begin to understand herself and her world once she remembered her familiar, her spirit (118–120).

In *The Color Purple*, which is dedicated to "the Spirit," and *The Third Life of Grange Copeland*, Spirit/Love is also transformative and transcendent. It allows those characters who remember and embrace it within themselves to not only survive, but "survive whole." Love empowers them to see through illusions to truth: racist whites created brutal conditions under which blacks lived, but they weren't gods that were responsible for every choice Grange made. Sexist males assumed themselves superior and behaved accordingly, but their domineering behavior was not indicative of the value of the lives of those they would oppress, repress, or destroy. Walker emphasizes in *Sent by Earth* that hatred, like war, is never the answer or response to any problem or any situation, including situations involving oppressive tactics. In discussing these ideas, she makes reference to Buddhist monk Thich Nhat Hanh, who taught young people caught in the violence of the Vietnam

War that "hatred will not cease by hatred. By love alone is it healed." He recommended that they "prepare to die without hatred," that compassion and forgiveness were the responses to choose: "Even if you are dying in oppression, shame, and violence, if you can smile with forgiveness, you have great power" (33, 34). In his poem titled "Recommendation," Thich Nhat Hanh wrote that "man is not our enemy" (33). "Our enemy," he taught, "is our anger, hatred, greed, fanaticism, and discrimination against (each other)" (33).

Alice Walker and Thich Nhat Hanh suppose that colonialism, racial and political apartheid, patriarchy, sexism, environmental exploitation, and any and all forms of domination will end when humankind moves toward the development of mature relationships. Within mature relationships, explains Thich Nhat Hanh, "there is always compassion and forgiveness" (34). Walker sees such relations as a critical component of a healthy and holistic understanding of the world. She states, "Every thought, every act, every gesture, must be in the direction of developing and maintaining a mature relationship with the peoples of the planet; all thought of domination, control, force and violence must be abandoned" (34). It is necessary, therefore, to take responsibility for one's thoughts, choices, and actions. It is necessary to resist collusion with the forces of domination.

In her fiction, Walker shows that it is necessary to be mindful of the ways in which one becomes complicit with forces of domination. In *The Third Life of Grange Copeland*, Brownfield colludes with the "forces of domination" as he intentionally sabotages every plan Mem thinks of to create a less onerous and more commodious life for her family, forcing them all back into the sharecropper's nightmare they had but briefly escaped. Just as Brownfield resented Mem's ability to create what he despaired of achieving, in *The Color Purple*, Celie resents Sofia's fearlessness and courage not only to speak up for herself but to physically fight to protect herself. As Celie was beaten into submission, she advises Harpo to do the same to Sofia. Later in the novel, Samuel is prepared to help the Olinka remain free from colonial control by joining with the *mbeles* and escaping into the forest. But Nettie cautioned his enthusiasm, as there were those among the Olinka "who want[ed] bicycles and British clothes. Mirrors and shiny cooking pots. They want to work for the white people in order to have these things" (*CP* 233).

In *Sent by Earth*, Walker explicates her philosophy further, explaining the necessity to take responsibility to see the connection between war and "our dogs of war," that is, our endless and thoughtless consumption. "Some of our own war dogs, we have to own," states Walker, "are paying taxes that will be used to destroy people almost identical to us. Many of our war dogs are connected to heating our homes and driving cars" (*Sent* 19–20). Walker writes, "We, as Americans, have a hand in each nation's fate, but we tend to look only at the hand the news media shows us, constantly." It is necessary to be honest she implores, as "the soul loves awareness. . . . The soul wants to know the truth; what is really going on" (*Sent* 48, 49).

According to Walker in *We Are the Ones We Have Been Waiting For*, what is going on in the world can be described as "the worst of times." There is continuous warfare, she reports, and ecological imbalances that threaten the only home known to be hospitable to humankind (1). In *Overcoming Speechlessness*, Walker recounts the genocidal war endured by the people of Rwanda and eastern Congo. She recalls for the reader that the Tutsi and Hutu people of the region lived together peacefully before German and Belgian colonization. During their occupation in the 1800s, the Belgians created dissension between the two groups by declaring the Tutsi to be more intelligent than the Hutu and more phenotypically European. Therefore the Tutsi were perceived to be superior and the Hutu inferior (18). When the Belgians left over a century later, they vested the Hutu with official governing authority. The tension this generated culminated in the Rwandan Genocide of 1994.

Overcoming Speechlessness also chronicles Walker's visit to Palestine/Israel. Just as Belgian colonialists destroyed the relations between two groups who lived together amicably on common land, British colonialists destroyed the stability of the Palestinian people by forcing them to cohabitate with another group of people on Palestinian land. Ending their occupation of Palestine, the British contrived a plan to resettle European Jews who had been dislocated from their homes in Germany and elsewhere and had survived the Holocaust (19). The outcome has been "never-ending 'conflict'"(23). This pattern of colonial divisiveness and partitioning has had the effect of all colonialist projects—separation, suffering, the diminishment of the human spirit. Walker informs the reader that she traveled to Gaza—a parcel of land that recalls the barren strip of land on which the Olinka were relocated—"to bear witness" to what remained after the Israelis bombed the place and its people, "a missile landing every twenty-seven seconds for twenty-two days" (46). She, her companion, and members of CODE-PINK, an antiwar organization, saw demolished homes, schools, hospitals, factories, lemon and olive tree groves, and environmental pollution from the bombardment (61–62, 67). She wanted to bear witness, too, because most Americans are uninformed and, moreover, she writes, "have been deliberately misled by our government and by the media" about affairs in the Middle East, especially in relation to Palestine and Israel (23). And she wanted to bear witness to the similarities between the struggles of the Palestinian peoples and those of African Americans. "What is happening here feels very familiar, I tell them. When something similar was happening to us in Mississippi, Georgia, Alabama, and Louisiana, I say, our parents taught us to think of the racists as we thought of any other disaster: to deal with that disaster as best we could, but not to attach to it by allowing ourselves to hate" (56). A Palestinian woman responds, "We don't hate Israelis, Alice. . . . What we hate is being bombed, watching our little ones live in fear, burying them, being starved to death, and being driven from our land. We hate this eternal crying out to the world to open its eyes and ears to the truth of what is happening, and being ignored. Israelis, no" (57).

In "The Gospel According to Shug" in *The Temple of My Familiar*, verse fifteen reads: "HELPED are those who strive to give up their anger; their reward will be that in any confrontation their first thoughts will never be of violence or of war." The last verse, verse 27, reads: "HELPED are those who *know*" (288, 289). Walker wants humankind to know that what happens to one happens to all. "No matter how hidden the cruelty, no matter how far off the screams of pain and terror, we live in one world, we are one people" (18). The rape of Celie is the clear-cutting of the land. The colonization and partitioning of Africa is the colonization and partitioning of the Americas. Native American reservations in the United States are refugee camps in the West Bank and Gaza. The Rwandan Genocide is the Jewish Holocaust. As all domination is one, there is only one response to the problem of domination:

> One Earth
> One People
> One Love (*Sent By Earth* 54)

As Walker describes the first years of the twenty-first century as the worst of times, she also describes them as "the best of times" because, she writes excitedly, "*We live in a time of global enlightenment.*" With advanced telecommunications, satellites, and the advent of the Internet, what can remain hidden? Human beings are free to know. We are free to explore every crevice on the globe and "free to explore previously unexplored crevices in our own hearts and minds" (*We Are the Ones* 1, 2). In spite of how leaders manage the news, information is yet accessible. Oppression and suffering will be exposed. Even though many may find it difficult to break the chains of greed, says Walker, "no longer will we be an inarticulate and ignorant humanity, confused by our enslavement to superior cruelty and weaponry" (2). We can know the truth Walker writes and that truth will allow us to withstand and transcend domination in any form. As humankind actively discovers and remembers its familiar, decolonization of the human spirit occurs. "And what is the result of decolonizing the spirit?" Walker asks:

It is as if one truly does possess a third eye, and this eye opens. One begins to see the world from one's own point of view; to interact with it out of one's own conscience and heart. One's own "pagan" Earth Spirit. We begin to flow, again, with and into the Universe. And out of this flowing comes the natural activism of wanting to survive, to be happy, to enjoy one another and Life, and to laugh (226, 227).

Works Cited

Hurston, Zora Neale. *I Love Myself When I Am Laughing, and Then Again When I Am Looking Mean and Impressive*. Old Westbury, NY: Feminist, 1979.

Spalding, Phintzy, and Harvey H. Jackson, Eds. *Oglethorpe in Perspective: Georgia's Founder after Two Hundred Years*. Tuscaloosa: U of Alabama P, 1989.

Walker, Alice. *Anything We Love Can Be Saved: A Writer's Activism*. New York: Ballantine, 1997.

_____. *The Color Purple*. Orlando, FL: Harcourt, 1982.

_____. *In Search of Our Mothers' Gardens*. San Diego: Harcourt, 1983.

_____. *Overcoming Speechlessness: A Poet Encounters the Horror in Rwanda, Eastern Congo, and Palestine/Israel*. New York: Seven Stories, 2010.

_____. *Sent by Earth: A Message from the Grandmother Spirit, After the Attacks on the World Trade Center and Pentagon*. New York: Seven Stories, 2001.

_____. *The Temple of My Familiar*. San Diego: Harcourt, 1989.

_____. *The Third Life of Grange Copeland*. New York: Harcourt, 1970.

_____. *We Are the Ones We Have Been Waiting For*. New York: New Press, 2006.

_____. *The World Has Changed: Conversations with Alice Walker*. Ed. Rudolph P. Byrd. New York: New Press, 2010.

The Myopic Eye in Alice Walker's "The Flowers"

Antoinette Brim

> There was a world in my eye. And I saw that it was
> possible to love it: that in fact, for all it had taught me of
> shame and anger and inner vision, I did love it.
>> (Alice Walker, "Beauty: When the Other Dancer Is the Self")

> If you can see, look.

>> (Jose Saramago, *Blindness*)

Alice Walker's concise short story, "The Flowers," explores a ten-year-old girl's somewhat narrow and immediate or "myopic" view of the world. Walker's young protagonist, aptly named Myop, is initially focused upon her own creative power. She is quite the budding artist, as she curates beauty, composes music, and orders nature. However, when her gaze falls upon a lynching rope, Myop's focus hones in on the ugliness that is the inescapable encroachment of racism into her young existence. Though the story is very short, what is implicit in Walker's imagistic text is the complex struggle that occurs when one juxtaposes beauty with the grotesque. While the grotesque can contain elements of beauty, as the reader finds in Walker's descriptions, the grotesque can sometimes overshadow beauty and thereby create for itself a type of permanence. Beauty, in its multiple manifestations, can then be supplanted by fear, a result of experiencing the grotesque. Subsequently, the beauty that Myop formerly enjoyed and herself created is, like her own innocence, imperiled. This causes the reader to question whether beauty, creative power, and innocence will be lost to Myop henceforth, only to be replaced by fear as racism becomes her focus in the future or if Myop's gaze will return solidly to her art.

Early in the story, the reader cannot help but be struck by Myop's innocent and exuberantly contented nature. She is not weighed down by her family's apparent poverty. Instead, the language of the story's early paragraphs describes a pastoral, almost Eden-like landscape and existence in which Myop plays. Myop does not yet understand that her social standing is an impediment. Instead, she "turn[s] her back on the rusty boards of her family's sharecropper cabin" (Walker 404). The image of the young girl turning her back on the symbol of institutionalized postslavery enslavement is a powerful one. This suggests that Myop feels free to exercise her own power to determine her own future. She can turn her back and walk away. Additionally, her perception of her present is one of ownership and freedom. She feels free enough to "[strike] out at random chickens she liked," and she is bold enough to pound "out the beat of a song on the fence around the pigpen" (404). There is no evidence of timidity in Myop. There is no indication of shame, no sense of deprivation.

Myop is buoyant as she skips "lightly from hen house to pigpen to smokehouse" (404). Myop's joy "that the days had never been as beautiful as these," illustrate that the ten-year-old finds beauty in her humble surroundings (404). She becomes its curator. The simple harvest offers Myop "a golden surprise" each day (404). It is Myop who scouts out the flowers to be gathered and then arranged. It is Myop who discerns what beauty is. The fact that she finds beauty all around her in her world cannot be overstated, especially since the outside world that Myop must one day negotiate will attempt to redefine notions of beauty for her. Even so, initially, Myop makes these determinations for herself. Her world is beautiful and Myop has dominion over this beauty.

The reader might assume that finding pastoral beauty in a depressed rural environment is a by-product of Myop's innocence and that her view is narrow because all she knows is the farm and the surrounding woods. Therefore, she finds beauty that has at its heart the comfort of familiarity and, subsequently, safety. The reader might also gather that beauty resides in the simplistic, uncomplicated life of those insulated from the regimented rules of Jim Crow. Therefore, Myop's depressed rural environment acts as a barrier or shield that protects Myop's innocence. The reader might ask whether Myop's grasp on beauty and her assertion of her own power are inspired by innocence or ignorance. However, a study of Walker's larger body of work would suggest that it is Myop's own innocence and inner beauty that reflects onto and thereby illuminates the landscape. For example, in Walker's story "Everyday Use," the loving care that Mama and Maggie take to prepare their home for the arrival of the prodigal Dee, transforms the sparse house with no lawn into a home of welcome. Its contents—the butter churn with the hand-whittled dasher, the benches replete with rump prints, and the coveted quilts made of salvaged clothes—become priceless artifacts that remain in everyday use (2437–42). It is the warmth of the characters and their intrinsic goodness that cast the glow onto the setting, not ignorance or romanticized poverty.

The importance of a young girl's ability to discern beauty for herself is a recurring theme for Walker. Her examination of its connection to self-determination and a sense of individual power extend past Walker's fiction and into her memoir "Beauty: When the Other Dancer Is the Self." Like young Myop, Baby Alice has a strong sense of her own power. Even though "this is before the word 'beautiful' exists in people's vocabulary," Baby Alice knows that she is favored for her beauty (362). Even at two and a half years old, Baby Alice stands and proclaims "hands on hips, before [her] father. 'Take me, Daddy. . . . I'm the prettiest!'" (362). What follows next, in this essay, is a litany of major and minor accomplishments that win young Alice accolades from the grown-ups around her, but that do not surprise young Alice herself. She expects to be successful in her every endeavor because she has defined herself as beautiful and thus worthy (362).

Unfortunately, like Myop, Baby Alice's perception of herself and her place in the world changes in a day. For each girl, the change in her notion of 'self' is heralded by a change in her own eye. Young Alice no longer feels beautiful and thereby invincible when her eye is damaged by an accidental shooting from her brothers' BB gun. Subsequently, she is disempowered for many years (361–70). Myop's beautiful world is tainted by the discovery of the corpse of a lynched man in her wooded Eden. The visual shift from one's connection to beauty and self to notions of the grotesque put the girls outside themselves and into a strange and new world. Therefore, their sense of self and individual power is shaken and even momentarily lost to them.

Since each girl is relatively young, her viewpoint is myopic. There is no experiential knowledge to provide balance; therefore what each girl sees becomes all she can see. For instance, young Alice is still capable of great achievement. The loss of the sight in one eye does not diminish her intelligence or ability. However, it is the focus on the clouded cataract in her wounded eye that she focuses upon. It becomes the object of focused loathing that renders it her "grotesque." It is sadly ironic that the seeing eye's focus on the blind eye obscures young Alice's view of her own self-worth. Subsequently, the reader of "The Flowers" is left to wonder if Myop, like young Alice, will enter an epoch of intense focus on her version of the grotesque and if she, like the adult Alice, will be able to reclaim her own mastery of and the ability to create beauty.

The blinded eye of the anonymous lynching victim becomes Myop's entry into the world of the grotesque. She both literally and figuratively steps "smack into his eyes" (405). Literally, Myop's "heel became lodged in the broken ridge between brow and nose" (405). However, metaphorically, it is as if, Alice-in-Wonderland-like, she has fallen into a world of altered perspective and consequence. Critic Wolfgang Kayser explains in *The Grotesque in Art and Literature*:

> The grotesque is a structure. Its nature could be summed up in a phrase that has repeatedly suggested itself to us: *THE GROTESQUE IS THE ESTRANGED WORLD*. But some additional explanation is required. For viewed from the outside, the world of the fairy tale could also be regarded as strange and alien. Yet its world is not estranged, that is to say, the elements in it which are familiar and natural to us do not suddenly turn out to be ominous. (184)

Even though Myop is a child and subsequently incapable of the foresight that experience brings, the reader accepts Myop's narrow and immediate perspective of her world. She is the reader's lens. It is a credit to Walker that Myop seems to be a credible character, despite her age. Perhaps, this is to be credited in part to how child-like innocence is widely valued and its loss is generally seen as an inevitable violation to be staved off for as long as possible. The reader wants to revel in the fairy tale wash that Walker has applied to Myop's modest world and this day in particular. As Kayser suggests, while the world of the poverty-stricken sharecropper's daughter may be somewhat strange and not relatable to the reader, the reader can relate to the joy of a summer day and the freedom it affords a precocious little girl. Therefore, readers willingly join Walker's Myop as she begins her day of adventure with the optimistic expectation reserved for the innocent. Subsequently, when Myop stumbles into the eye of the lynching victim, both the reader and Myop have stumbled into the estranged world. Kayser expands on this notion:

> *Suddenness and surprise* are essential elements of the grotesque. In literature the grotesque appears in a scene or animated tableau. Its representations . . . do not refer to a state of repose but to an action, a "pregnant moment" . . . a situation that is filled with ominous tension. (184)

The discovery of the corpse is clearly sudden and unexpected for young Myop who gives "a little yelp of surprise" upon seeing its "naked grin" (405). Additionally, the scene derives much of its power from the juxtaposition of the ten-year-old girl (for whom the reader has come to have an affinity) with the decomposing body of the lynching victim. They become the tableau of which Kayser speaks in his explanation of the grotesque. Actually, what the reader "sees" within the text, is a *tableau vivant* or "(from French, literally, living picture): a depiction of a scene usually presented on a stage by silent and motionless costumed participants" ("tableau vivant"). This is much like the disturbing images of the lynching postcards catalogued in James Allen's book and exhibit entitled *Without Sanctuary*, where the living and the dead are frozen in scenes of the mundane and macabre juxtaposed. In Allen's collection, the lynched swing in the breeze above picnickers or gentle streams. Their dead eyes gaze off into unclouded skies. In Walker's story, the corpse of the lynched man rests upon layers of rich earth, his eyes absent and not seeing the child holding a carefully curated bouquet of flowers above him.

While there is a moment of shock and perhaps silence, there is no repose. In both "The Flowers" and *Without Sanctuary*, there is no repose for the dead who remain exposed and vulnerable in the scene and no repose for the observer who must now decide what to do with the images that cannot be unseen. This provides the ominous tension that Kayser writes about and Allen relates in his *Without Sanctuary* narrative:

> It wasn't the corpse that bewildered me as much as the canine-thin faces of the pack, lingering in the woods, circling after the kill. Hundreds of flea markets later a trader pulled me aside and in conspiratorial tones offered me a second card, this one of Laura Nelson, caught so pitiful and tattered and beyond retrieving—like a child's paper kite snagged on a utility wire. The sight of Laura layered a pall of grief over all my fears.

Myop studies the man she finds. Like Allen, she wants to ascribe a modicum of humanity to the victim she stumbles upon. She unearths him, finds that once "he had been a tall man" (405). She sees that he once had "large white teeth . . . long fingers, and very big bones" (405). Once, he had worn "blue denim" overalls (405). There must be simultaneously a strange anonymity and familiarity that Myop finds in his appearance. Though she does not recognize the man, what she sees of him must be very much like the men that populate her world, big men who farm in similar overalls and who grin showing big white teeth. Perhaps that is why she is unafraid at this point; she even stands still holding her bouquet of flowers. Living on a farm, surely Myop is familiar with the inevitability of death. However, it is when she reaches to pick the wild pink rose that she unearths the grotesque truth of her find:

> Very near where she'd stepped into the head was a wild pink rose. As she picked it to add to her bundle she noticed a raised mound, a ring, around the rose's root. It was the rotted remains of a noose, a bit of shredding plow-line, now blending benignly into the soil. Around an overhanging limb of a great spreading oak clung another piece. Frayed, rotted, bleached, and frazzled—barely there—but spinning restlessly in the breeze. (405)

The small wild rose is metaphorically a nod to Myop's own innocence. The rose is small, uncultivated, thriving and without thorns. And, as most wild roses, it is the pink generally associated with little girls. Most troubling is that its roots are bound by the noose suggesting that Myop's ability to thrive may also be challenged by the constrictions of racism. After all, had the little wild rose continued to grow there, at some point its life-sustaining root system would have been choked off. Even more problematic is that Myop realizes that what she has stumbled upon is not a natural death. The intersection of the rose and the rope signals perhaps the end of Myop's innocence and her entry into the world of a burgeoning black young woman who must somehow thrive despite the ropes that may tie and bind. Whatever Myop may have heard whispered amongst the old folks in the cabin about lynching and racial hatred has now come into sharper focus. It has encroached on her safe space. It has found her. Kayser explains:

> We are strongly affected and terrified because it is our world which ceases to be reliable, and we feel that we would be unable to live in this changed world. The grotesque instills fear of life rather than death. Structurally, it presupposes that the categories which apply to our world view become inapplicable. The various forms of the grotesque are the most obvious and

pronounced contradictions of any kind of rationalism and any systematic use of thought. (184)

When Myop lays down her flowers, she is performing the time-honored ritual most associated with paying homage to the dead (405). It is an act of reverence and sacrifice. However, when the description of this act is so closely followed with the one-line paragraph, "And the summer was over," the scene explodes with resonance (405). It isn't the corpse that sends Myop figuratively into the eye of the condemned man. It is the noose and subsequent revelation that the violence of racism has invaded her relativity safety. Myop is only a mile or more from her house and has been this far from it often (404). And even before she stumbles into the lynched man, she feels how "the strangeness of the land made it not as pleasant as her usual haunts. It seemed gloomy in the little cove in which she found herself. The air was damp, the silence close and deep" (405). Already the landscape had begun to shift away from her. She sensed it earlier and she had wanted to "circle back to the house, back to the peacefulness of the morning." But it was then that she discovered the body. This is what makes Myop's world unreliable. She can no longer wander this far from home again without a sense that her adventure may have an ominous outcome. Like the "tiny white bubbles" that "Myop watched disrupt the thin black scale of soil" (404), the encroachment of white racism and violence has disrupted the thin layer of protection that the little girl's community has come to trust. Henceforth, young children will be made to stay close to home. Indeed, the summer is over.

More immediate is that the summer day no longer belongs to Myop. She is no longer the composer of songs or curator of bouquets. She is now the little girl who found the corpse. The day now belongs to the corpse's naked grin. When she arrives home, her family and the community at large will convene to discuss what has happened. Perhaps families with lost men folk will come to Myop's woods in hopes of identifying the body and in so doing, trample the wildflowers.

Walker's use of flowers as image and symbol, whether wild or culti-vated, pervades her work. Upon reading Walker's essay, "In Search of Our Mothers' Gardens," the reader might attribute this to her mother's gardening prowess, which rendered her mother, "radiant, almost to the point of being invisible—except as creator: hand and eye" (241). The reader sees this budding artistry in young Myop, who carefully chooses amongst the wildflowers for her bouquet. Myop's character is a study in both hand and eye. Her myopic perspective blazes with in-tensity, scrutiny, and discernment. Her eye discerns which flowers are appropriate for her work of art. Her hand determines their placement. She is both intent upon and content to spend the better part of her sum-mer day, not playing with friends, but carefully creating a bouquet of flowers. The reader must surmise that Myop's flower gathering is more than an idle day in the woods. Myop is a budding artist. Her home will become her gallery. Walker reminisces, "my mother adorned with flowers whatever shabby house we were forced to live in" (241). The reader expects that, like Walker's own mother, Myop will adorn her family's modest sharecropper's cabin with her art. The impact of this is made clearer as Walker further explains:

Whatever she planted grew as if by magic, and her fame as a grower of flowers spread over three counties. Because of her creativity with her flowers, even my memories of poverty are seen through a screen of blooms—sunflowers, petunias, roses, dahlias, forsythia, spirea, delphini-ums, verbena . . . and on and on. (241)

The introduction of beauty into the landscape of poverty and oppres-sion is life-giving and soul-fortifying. What Myop does by curating beauty and introducing it into the otherwise bleak milieu of her fam-ily's cabin is not only integral to her own development as a person and budding artist, but also to her development as a member of her house-hold and as a member of the larger community. Walker describes her mother's gardening as the work that "her soul must have" (241). Early in the story, Myop is self-possessed. She is free to follow her ten-year-old ambitions. And had the wildflower bouquet made it home, perhaps Myop would have been lavishly praised, though on a smaller scale than Walker's mother, an artist in full bloom, was. Walker writes:

> And I remember people coming to my mother's yard to be given cuttings from her flowers; I hear again the praise showered on her because whatever rocky soil she landed on, she turned into a garden. A garden so brilliant with colors, original in its design, so magnificent with life and creativity, that to this day people drive by our house in Georgia—perfect strangers and imperfect strangers—and ask to stand or walk among my mother's art. (241)

Though Myop is a child, her place in the world of artistry cannot be overstated. Children take their affinities, abilities, and early life experiences into their adulthoods and thereby fashion their lives from them. As pivotal as the discovery of the corpse and the lost summer will be to Myop going forward, the solace and creative power she derives from her art will also be—if it is nurtured.

Walker is very aware of the power of community and its relationship to the artist. In "The Black Writer and the Southern Experience" she writes, "what the black Southern writer inherits as a natural right is a sense of community" (17). And though the literary stage of "The Flowers" is primarily occupied by Myop and the lynched man, the aura of her family and community suffuse the story as well. Consequently, the connection between Myop as the artist and her community must be made.

The connection of the artist to the community is widely discussed, researched, and written about. Sandra L. Bloom of Drexel University's School of Public Health emphatically asserts in "Bridging the Black Hole of Trauma: The Evolutionary Significance of the Arts" that *"artistic performance is the bridge across the black hole of trauma, the evolved individual response and group response to the tragic na-*

ture of human existence." Additionally, she asserts that art is a form of dissociation. That is, humans reorder their world in response to trauma, both immediate and ongoing. According to Bloom, "human beings alter their reality with such consistency and frequency that we are forced to conclude that this capacity is innate and must therefore have significant survival value." Reflect upon how Walker's mother brings beauty into her shabby home and outside it when she plants "ambitious gardens . . . with over fifty different varieties of plants that bloom profusely from early March until late November" (241). Consider how Mama and Maggie cover their old table with a feast that suggests wealth and abundance, though the reader understands that all of that food must have come at great cost to the poor women (2437–42). Their art, whether horticultural or culinary, is a form of dissociation; these women have altered their worlds to create pockets of beauty and joy for themselves, their families, and communities. Art then becomes both remedy and shield.

Myop, her family, and surrounding community live in a state of ongoing trauma. As sharecroppers, they live in a form of poverty that is self-perpetuating. As Trudier Harris explains in her entry, "Sharecropping":

Without land of their own, many blacks . . . worked a portion of the land owned by whites for a share of the profit from the crops. They would get all the seeds, food, and equipment they needed from the company store, which allowed them to run a tab throughout the year and to settle up once the crops, usually cotton, were gathered. When accounting time came, the black farmer was always a few dollars short of what he owed the landowner, so he invariably began the new year with a deficit. As that deficit grew, he found it impossible to escape from his situation by legal means.

Farming is difficult at best. The best farmer is often at the cruel mercy of the weather, insects, and temperamental seed. The payoff is the harvest that the farmer nurtures into maturity. However, when the fruits of one's labors belong to another and seasonally fall short of provision, a collective despair falls over the household and community.

Communities rely upon individual prosperity to thrive. Without prosperity, no new buildings are built. Commerce is limited. Education becomes secondary to survival. Even more problematic is the psychic trauma the communities endure. Men feel inadequate to provide for their families. Women fret over their ability to feed and clothe their children and lament the children yet unborn. Though Myop is still innocent, she is not immune to the effects of this trauma. Even if she cannot name it, she is most assuredly viscerally aware of it. No member of a community is immune to this "emotional contagion" or "emotional convergence," as Bloom refers to it. In her article, she cites Hatfield:

> We respond to each other's emotional state within one twentieth of a second and in that time our physiology is changed and our bodies become synchronized to the emotional state of the other. This happens outside of our conscious awareness and is beyond our ability to control. (Bloom)

It is then necessary that a "social species . . . erect such social obstacles to the integration of post-traumatic experience" into their communal fabric (Bloom). Subsequently, art as dissociation equates to art as survival. This renders Myop's narrow focus on her own creative ability to discern, curate, and possess beauty more than just child's play. Her potential to offer this gift to her community could alter its psychic landscape just as Walker's mother's seemingly magical garden does.

Finally, if the reader were to personify the flowers that little Myop lays beside the lynching victim, they might represent the varied and beautiful young women of Myop's community. The pink wild rose would be Myop herself: poignantly thriving, but ensnared in a social political structure that threatens her community and her autonomous selfhood. The lynching rope killed the man, but it looms large in its ability to magnify a community's fear and perhaps stymie its ability to clothe itself in respite beauty. The ferns she gathers might be the elder women—they, too, joined on one flexible stem of shared identity and origin, their combined fronds, a legion of legacy and legend. All of the other wild flowers would be individuals, resilient and uniquely beautiful. But then to have this bouquet of women laid down beside the corpse of a lynched man conjures up the voices and spirits of widowed women, orphaned children, and sobbing mothers whose menfolk were taken from them.

The reader leaves Myop looking down into the tableau: a sculpture of sorts in the form of a decapitated corpse fashioned by mob-driven hate and violence. Lying nearby is her own earthy artistry in full bloom, a simple bouquet of wildflowers. So much depends upon whether little Myop can climb out of the eyes she has stepped smack into on this summer day. Should the fear fueled by this grotesque scene become the locus of her myopic perspective, she will surely lose herself and her creative power. Her thoughts will only be of how she will survive this newly estranged and unreliable world. Her shield of artistic endeavor will be lowered, leaving both Myop and her community exposed to an existence of continued and unmitigated internalized trauma. If the grotesque estrangement created by the lynching party endures, beauty in its multiple manifestations will then be supplanted by fear. Myop and others like her will lose their innocence. The reader might wonder why so much should depend upon Myop, this one little girl on this particular summer day. Simply stated, Myop is an "everygirl." Every girl will either relinquish her innocence or have it wrested from her. Every little girl will lift her gaze outward into the world that lay past the relative safety of her home and community. Myop, this seedling of a child, can still grow in many directions: as disoriented as Dee, timid as Maggie, resilient as Alice. And her family and community can be made the better or worse for it.

Works Cited

Allen, James, and John Littlefield. *Without Sanctuary: Photographs and Postcards of Lynching in America.* Collection of James Allen and John Littlefield, 2000–2005. Web. 5 July 2011.

Bloom, Sandra L.. "Bridging the Black Hole of Trauma: The Evolutionary Significance of the Arts." *Psychotherapy and Politics International* 8.3 (2010): 198–212.

Harris, Trudier, "Sharecropping." *The Oxford Companion to Women's Writing in the United States.* Oxford: Oxford UP. *Modern American Poetry: About Sharecropping.* U of Illinois, 7 Jul 2011. Web. 9 Mar. 2012.

Kayser, Wolfgang. *The Grotesque in Art and Literature.* Morningside Ed. New York: Columbia UP, 1981.

"Tableau vivant." *Collins English Dictionary: Complete and Unabridged.* New York: Harper, 2003.

Walker, Alice. "Beauty: When the Other Dancer Is the Self." *In Search of Our Mothers' Gardens.* Ed. Alice Walker. Orlando: Harcourt, 1983. 361–70.

_____. "The Black Writer and the Southern Experience." *In Search of Our Mothers' Gardens.* Ed. Alice Walker. Orlando: Harcourt, 1983. 15–21.

_____. "Everyday Use." *The Norton Anthology of African American Literature.* 2nd Edition. Ed. Henry Louis Gates Jr. and Nellie Y. McKay. New York: Norton, 2004. 2437–42.

_____. "The Flowers." *Reading and Writing about Short Fiction.* Ed. Edward Proffitt. New York: Harcourt, 1988. 404–5.

_____. "In Search of Our Mothers' Gardens." In Search of Our Mothers' Gardens. Ed. Alice Walker. Orlando: Harcourt, 1983. 231–43.

Sexuality and the Healing of the Self: *The Color Purple, Possessing the Secret of Joy*, and *By the Light of My Father's Smile*

Karla Kovalova

Perhaps no other African American writer has polarized her readers to the extent that Alice Walker has done with her controversial novels *The Color Purple* (1982), *Possessing the Secret of Joy* (1992), and *By the Light of My Father's Smile* (1998). While praised by feminist critics as important works in the category of women's liberation fiction, the novels attracted harsh criticism for three perceived flaws: a negative portrayal of black men in America, cultural imperialism, and a pornographic/gynecological description of female sexuality, respectively.[1] The subtext of the criticism could hardly be missed: Walker has gone dangerously too far in her fictional reconstruction of black female subjectivity and history.

Described aptly as "[a] woman walking into peril" (Dieke 1), Walker has always chosen for her "route to truth" a path through "the forbidden" (Christian 40). Committed to "the spiritual survival, the survival *whole* of my people. But beyond that to exploring the oppressions . . . and the triumphs of black women" (*In Search* 250), she has insisted, in her writing, on challenging, in her eyes, the three major blocks to black women's well-being and growth: the patriarchal system, white supremacy, and Western religion. Influenced by indigenous spiritualities, particularly African and Native American, she has further rejected Western dualism, i.e., the belief in the separateness of body and mind, to espouse a more holistic understanding of the self and the place of humans in the sacred web of life, thus expanding her womanist[2] concept of personal wholeness to not only global unity, but universal unity. It is within this paradigm that she reclaims sexuality as a sacred practice wedded to both personal wholeness and humans' bond with nature, divinity, and Creation, thus integrating the personal, sexual, and spiritual into a whole. *The Color Purple, Possessing the Secret of Joy*, and

By the Light of My Father's Smile engender this vision as they unveil women's erotic freedom not only as a site of women's oppression, but also as a site of empowerment, a path to healing, redemption, and reconciliation. The novels' radical call to black women to reclaim their bodies and the joy that they can experience through them in order to liberate themselves from the patriarchal order, which has denied them the right to full selfhood, is precisely what constitutes Walker's dangerous act of "going too far," an act threatening to undo the order as it stitches together fragments of the female self.

In this respect, *The Color Purple*, Walker's third novel, serves as a fitting model. Set in the 1940s in the American South, it tells a story of the transformation of Celie, a poor, uneducated black woman who, as Tuzyline Jita Allan observes, is "locked within a cultural text that defines her as an object" (83) at the beginning of the novel. Repeatedly raped since the age of fourteen by her stepfather with whom she has two children, both taken away from her, and later "sold" by him into marital slavery to endure more violence from her husband, Celie is initially portrayed as a victim whose womanhood as well as subjectivity has been denied to her. A silenced woman forced into utter submission, she has no sense of herself as a human being; her body and spirit have been broken by the patriarchal law represented in the novel by her stepfather and her husband, respectively. To reclaim her wholeness, Walker insists that Celie must find guidance and sustenance in bonding with black women, who can help her liberate herself from the bondage preventing her from spiritual growth and self-realization, and enable her to become a subject with her own voice.

Robbed of her mother, who, weak from childbearing, died too soon, and separated from her sister Nettie, the only person who ever cared for her, Celie has no one to confide in about her abuse. Voiceless, she writes letters to God, obeying her stepfather's imperative—"*You better not tell nobody but God. It'd kill your mammy*" (11)—while breaking the silence associated with victims of sexual abuse. But the patriarchal God remains silent, giving her no sign of advice about how to liberate herself from the yoke of oppression, reinforcing Celie's belief that, as a poor black woman, she deserves her fate. Consequently, accepting the position of the victim, Celie blindly perpetuates the violence done to black women by advising her stepson Harpo to beat his strong-minded wife, Sofia. As she later admits, justifying the "sin" of her act, it was because she was jealous of Sofia's resilience: "you do what I can't . . . Fight" (46).

Paradoxically, the betrayal marks the end of Celie's submissive loneliness, for the confrontation with Sofia that follows sparks a genuine sisterhood between the two women who reconcile over quilting. For Celie, quilting represents "the crucial initial act of redemption" (Elsley 166). As Judy Elsley explains:

> Celie and Sofia's quiltmaking is a process of healing because they are no longer passive victims who are torn. Quiltmaking turns being torn into tearing, turns object into subject. Active creation replaces passive victimization as the two women, their sisterhood reaffirmed, set about constructing a pattern of their choice out of the fragments of their lives. Celie's decision to make the quilt is thus the turning point in her life because it is the first step to her empowerment via connection with other women. (167)

While the importance of Celie's newly developed friendship with Sofia cannot be underestimated, it is not until Celie engages in a relationship with Shug Avery, who becomes her "surrogate mother," friend, and a lover, that she can find the necessary strength to fight the oppressive patriarchal system, and assume responsibility for her own life, thereby becoming a subject in her own right. For Shug enables her to reclaim not just the fragments of her life but also her own body and erotic freedom, allowing her to love and accept herself as a whole person.

Bearing a resemblance to her literary foremother Zora Neale Hurston, Shug is *the* embodiment of Walker's womanist philosophy— audacious, assertive, and in love with men, women, and life—she incarnates the triumph of black woman's independence and resilience. Celie's initial meeting with her, however, like the incident with Sofia, is devoid of the warmth of sisterhood embedded in the term "woman-ist." Sick with fever and jealous of Celie's marriage to Albert, Shug insults Celie with a mean comment: "You sure *is* ugly" (50, emphasis in the text), betraying both Celie's love and admiration for her and one of the key womanist tenets, that of loving and appreciating other black women. It is not until after Celie bathes Shug's sick body, combs her hair, and restores her back to health with her food that they establish a unifying bond, opening doors to a life-long intimacy that will be con-stitutive of Celie's healing of both her broken spirit and abused body.

While Celie aids Shug in gaining back physical strength, Shug in turn enables Celie to experience "spiritual rebirth"; as "a surrogate mother," she gives her a sense of self, belonging, and being loved (Barker 55, 58). First, Shug dedicates a song to her that, describing Celie's life, articulates all the wrongs a man does to a woman under the patriarchal order. The song has a therapeutic effect: it validates Celie's experience while simultaneously cleansing her of the false belief that she, as a black woman, deserves the position of the lowest. Moreover, being the first thing that someone made and named after her, the song awakens in Celie a sense of self-worth. Shug also intervenes when Celie confides that Albert, whom she calls Mr. _____, beats her for not being Shug. This second manifestation of caring about Celie rein-forces her sense of self, that she is worthy of humane treatment, which is boosted further by Shug's support of Celie's pants business, encour-aging her creativity and self-actualization. Finally, Shug shows Celie where Mr. _____ has hidden letters sent to her by Nettie, allowing her to reconnect via the written word with the family she thought she had lost, restoring her sense of kinship and belonging.

The discovered letters mark the beginning of Celie's ability to speak in her own voice and claim her female subjectivity. Finding the courage to curse Albert who has attempted to control her life, she "reject[s]," as Rudolph P. Byrd observes, "the passive stance of the victim and . . .

---

assume[s] the aggressive, defiant stance of the warrior" ("Spirituality" 376), or, as Catherine A. Colton argues, becomes "her own conjure woman" (37), who knows the power of the word. This transformation is largely enabled by Celie's newfound understanding of God, in which she replaces the patriarchal male God, to the plight of poor colored women, with a new image that encompasses everybody's experience. As Shug enlightens her:

> God is inside you and inside everybody else. You come into the world with God. But only them that search for it inside find it. . . . God ain't a he or a she, but a It. . . . God is everything . . . Everything that is or ever was or ever will be. And when you can feel that, and be happy to feel that, you've found It. [. . .] that feeling of being part of everything, not separate at all. (177–78)

Shug's radical understanding of the divine, which rejects institutionalized Christianity in favor of one's inner experience, underlines Walker's concept of human oneness with the universe and allows Celie to discover that she is also part of Creation like anyone else. Moreover, it enables her "to git man off her eyeball" (179) and "to conjure up words . . . that can 'activate the power' of her new interconnected, more African worldview" (Colton 37).

Celie's transformation from a self-negated object to a subject with her own voice, however, cannot be complete without the healing of Celie's long abused body, the key to which, as Walker suggests, lies in its suppressed sexuality. Having endured repeated rape by her stepfather and selfish marital sex imposed on her by her husband, which always felt as if "he [was] going to the toilet on [her]" (79), Celie initially seems devoid of sexual desire; her lack of libido being underscored by her premature menopause. Yet contrary to her stepfather's claim that she is sexually "spoiled" (17), for Shug, she is "still a virgin" (79) because she has never known sexuality as a site of pleasure and has been kept ignorant about the sexual functions of her body. To fill the void, Shug initiates her into the secret knowledge of both: "Listen . . . right down there in your pussy is a little button that gits real hot when you do you know what . . . It git hotter and hotter and then it melt. That the good part. But other parts good too . . . Lot of sucking go on, here and there . . . Lot of finger and tongue work" (79). Handing her a mirror in which Celie can see, for the first time, her sexual parts, Shug enables Celie to accept her body as her own. Celie's exclamation, "It mine" (79), referring to the discovery of her clitoris, is her first step toward its reclamation.

Shug's initiation also enables Celie to experience, for the first time in her life, sexual desire and lesbian love, which to Celie, "feel like *heaven* . . . not like sleeping with Mr. _____ at all" (110, emphasis mine). In some ways, Celie's discovery of the pleasure of physical intimacy "complete[s] her spiritual journey toward selfhood," for "this is the first time Celie . . . feel[s] secure and loved" (Barker 61)—whole (and healed) both in body and spirit. Her lesbian relationship with Shug represents a sexual rebirth for Celie, a window into a world of love, in which black women can blossom and experience "feminine jouissance," an erotic freedom of which the color purple can be understood a symbol (Abbandonato 306). This world cannot, however, exist under male domination but, as Walker insists, must be re-created on the basis of equality. While a lesbian relationship that reinforces the richness of female bonding can serve as a model in this respect—or can sometimes be, as it is for Celie, the only choice, given the history of men's abuse of women—Walker does not imply that lesbianism should be the norm for black women. A true womanist, like Shug, loves sexually (or not) both men and women, and does not restrict her choices to either-or; instead, she embraces all possibilities that celebrate and affirm life.

This is most evident in Shug's reconceptualization of the patriarchal God, which enables Celie to make the final step toward ultimate wholeness: to believe herself part of Creation, "free and equal to anyone and anything" (Barker 61). With this knowledge Celie is able to accept and love herself regardless of her family background—her lynched father, deranged mother, and rapacious stepfather—and to appreciate the wonder of simply being in the world. Her words, "I'm pore, I'm black, I may be ugly and can't cook . . . But I'm here" (187), are a poignant expression of Celie's spiritual triumph, i.e., her celebration of her whole self: liberated and free to enjoy the physical pleasures of life.

Unlike Celie, whose journey to selfhood has led her to embrace life and rejoice in it, Tashi, the protagonist of Walker's fifth novel, *Possessing the Secret of Joy*, faces at the end of her own journey death for the murder of the national *tsunga* (Walker's invented term to designate a woman circumciser). Yet despite what seems a tragic ending, the novel, just like *The Color Purple*, does not portray its heroine as a mere victim; rather, it seeks to liberate the black female by celebrating her dignity and agency, showing her, as Lauret observes, as a "warrior who uses her own suffering to help eliminate that of others" (162). As Tashi estimates her accomplishment, dying: "I am no more. And *satisfied*" (264, emphasis mine).

The novel, tellingly dedicated to the "blameless vulva," presents a story of a rehabilitation of an African woman who submits, of her own will, to the ritual of excision (female genital mutilation) and, traumatized, searches for an understanding of the roots of her pain. Although explicitly concerned with African female experience, the novel establishes a clear link to African American culture via the protagonist's marriage to an African American (one of Celie's two children who had been taken away) and the sisterhood invoked in its note to the reader, in which Walker explains: "I have created Olinka as my village and the Olinkas as one of my ancient, ancestral, tribal peoples. Certainly I recognize Tashi as my sister" (283). This sisterhood, claimed on the grounds of the historical fact of the transatlantic slave trade, also enables Walker to claim the sensitive subject of female genital mutilation as her concern; her act, however, is seen as problematic for Africans, who view the novel as yet another case of Western arrogance for its implication that African women cannot speak for themselves.[3]

Initially, Tashi belongs to an African tribe that considers women's genitals unclean, and which ritually excises girls' genitals to initiate the girls into womanhood and ensure their marriageability. With her mother under the influence of American missionaries who denounce the practice of "bath" as barbaric, and the death of her older sister Dura, who bled to death as a result of it (the memory of which Tashi was made to repress), Tashi was not circumcised at puberty. Yet as an act of rebellion against the oppressive colonial rule, she eventually chooses to undergo female genital mutilation to be "Completely woman. Completely African. Completely Olinka" (61). In doing so, she blindly follows the rhetoric of the Leader of her tribe, who advocates resistance by "keep[ing] ourselves clean and pure as we had been since time immemorial" (119). As she learns much later from the *tsunga*, who reveals to her the truth about the role that women were expected to play in the liberation movement—cooking, cleaning, and providing sex for male soldiers, "keeping the tribe intact was, in reality, only a metaphor for keeping the women under control" (Simcikova 31).[4]

The result of Tashi's circumcision or "hidden scar" (*Possessing* 66) between her legs is detrimental. With her external genitals removed and her flesh sewn tight, "it now took a quarter of an hour for her to pee. Her menstrual periods lasted ten days. She was incapacitated by cramps nearly half the month . . . There was the odor, too, of soured blood, which no amount of scrubbing . . . ever washed off" (64). Instead of bringing the bliss of feeling more complete, the circumcision results in a triple subtraction as it destroys Tashi's body, the quality of her life, and her marriage in the United States. With each sexual act, she experiences nothing but excruciating pain, inevitably making her husband, Adam, an aggressor. In addition, her miraculous pregnancy (it took several months just to penetrate her) turns into a horror: due to the lack of space in her womb necessary for the growth of the child and the subsequent traumatic labor and delivery, their son is born mentally disabled. Fearing the same result with her second child, and unable to accept the option of a Caesarian section that would ease the childbirth for the trauma of having to be cut and sewed again, Tashi resorts to abortion, destroying the life of a daughter she would have loved to nurture under different circumstances (217).

Robbed of her physical *whole*ness, being left with, what Western medical doctors refer to ironically as a "hole," Tashi soon begins to lose her mind as well: she suffers from recurring nightmares in which her repressed memory of her sister's death comes to haunt her, screaming her pain into her ears. Attempting to mutilate herself in sleep, she must resort to psychotherapy to achieve psychical healing. With the help of two psychoanalysts, a European male, Carl Jung/Mzee, and an African American female, Raye, she is, eventually, able to confront the repressed pain and access her cultural memory. However, it is not until Adam's son (with his lover Lisette) Pierre, a cultural anthropologist, helps Tashi decipher the meaning of the ritual's symbolic language that she comes to understand the deep-rooted significance of the practice of female genital mutilation and the religious mythology on which it is based:

> Man is God's cock.... It drops the seed.... But its offspring ... It cannot identify.... The *tsunga*'s stitch helps the cock to know his crop ... the *tsunga* though herself a woman ... helps God ... Woman is queen.... If left to herself, the Queen would fly.... But God is merciful.... He clips her wings.... That is why He created the *tsunga.* (230–232)

Having gained the knowledge of how her tribe has *blinded* its women into accepting their fate as part of a tradition sanctioned by their ancestors, and therefore sacred, Tashi also comes to understand how the practice of female genital mutilation keeps women subordinate to men, denying them the right to full selfhood and subjectivity. Helping to maintain the system that views female sexuality as unrestrained and dangerous if not under check, the practice is perpetuated "to control women's reproduction and sexuality" (Simcikova 33) and turns women into living objects to be used by men.[5] To break away from the oppressive system (upheld by the means of women's/mothers' collaboration and a set of taboos regarding the functions of the body and a verbal expression of suffering), Walker insists that women must repossess full control over their bodies and sexual organs that "identify the self" (Warren and Wolff 15), and reclaim "the blameless vulva" and the sexual pleasure they can experience through it. As she expresses her belief through the metaphor of "sexual blindness in *Warrior Marks: Female Genital Mutilation and the Sexual Blinding of Women* (1993), a book thematically related to her novel: "Without the clitoris and other sexual organs, a woman can never see herself reflected in the healthy, intact body of another. Her sexual vision is impaired" (19).

Having experienced highly pleasurable clitoral orgasms during sex with Adam before her circumcision and their subsequent marriage to him, Tashi can remember her full sexual vision, which she has irretrievably lost after her "bath." Realizing the full extent of the damage that she has voluntarily inflicted on herself and that has been forced upon other innocent girls, she seeks revenge and punishment of those who have helped to perpetuate the practice and thus returns to Africa to kill M'Lissa, the *tsunga* of the Olinka tribe. Tashi's physical journey to the actual location of the origins of her wound (as opposed to her psychotherapeutic access to it via memories) marks, just like Celie's discovery of her sister's letters, the beginning of Tashi's transformation from a passive victim to a warrior who is ready to take up her arms for justice. It is this transformation that gives her the strength to write a sign of protest: "If you lie about your own pain, you will be killed by those who will claim you enjoy it" (106), consciously breaking the major taboo/commandment among the Olinkas—never tell about your suffering. The journey also allows her to reintegrate the African part of her into her Americanized self and thus accept it as constitutive of her complex identity, as evident in the title of the last chapter: "Tashi Evelyn Johnson Soul" (Lauret 173).

This reintegration happens after Tashi confronts M'Lissa and is forced to hear her story, which reveals "a commonality of experience

---

and identity" between them (George 363). She learns that M'Lissa herself is a victim of genital mutilation whose mother, also a *tsunga*, secretly believed in a woman's right to sexual pleasure and had tried to protect her daughter's womanhood by hiding a doll, a clay image of a smiling woman touching her genitals, in a tree in the forest. When other women found out that M'Lissa had been circumcised only lightly, they completed her mutilation to the point of leaving her with a permanent limp. Scarred both physically and psychically, M'Lissa became emotionally numb, ignorant to the pain she was inflicting on other women while perpetuating the tradition that destroyed her own life. In doing so, she was trying to forget the abandoned crying child (herself), who, she tells Tashi, "is still crying" and "has been crying all *our* tears" (218, emphasis mine). M'Lissa thus acknowledges the collectivity of this African female experience.

To put a stop to the ongoing tradition of crippling women, Tashi finds the courage to enact her struggle and kill M'Lissa, the executor of the ritual. Her act, although legally and morally wrong from the Western point of view (though expected in the tradition of *tsunga*), is, as Lâle Demirtürk points out, liberating in its determination "to change a situation that prevents the African female self from blossoming into wholeness" (36). Moreover, Tashi's execution—the consequence of her act of resistance—liberates her in "a spiritual transcendence of the life-long pain," reconciling her "to the ancient African women's vision of freedom" (36). For as Tashi discloses her freshly gained knowledge in her letter from jail: "these women . . . in their own ancient societies they owned their bodies, including their vulvas, and touched them as much as they liked . . . early African woman, the mother of womankind, was notoriously free!" (276). To acknowledge a connection to her, before her execution, Tashi gives to her spiritual daughter Mbati "a little sacred figure of Nyanda" (270), a doll signifying African female subjectivity and sexual freedom. In passing on her secret of joy, she can reconcile her imminent death and nurture hope that one day future generations of black women will be able to claim it for themselves.

Perhaps to test the waters and to see if the current generation is ready to accept the legitimacy of female sexual freedom, the first chapter of Walker's sixth novel, *By the Light of My Father's Smile: A Story of Requited Love, Crossing Over, and the Sexual Healing of the Soul*, closes with a highly erotic scene of two black women making love:

> Pauline's mouth captures the whole of Susannah's vulva. There is no little corner of it that at first escapes. It is as if she would suck out the womb and, indeed, she appears to dive for it with her long whining tongue. Only now, at this, the whining tongue sings, and Susannah *feels herself mounting to the clouds*, and tries to slow herself down from arriving there. (13, emphasis mine)

While antithetical to Tashi's experience of excruciating pain and somehow reminiscent of Celie's experience of sleeping with Shug, which, as noted earlier, felt "like heaven," the scene highlights the power of female sexual freedom and the bliss one can experience through it. Yet contrary to our expectations, the novel stops short of being a celebration of the victory of female sexual freedom. For ironically, the somewhat (porno)graphic description is given by Mr. Robinson, Susannah's late father, who, in the bodiless form of a non-Christian angel, is forced to witness it as a way to punish him for brutally suppressing Susannah's sister's positive expression of sexuality.

While structured as the tale of a father's redemption, the novel, a tribute to Eros, the Greek god[6] of erotic love and life energy, tells, essentially, the story of two sisters, Magdalena and Susannah, who due to their father's internalization of "the rigid patriarchal notion of a daughter's virginity," are prevented from spiritual growth and the right to wholeness (Simcikova 41). An open critique of "controlling images" aimed at restraining women's sexuality, and the impact of Christian dogmas on parental education of girls, the novel calls for fathers' affirmation of their daughters' sexual lives while celebrating the sacredness of human sexuality as depicted in the practice of the mixed-race

Mundo tribe. Manuelito, a member of the tribe and Magdalena's lover, explains the deeper implication of sexuality while conversing with Mr. Robinson: "it is when making love that we make life" (153).

Having a mutually satisfying and energizing sexual relationship with his wife Langley, in whose presence he finds much needed grounding, Mr. Robinson understands the import of sexuality in one's life. Yet in his hypocrisy, he cannot acknowledge and affirm sexuality in his teen-age daughter Magdalena, who appears to him as incomprehensibly wild. Comparing her to her sister Susannah, whom he finds pure, he sees her as a tramp whom he must tame. To suppress her sexual desires, he beats her with a belt, causing her physical as well as psychical wounds. Magdalena describes the irreparable damage to her life with the following words:

> He'd taken the moment in my life when I was most secure in its meaning. The moment my life opened, not just to my family and friends, but to me myself. The moment when I knew my life was given to me for me to own. He took that moment and he broke it into a million bits. He made it dirty and evil. . . . The man wrecked my life. (116–17)

The incident proves to have far-reaching effects. After witnessing her sister's punishment, Susannah is, for years, "crippled in a place that should be free" (28), unable to imagine ecstatic sex without feeling guilt. Moreover, she estranges herself both from her father, whom she used to adore, and her sister, whose presence reminds her of his brutality.

As Walker explains, Mr. Robinson's understanding of his daughters' sexuality is largely informed by Christian attitudes to it, which he espouses as part of his role as a mock-minister and priest among the Mundo, the subjects of his anthropological research. Having internalized the "ideas, beliefs, edicts, that had been put into practice" before he was born (30), he wants Magdalena to conform to his "constructed model of femininity" of "daddy's little girl" (Simcikova 42), thus confining her "to a perennial state of virginity" (Byrd 721).

For Walker, the traditional Western Church has "proven to be an agent in women's subordination" (Simcikova 30). Branding female sexuality as evil (and confining sex to the purpose of procreation only), it has denied women their right to sexual pleasure while constructing "controlling images," such as those of "virgin" and "whore," to keep women's sexuality under control (41). In the novel, Walker gives several examples of the church's negative impact on women's lives—Pauline's mother died of bearing children while Suzanne's friend Irene, who was born as a result of rape and whose mother also died in childbirth, was considered "God's punishment for her mother's sin" (51) and, as such, is exploited as a servant to the church. Moreover, it has "diminished the importance of sexuality in favor of 'higher' spiritual enlightenment" (40). To provide a corrective, Walker invents the Mundo tribe, whose egalitarian spirituality, in many ways akin to womanism, provides a positive alternative, wedding the sexual and the spiritual into a whole.

As Manuelito explains to Mr. Robinson, the Mundo believe that sexuality is "an integral part of their lives" to be enjoyed by both sexes; the sexual act between two persons is considered sacred (42). Knowing that both men and women are "inseparably connected to nature" through the Moon, whose light they understand as an approving smile of their Father blessing their sexuality, the Mundo approach sexuality with reverence, as "a celebration of Life itself, a praise of God who is 'Nature and Earth itself'" (106). This is evident in the wedding ritual the Mundo practice, in which the parents kiss the sexual organs of their children to bless them, the kissing being in sharp contrast to the idea that the sexual parts are unclean, sinful, and/or shameful parts of one's body to be cut out and/or never touched.

The sacredness of sexuality can also be seen in the description of Magdalena's lovemaking with Manuelito, in which she feels "[her] whole self seen" when he "whisper[s her name] against her clitoris"

(*By the Light* 24). Unlike Tashi, who, as argued earlier, "[w]ithout the clitoris and other sexual organs . . . can never *see* herself reflected in the healthy, intact body of another," Magdalena experiences more than a good "sexual vision"; her act of lovemaking "becomes a praise of her body" (Simcikova 43): "Everything we did pleased me. . . . Worshipped is how it felt. To know myself so thought of, so cared about . . . [to] feel in myself and in my response to Manuelito such depths of trust and desire *caused me to feel innately holy*" (*By the Light* 25, emphasis mine).

Just like Celie during her sexual act with Shug, and Susannah in her ecstatic orgasm with Pauline, Magdalena is able to experience the most powerful moment of all: a connection to the divine, "a cosmic consciousness," i.e., the feeling of oneness with the whole universe. It is precisely this experience that Mr. Robinson takes away from her, and by extension, from all daughters, in his punishment of her. Ignorant about the spirituality of the Mundo, whom he considers too poor and small in numbers to have any coherent and valuable set of beliefs that could compete with Christianity, he denies her spiritual nourishment available through the sacredness of a sexual union. To understand his mistake and realize the fallacy of Christian superiority and absurdity of women's confinement into rigid categories (ironically, the supposedly "sluttish" Magdalena turns out to have only one lover in her life while the "pure" Susannah enjoys a rich, promiscuous life), he must die and find himself in the Mundo realm of the dead.

In death Manuelito joins Mr. Robinson and helps him transform into a man with "his belief in woman" (156): a man who appreciates women, considers them equal and affirms their sexuality. Repenting for his sin, he hosts a wedding ceremony for Manuelito and Magdalena so she can "face eternity reconciled and complete" (148), finally acknowledging and blessing her sexual love. His redemption, signifying the legitimacy of black women's right to sexuality, however, seems simultaneously to cast a shadow over it, for the fact that Mr. Robinson and Magdalena do not reconcile until after their respective deaths, diminishes, to a large extent, the import of their reconciliation, while also erasing black female agency. And yet Walker does not undermine her own beliefs. If Magdalena's story means that perhaps the real, large-scale sexual reconciliation between fathers and daughters and by extension, men and women, cannot yet happen in the real life because the men believing in women are still few, like the members of the Mundo tribe, it also highlights "the value of forgiveness" and "the restorative value of ritual . . . challeng[ing] us to create new rituals . . . that will bring about reconciliation between the violated and the violator" (Byrd 722). Moreover, the novel "challenges us to create new rituals" (722) to restore the sacredness of sexuality and with it, our original bond with nature, divinity and Creation, and egalitarian way of being in the world. Finally, joining *The Color Purple* and *Possessing the Secret of Joy*, it calls for "the liberation of women from all forms of oppression which would deny them access to the knowledge and power of the body and the erotic" (722) and testifies, through the example of Suzanne/Pauline, that the liberation can, indeed, happen.

Notes

1. For a good summary of the controversy surrounding *The Color Purple*, see, for example, Jacqueline Bobo's "Sifting Through the Controversy: Reading *The Color Purple*." For an insight into why *Possessing the Secret* of Joy may elicit opposing reactions, see, for example, Olakunle George's "Alice Walker's Africa: Globalization and the Province of Fiction." For a discussion on how *By the Light of My Father's Smile* may polarize reviewers, see, for example, David Streitfeld's "Walker on the Wild Side, Again."

2. For a definition of Walker's concept of womanism see the preface to *In Search of Our Mothers' Gardens* (1984).

3. See, for example, Omofolabo Ajayi's article "Transcending the Boundaries of Power and Imperialism: Writing Gender, Constructing Knowledge."

4. The author wishes to acknowledge that some of the insights in this article come from her book *To Live Fully Here and Now: The Healing Vision in the Works of Alice Walker*, which deals in more detail with the issues of reclamation of the body in *Possessing the Secret of Joy* and reclamation of sexuality in *By the Light of My Father's Smile*.

5. For Walker, as I explain in *To Live Fully Here and Now*, female genital mutilation, as an example of male domination, cannot be seen as a phenomenon restricted

only to African societies but rather as a global issue. Tashi comes to understand this as she is introduced by her African American psychoanalyst Raye to Amy Maxwell, a white American woman who was also circumcised for touching herself as a little girl. As Walker further asserts in an interview with Pratibha Parmar, in a patriarchal society "it's . . . about shaping a woman in the image that men think they want" (*Warrior Marks* 276). In this light, "Tashi represents a 'universal woman' who is crippled because of her society's idea of what she is supposed to be like. While in some cultures, men require changes in women's genitalia, in other cultures, they set preferences for women's outer appearance" (Simcikova 34), hence the blossoming of plastic surgery, and the diet and fitness industries.

6. The novel contains several references to Greek as well as Biblical mythology. For a discussion of some of them, see Lauret.

Works Cited

Abbandonato, Linda. "Rewriting the Heroine's Story in *The Color Purple*." *Alice Walker: Critical Perspectives Past and Present*. Ed. Henry Louis Gates Jr. and K. A. Appiah. New York: Amistad, 1993. 296–308.

Ajayi, Omofolabo. "Transcending the Boundaries of Power and Imperialism: Writing Gender, Constructing Knowledge." *African Women and Imperialism*. Eds. Obi Nnaemeka and Ronke Oyewumi. Trenton: Africa World, 1997.

Allan, Tuzyline Jita. *Womanist and Feminist Aesthetics: A Comparative Review*. Athens: Ohio UP, 1995.

Barker, E. Ellen. "Creating Generations: The Relationship between Celie and Shug in Alice Walker's *The Color Purple*." *Critical Essays on Alice Walker*. Ed. Ikenna Dieke. *Critical Essays on Alice Walker*. Westport: Greenwood, 1999. 55–66.

Bobo, Jacqueline. "Sifting Through the Controversy: Reading *The Color Purple*." *Callaloo* 0.39 (1989): 332–42.

Byrd, Rudolph P. Rev. of *By the Light of My Father's Smile*. *African American Review* 33.4 (1999): 719–22.

_____. "Spirituality in the Novels of Alice Walker: Models, Healing, and Transformation, or When the Spirit Moves So Do We." *Wild Women in the Whirlwind: Afra-American Culture and the Contemporary Literary Renaissance*. Eds. Joanne M. Braxton and Andrée Nicola McLaughlin. New Brunswick: Rutgers UP, 1990. 363–78.

Christian, Barbara. "The Black Woman Artist as Wayward." *Alice Walker*. Ed. Harold Bloom. New York: Chelsea, 1989. 39–58.

Colton, Catherine A. "Alice Walker's Womanist Magic: The Conjure Woman as Rhetor." *Critical Essays on Alice Walker*. Ed. Ikenna Dieke. *Critical Essays on Alice Walker*. Westport: Greenwood, 1999. 33–44.

Demitürk, E. Lâle. "The Black Woman's Selfhood in Alice Walker's *Possessing the Secret of Joy*." *Journal of American Studies of Turkey*. 2(1995): 33–36. *AKE Department of American Culture and Literature*. Hacettepe Universitesi, n.d. Web. 27 Mar. 2012.

Dieke, Ikenna, ed. *Critical Essays on Alice Walker*. Westport: Greenwood, 1999.

Elsley, Judy. "Nothing can be sole or whole that has not been rent": Fragmentation in the Quilt and *The Color Purple*." *Critical Essays on Alice Walker*. Ed. Ikenna Dieke. Westport: Greenwood, 1999. 163–70.

George, Olakunle. "Alice Walker's Africa: Globalization and the Province of Fiction." *Comparative Literature* 53.4 (2001): 354–72.

Lauret, Maria. *Alice Walker*. London: Palgrave, 2000.

Simcikova, Karla. *To Live Fully Here and Now: The Healing Vision in the Works of Alice Walker*. Lanham: Lexington, 2007.

Streitfeld, David. "Walker on the Wide Side, Again." *The Washington Post* (11 Oct. 1998): X15.

Walker, Alice. *By the Light of My Father's Smile*. New York: Ballantine, 1998.

_____. *The Color Purple*. New York: Washington Sq., 1983.

_____. *In Search of Our Mothers' Gardens*. San Diego: Harvest, 1984.

_____. *Possessing the Secret of Joy*. New York: Harcourt, 1992.

_____. *The Warrior Marks: Female Genital Mutilation and the Sexual Blinding of Women*. New York: Harcourt, 1993.

Warren, Nagueyalti, and Sally Wolff. " 'Like the Pupil of an Eye': Sexual Blinding of Women in Alice Walker's Works." *Southern Literary Journal* 31.1 (1998): 1–16.

Living Spaces for Learning in Alice Walker's
*The Temple of My Familiar*_____

Toni Wynn

> "Last night I dreamed I was showing you my temple," said Miss Lissie. "I
> don't know where it was, but it was a simple square one-room structure,
> very adobe or Southwestern-looking, with poles jutting out at the ceiling
> line and the windows set in deep. . . . I remembered going there for the
> ceremonies dressed in a long white cotton robe. . . . Anyway, my famil-
> iar—what you might these days, unfortunately, call a 'pet'—was a small,
> incredibly beautiful creature that was part bird. . . part fish . . . and part
> reptile. . . . Its predominant color was blue, but there was red and green,
> and flecks of gold and cerise. And purple."
>
> (Alice Walker, *The Temple of My Familiar*, 118–19)

Alice Walker cares about how interconnected we are (and were)—not
just with one another, but also with nature and all of its forces. Walker's
approach to her writing—fiction, poetry, and essays—is a holistic one
where few roads remain unexplored. Walker is disinclined, however,
to promote the patriarchal Judeo-Christian perspective. "I do understand that my worldview is different from that of the critics. . . . [T]hey
are defending a way of life, a patriarchal system, which I do not worship" (*World Has Changed* 78–85). That perspective is, in her opinion, overrepresented and infused with a kind of power, which quashes
less-represented voices. Walker's womanist spiritualism is a spectrum
away; the author's feminism and blackness are the lenses through
which she interprets religious concepts. In *The Temple of My Familiar*,
Walker references the Holy Ghost "who at one time was the Female in
the Deity" (147). There is historical precedent in regard to the feminine
in spiritual beliefs and practices. For example, many think of the dove
as being divine and female, representing love and fertility. Both Ishtar
in the ancient Middle East, and Aphrodite in ancient Greece were represented by the dove.

The Book

The Temple of My Familiar chronicles the present and past lives of seven people: Carlotta and Arveyda, Lissie and Hal, and Fanny Nzingha and Suwelo, three couples in long-term relationships who travel geographical and life paths that come to intertwine; and Mary Jane, whose own life and that of an ancestor unlock a different future for some of the novel's characters. The characters travel great distances in search of wholeness and peace of mind. This quest and tragicomic explorations of relationships with loved ones and Earth could be said to be what the novel is "about." All of the main characters in *Temple* are artists or teachers (or both).

Walker employs magical realism in the novel to shift through time and space. Magical realism is an approach in art and literature where the artist weaves elements of myth and dreams into realistic narratives or subject matter. In *Temple*, time does not progress in a linear way. Walker manipulates the representation of time—by portraying ancestral teachings as occurring in real time, for instance—to support the story. The character Lissie is the primary shape-shifter who bears witness to evolution of human ethics and spirit over the course of millennia, even though much of the novel takes place in the late twentieth century.

Walker published *The Temple of My Familiar* in 1989, seven years after her classic work, *The Color Purple*. Although Walker fit *Purple* with a more linear plot, the self-determination of her female characters pervades both books. Providing continuity between the two novels, Fanny Nzingha is the granddaughter of *The Color Purple's* main character Celie. Shug, Celie's partner in both novels, lends additional heft to Walker's enthusiasm for matrilineal strength, particularly through her "gospel," presented in *Temple* on a pamphlet illustrated with her familiar: elephants.

Alice Walker's Messages about Spaces and Places

The use of the word "temple" in the novel's title points the reader to Walker's emphasis on place. Although we can consider the body to be a temple, one's most personal vessel for self-care and respect, I would like to cast Walker's temple as the physical space that her characters (and their familiars) use and where they reside. A temple is a building devoted to worship, a sacred place apart from other places. Although none of the spaces described in this essay is a place of organized religious worship, many places—some wild, some domestic—have a vaulted stillness that invites contemplation. Temples can be ornate or simple in their construction and design. Those who use the space determine its efficacy. What does the character come to the temple for? What does she or he leave with? With the assistance of an architect's renderings that offer a nonverbal view of two of Walker's characters' spaces, this essay tours these "temples," moving the reader through them and their connection with the characters in *The Temple of My Familiar*.

In a sense, it seems wrong to write about place. Place is something—a landscape, street, neighborhood, village, city, workplace, home—to experience viscerally, by being there, or through sensation. Verbal description puts us at some remove. In *The Temple of My Familiar*, however, Alice Walker describes a succession of places that feeds the reader like essential sustenance, and maps the novel's characters like a breadcrumb trail. Place fills some gaps that Walker leaves in the characters themselves: trees, interior hallways, patios, cramped rooms, even a yurt nourish the reader.

The characters in *Temple* most often work with, not against, their physical spaces. Often in literature, and especially in pop culture, characters struggle to overcome the spaces they are situated in. In the pop song "Beautiful" from her 2001 release *Acoustic Soul*, singer-songwriter India.Arie sings, "these walls are closing in on me . . . I need to find a place where I can breathe . . . I wanna go to beautiful, beautiful, beautiful." That struggle is emblematic of what the character is capable of, creating place-as-metaphor: The place itself ("these walls") stands in for the life the character struggles to escape. Consider where you are now, reading this. Perhaps your environment helps define you. If a novel was being written around you, how would your environment figure, if at all?

The Familiars

In this novel, Walker sometimes assumes the role of a fabulist—a writer of fables. *Temple* is a novel that uses fable as a device to inform the reader of origin and history. A fable uses nonhuman creatures, usually animals, to illuminate a moral. The element of animals and familiars moves parts of the novel strongly toward fable. According to the *Merriam-Webster Unabridged Dictionary*, a familiar is "a supernatural spirit often embodied in an animal and at the service of a person."

In the first edition printing of the novel, each of the book's six parts carries the emblem of a mythical or real bird or animal. The dust cover is a close-up of a peacock feather; a colorful picture of a lion in a garden is inset on the front cover. These creatures are the alpha familiars of the book's title. These symbolic stewards accompany the characters and the reader through the narrative, and would be of minimal interest if the novel's title did not draw the reader's attention to them. Walker sometimes only casually associates a familiar with a character, such as a brief reference to Shug, Celie's partner from *The Color Purple,* liking elephants and turtles. In other instances, such as Miss Lissie's series of paintings of lions, the association between a creature and a particular character is more overt. Along with the familiars, each landscape, whether interior or exterior, conveys information that works in concert with each character and her or his intent.

Part One: The Peacock

The peacock is the familiar for part one of *Temple*. The peacock represents love and beauty, royalty, and immortality, and is linked to paradise and resurrection. Its eyes are likened to stars. Birds are familiars for Celie, the free-spirited Fanny's grandmother. Celie and Shug had an intimate, but not romantically exclusive relationship in *The Color Purple*. In *Temple* they are elders whose relationship is malleable and dynamic. "Bird" is Celie's nickname. Feathers appear and reappear throughout the novel. For Carlotta's mother and grandmother, both South American women named Zedé, bird feathers enable them to make a living creating feathered capes for performers and festivals (154).

The early part of the novel features Miss Lissie, "the one who remembers everything" (52). Lissie is a woman/being who narrates stories from her past lives. Walker employs fable and magical realism most often through Lissie and her stories. Miss Lissie's perspective encompasses "hundreds of lifetimes," some of which she lived in wild and wooded areas. Miss Lissie's lives have the most weight; all other characters in the novel are measured against her canvas. Inevitably, Lissie moves through a major array of landscapes. Going back to the future in the novel, one of the more notable spaces is one of the last spaces the reader knows Lissie to inhabit. The house she shares with Mr. Hal is simple, but the landscape and their eternal soul connection are not. The metaphor that the person may be uncomplicated, but her or his life is complex is difficult to dismiss.

Outdoor Spaces

Lissie describes a life she lived as a pygmy in a forest. Early in her description of this magical place, Walker's temple reference surfaces: Lissie says, "the trees then were like cathedrals" (84). Those trees were home, quiet and safe, especially as the "cousins," who this reader thought of as apes, dwelled in them. This is not a new reference; countless journalists and travel writers have described the redwood forests of Northern California similarly, in awe of their majesty and quiet. Walker's Lissie, as her child-self, establishes the forest as a place of trust, growth, and, importantly, of relationships. As a woman who has "lived" generations of "oppression," her one reference for peace is a forest, and she treasures the largely nonverbal relationships she observed taking place among the apes there.

Walker employs outdoor spaces throughout part one. Suwelo and Fanny, divorcing, discuss being unmarried while "among the roses" in the garden behind their home. "The rosebushes had already been pruned and the branches burned" (138). The condition of the rosebushes in the garden—pruned in preparation for summer flowering—presents Fanny's estranged spouse and the reader with a metaphorical fait accompli: Fanny has made up her mind about what to leave: the marriage; and what to keep: the loving relationship with Suwelo. The relationship will flower again, with time.

Carlotta's mother, Zedé, tours the South American "old country," reestablishing herself in the village that has evolved from the rough prison where Carlotta was born. She marvels at a compound by the river that is lush with peacocks and avocado, mango, and coconut trees. That peaceful life is contrasted with their housing in a cramped apartment over a grocery store upon their sudden emigration to San Francisco. Mr. Hal, Miss Lissie's best friend, describes his father's upbringing on a plantation on a barrier island in the American South. Walker describes the island as being much more pleasant and temperate than the mainland where the white people lived most of the year. Walker suggests that the value of living largely outdoors is a generous freedom of spirit, connection to the earth, and peace of mind.

Uncle Rafe's Baltimore Row House

The most significant interior space in part one is the Baltimore row house Suwelo inherits from his Uncle Rafe. This is where the reader gets to know Suwelo, and the character gets to know himself. The three-story house is orderly and still, a mirror for Suwelo's self-regard when he arrives there to put the house up for sale. Suwelo allots a week to take care of his uncle's business, but stays for months.

Although its exterior is gentrified, the house's interior is as Suwelo remembers it from his childhood, when he was known as Louis Jr. The house has high ceilings and is filled with photographs, vintage furniture, and chandeliers. There is no garden, but the grassy yard is neat and trimmed. There is a huge oak tree that shelters the yard and those of two of his neighbors. Under the oak is "an ugly metal fake 'barn' that his uncle must have used as a toolshed" (31). This foreshadowing by Walker encourages the reader to anticipate something insincere in

Suwelo's character; indeed, it emerges later in the way he uses Carlotta while he and Fanny are estranged.

Early in the novel and in his time in the Baltimore house, Suwelo lingers on a high bed in the master bedroom across from the small austere room where Uncle Rafe slept. The bed, outfitted with ornate pillows and quality linens, comforts Suwelo, "his owlish eyes fixed on the fire" (33), and offers him a celibate place to simply relax. The owl reference comes back into play later in the novel as a protective night spirit.

As Suwelo cleans out Uncle Rafe's house from the basement up, he allows Mr. Hal and Miss Lissie, his uncle's closest friends, to enter his life. He spends most of his time listening to them, and getting beyond the remorse he feels about his relationships with his estranged wife Fanny and his lover Carlotta, whom he has not bothered to get to know or understand.

Part Two: The Griffin

Part two offers a griffin as a familiar. It has a lion's body, an eagle's head, a serpent's tail, and wings. A griffin is a good guardian: attentive, swift, brave, tenacious. Walker weaves Shug, Celie, and Nettie, Celie's sister from *The Color Purple,* into the story to describe the circumstances of Fanny's birth and rearing in the Atlanta area. These women are the bedrock of her family, at least until Fanny reacquaints herself with her mother, Olivia, Celie's daughter who was raised by Nettie and others in Africa. Geographically, Walker takes the reader from Georgia to Africa, London, Baltimore, and Northern California. This wide swath samples the characters' early lives, stories about their parentage, and the many ways that their beliefs shape them. The griffin guards these creation stories.

Ola's House in Olinka

Fanny sojourns with her mother, Olivia, to London, and then to Olinka, where she meets her father, Ola. As minister of culture, Ola has been imprisoned for being too outspoken. Ola is a dignitary, but a belligerent one. Ola picks Fanny and Olivia up at the airport in Olinka. He guides them through the town. It is Fanny's first time there. Ola's compound is brightly painted in a landscape of adobe walls adorned with abstract designs. Walker describes Ola's compound as being "painted in the loudest colors of all" (162), and asserts that San Franciscans would be drawn to its brightness. Ola's house is described as "simple," and "native-style," with four bedrooms, a large living room, two bathrooms, and a veranda that lines the inner courtyard. By now the reader has grown to expect Walker to provide gardens of flowers and vegetables in spaces where new ideas and perspectives take hold in her characters' lives. The bright colors and abstracts trumpet Ola's assertive nature and innovative use of theatre in his work. The design and the traditional materials used in his house speak to Ola's pride in and tie to the land.

Lissie and Hal's Baltimore Home

Early in the novel, before the reader knows much about Miss Lissie and Mr. Hal, Walker has Suwelo bid them farewell after selling Uncle Rafe's home and embarking on his trip back to California. It is a small and powerful moment in the book, marked by a particular kind of silence. The scene takes place in a studio of sorts, but the art making happens outdoors in Lissie and Hal's garden. Both elders paint at easels. Their subject matter is "the back of their own small, white-clapboard house, a large ivy-encircled pecan tree towering over its front, a garden along one side with flowers and fruits growing all together" (191). Suwelo is so lulled by this scene that he falls asleep in the middle of it (and Hal and Lissie paint him into their art). Walker uses the image of a circle and of a confluence of good things to punctuate a picture of two pictures. Lissie and Hal are at once distinct and interchangeable. Walker portrays their relationship as one so special—and eternal—that their self-portraits are painted by the other. Suwelo trusts their place and their company so well—despite this being his first visit to their house—that he falls asleep on their porch, which transmits his comfort in their presence. For an outdoor space in a large American city, this place is a cradle. Near the end of a lifetime together, Hal and Lissie have settled into a sweet, nurturing, quiet space, with a tree as a canopy to protect the quiet bliss found there.

Part Three: The Snake

The snake, known for its transmutation, eternal life, and relationship to female power, guards part three. Snakes, as represented on the symbol for medicine, can be toxic or ward off illness. A snake can symbolize elegance, curiosity, and deep thinking. In part three, Walker introduces a matrilineal white family that catalyzes the more central characters' transmutations throughout the story. The transmutation of Mary Ann Haverstock reaches its climax on the sea, via her boat *Recuerdo* ("I remember" in Spanish). The boat itself sheds its skin to become *The Coming Age,* thus moving from past to future in name and in destination. Through her "rescue" of Carlotta and Zedé from servitude in South America, the character Mary Ann Haverstock morphs into Mary Jane Briden. Mary Jane adopts the snake as her familiar: "The snake, which sheds its skin but is ever itself, and, because of its knowledge of the secret places of the earth, free from the threat of extinction, apparently uneradicable" (207). Mary Jane fakes her death and chooses to investigate the life of her great-aunt Eleanora in England. But it is Mary Jane's great-great-aunt Eleandra's (Elly's) journal that chronicles a long-ago trip to a stuffy museum in the United Kingdom. Emerging from the dust of the museum is a black woman or deity named M'Sukta, of the Ababa people of Africa.

M'Sukta at the Museum of Natural History

Walker depicts M'Sukta, a small African woman, as an installation in the Museum of Natural History in London. This is reminiscent of Saartjie Baartman, the South African woman who was the "Hottentot Venus" exhibit in the early 1800s. Walker precedes Mary Jane's discovery of M'Sukta with a lengthy description of a replica of her aunt

Eleanora's furnished room, located at a women's college in England. In this room, Mary Jane reads her great-great-aunt's diary. Mary Jane's ancestor is named Elly Burnham Peacock, keeping the bird familiar present in this part of the story. M'Sukta and a young boy had been part of an earlier installation on a lower floor of the museum. Possibly as a result of being in captivity and on constant display, the boy died. M'Sukta was relocated to a place in the museum that received less traffic and where she recovered from the child's death, and began to spin thread and cloth again.

There is an element of the "magic Negro" in the character of M'Sukta, although that term would not gain popularity until the 1990s. (Its origin is disputed.) The "magic Negro" character embodies a higher good, and creates the moment of catharsis and positive change that a pivotal nonblack character requires to fulfill her or his calling. M'Sukta does this for generations of women in Mary Jane's family. Mary Jane's great-aunt Eleanor is 100 years old when Mary Jane shows her old photographs during a visit. Although Eleanor cries silently as she is shown the hundreds of images, it is only the photo of M'Sukta that elicits a verbal response from the elder. Great-Aunt Eleanor's Aunt Elly came upon M'Sukta at the museum decades prior. M'Sukta's African habits and folkways caused Elly to feel "superficial." Shortly thereafter, Elly leaves her wealthy English family and relocates to Africa. Eleandra's grandniece and great-grandniece follow suit in subsequent generations.

At the Museum of Natural History, M'Sukta, a member of the matriarchal Balawyua or Ababa people, exists in an exhibit of colorful mud structures. There are three huts arranged at oblique angles, a granary, spindle, and looms. The ceiling is painted sky blue. On the wall is an Ababa saying, "THEY CANNOT KILL US, BECAUSE WITHOUT US THEY DIE" (229). The space M'Sukta inhabits in the museum is at once unpretentious, bright (contrasting to the drab museum and dry surroundings where Mary Jane reads the journal), temporal, and exotic. M'Sukta and the cloth she weaves animate the space and draw Mary Jane's ancestor, the writer of this journal entry, into M'Sukta's plight. Soon after, Elly is drawn into M'Sukta's culture, developing a predilection for Arabs and Africans. The elder Peacock is the first of the women in her family to venture into Africa and be changed. The snake transmutes.

Part Four: The Owl

The owl symbolizes part four. The owl is considered a protector, wise and learned. The owl connects with night and is related to death. Walker takes the reader from Uncle Rafe's house in Baltimore, where Suwelo continues to learn from Lissie and Hal, to San Francisco, Africa with the Olinka, Paris, and Northern California, where Suwelo and Fanny spend a summer in a yurt. Ola, Fanny's father, dies. Celie, Shug, and Olivia appear once again in a lighthearted scene where Fanny describes how the women named her.

Fanny and Suwelo's Yurt

Fanny and Suwelo's Northern California yurt is situated on top of a ridge on five acres of land. They grow a variety of vegetables, and a healthy crop of marijuana that they call "Big Women"—"tall, dark, and pungent" (248). The yurt, loaned to them seasonally by friends, is surrounded by forest, with its inhabitants of deer, birds, raccoons, and others. The owl flies and calls in the night air on the ridge, and Suwelo tacitly claims it as his familiar. Yurts are affiliated with nomadic cultures, especially the Mongol people in Central Asia. Fanny and Suwelo continue to move from place to place, separately and together, like nomads. Indeed, most of the novel's characters live in motion, embodying the energies of their familiars while learning all they can in the temporary places they inhabit.

Fanny and Suwelo occupy the yurt in the summers after their divorce. Wooden and round, the opening of the structure faces the rising sun. A valley of sheep ranches and vineyards spreads out below. Walker describes the structure as having "windows everywhere," but just enough room "to curse a cat" (277). Suwelo comes around to enjoying the enduring elements of his relationship with Fanny there. After the sting of her rejection of their marriage, they enjoy and appreciate one another in this structure with windows but no angles atop a ridge, dipping into a river and brushed by owls' wings.

Part Five: The Turtle

In part five, the turtle embodies Mother Earth, signifying strength and endurance, patience and wisdom. The turtle also stands for safety at sea. Part five takes place entirely in California's Bay Area. Carlotta, her husband Arveyda, her mother Zedé, Fanny, and Suwelo continue their intertwined story. Robin, Fanny's therapist, talks about spaces. Shug claims the turtle (and the elephant) as her familiar (154).

The turtle's reticent and retiring nature is emblematic of Fanny's life-stage at this point in the novel. She has left the large, more public stage of university teaching and administration, and strives to connect with people through the slow, physical work of massage therapy. Her workplace, Fanny's Massage Parlor, is small and located behind another building. Fanny shields herself and her clients with colorful vines and flowers. The tucked-away location makes plain Fanny's need to get away from the mainstream in order to move from an academic, cerebral mode into a physical appreciation of humankind.

Arveyda's Berkeley Bungalow

Arveyda's house in Berkeley, California, is first mentioned in part five. This space is most memorable. Described as "a spacious, low-slung acoustically perfect bungalow that jutted out of the hills over Berkeley and . . . inspired by houses designed by Frank Lloyd Wright" (290), the house epitomizes the digs of a cool, financially comfortable musician. Walker's use of the word "jutted" is assertive, masculine, and showy. "Low-slung" may be the way Arveyda wears his guitar or, perhaps, his pants. This house is anchored in the earth but extends horizontally from it, looking out at and moving into the world. Is it, in an area plagued with earthquakes, a building that will endure? Certainly, it is strong. Frank Lloyd Wright, a leading American architect of the early twentieth century, was known for his innovative and original designs, especially in housing and home furnishings; he inspired generations of architects and spawned many imitators. Lloyd Wright's repetitive patterns established a rhythm of their own. A musician like Arveyda could easily be drawn to such a designer. Wright used materials that blended with their surroundings, instead of standing in contrast to them. This sensitive and powerful gesture spoke to the architect's respect for nature.

Arveyda buys the house upon his return from Central and South America, which he toured with Carlotta's mother Zedé. The house has three levels, all displaying the sunsets beyond the Golden Gate Bridge. Carlotta has, meanwhile, been in a "cramped" apartment in nearby Oakland with her and Arveyda's three children, and in an equally cramped relationship with Suwelo. These dwellings—one expansive and lavishly equipped for a musician and the other undistinguished—mirror how their occupants see themselves.

Part Six: The Lion

Part six is the lion. Miss Lissie portrays herself with lion's eyes in one of her last paintings. The lion is known for kingship, courage, ferocity, strength, power, resurrection, and the sun. The reader returns to the Olinka people in Africa, the forest, Berkeley, and to a new space in Baltimore. There is a trip to Terre Haute, Indiana; to Sonoma County California, where the house appears to have wings because "each person must remain free" (395); and to Yelapa, Mexico. The essence of each central character, plus Husa the lion, Lissie's familiar in a past life, bring the novel to a close.

Homecomings

Miss Lissie dies. Mr. Hal describes her last few weeks as being "restless," with Lissie repetitively opening and closing windows in their house. They relocate Lissie's mattress onto the back porch, where she would rest, then rise and assume her place at the easel and paint. Lissie needs to be outdoors as much as possible, as fits an ancient spirit who learned from the "cousins" in the forest. Her last space (in this incarnation) is a single mattress, "a big fluffy cloud of white," on a porch of a house in Baltimore, shaded by a pecan tree and surrounded by flowers. She is in transition, ascending.

Arveyda's Berkeley house expands, as Carlotta and the children join their husband and father on the sprawling landscape. Carlotta establishes her space as the guest cottage on the property. She is not interested in cohabiting, but makes music with Arveyda and frequents the studio where they work on the ground floor of the main house. There is water, a ravine, and, in winter, a waterfall flowing through the property. The bridge over the ravine is the initial checkpoint to gain access to Carlotta's house. She is now a musician who plays bells and chimes; these instruments announce her potential visitors. If she does not respond negatively to the ringing bells by throwing rocks or shoes, the visitor proceeds to a gate with chimes. Carlotta mostly keeps this gate locked, but if it is not, the visitor sounds the chimes, proceeds, and strikes the chimes and bells at her door. Carlotta once lived her single-parent-of-three life in three-inch heels. By the end of the novel, she has shorn her head, like a monk or nun, and, with a lion's ferocity, focused on sharing her own musical gifts and talents.

Mr. Hal and Rose, an old friend, now reside at Mary McLeod Bethune Nursing Home in suburban Baltimore. Mr. Hal, who has lost his sight, is surrounded by Miss Lissie's art. Her last paintings are of the tree of life, where she depicts herself as a lion. In despair at how shortsighted he was with Lissie, Hal cries. He believes that, although they were so close as to be nearly symbiotic, Lissie grew closer to Suwelo's Uncle Rafe because Hal disallowed the deep magical symbolism that Lissie so often tried to communicate to him. After his tears and confession of grief to Suwelo, Hal stares at Lissie's last paintings, and his vision begins to return.

Fanny has moved into the yurt she once shared during summers with Suwelo. They confront one another there; argue about gender politics, shout, and cry. They come full circle, like the configuration of the yurt. They migrate back home to each other.

Suwelo and Fanny build a house based on the matriarchal Ababa people from M'Sukta's time. Walker describes it as "the first hetero-sexual household ever created" (395). Like a bird, it has two wings joined by a "body" in the center. The wings are self-contained units with bedroom, bath, a place for study, and a kitchen. The "body" was ceremonial space for the Ababa. Fanny and Suwelo use the airy, large area as a multipurpose space containing a loft, living room, kitchen-ette, and fireplace. Walker does not call it a "bird house," but it is not a stretch to do so.

The Takeaway

The takeaway from Walker's use of place in *The Temple of My Famil-iar* is that our environment extends and informs us. Walker's charac-ters in *Temple* are shaped and mirrored by the places in which they live and work and raise their children. This in itself is not particularly note-worthy. *Temple* is set apart by the architecture and landscapes Walker employs that often capture the souls of their inhabitants and offer the reader another way to "read" the novel. Walker models a way of being that instructs all of us to feel great responsibility and stewardship for our physical places in the world. We are not just here; we are here for a reason, and one of those reasons is to learn from and take care of our surroundings.

The familiars, symbolic and kinetic touchstones and guardians through stages of life, provide a backdrop for the novel that applauds the animal kingdom and ties it to a spirit world that offers teaching and solace. Walker goes to great lengths in her prose and poetry to commu-nicate her respect for animals and the natural world. Where the famil-iars in *Temple* are mythical, such as the griffin, the reader is reminded of the shifting realities of magical realism that the author employs when the "real" world is simply inadequate to explain its workings. The spaces provide the surroundings for the learning the familiars impart. Walker invites the reader to acknowledge and understand many levels of interconnectedness of body, mind, sprit, and nature in *The Temple of My Familiar*.

Works Cited

Arie, India. "Beautiful." *Acoustic Soul*. Motown, 2001. CD.

Cuddon, J. A. *A Dictionary of Literary Terms*. Revised ed. New York: Doubleday, 1976.

"Familiar." *Merriam-Webster Unabridged Dictionary*. Merriam-Webster, 2012. Web. 23 Mar. 2012.

Harris, Cyril M. *Dictionary of Architecture and Construction*. 4th ed. New York: McGraw, 2005.

Hellman, Louis. *Architecture for Beginners*. New York: Writers and Readers, 1988.

Leach, Maria, and Jerome Fried, eds. *Funk & Wagnalls Standard Dictionary of Folklore, Mythology, and Legend*. 1st ed. New York: Harper, 1984.

Petersen, Andrew. *Dictionary of Islamic Architecture*. New York: Routledge, 1999.

Rybczynski, Witold. *The Most Beautiful House in the World*. New York: Penguin, 1990.

Shepherd, Rowena, and Rupert Shepherd. *1000 Symbols: What Shapes Mean in Art and Myth*. London: Thames, 2002.

Walker, Alice. *In Search of Our Mothers' Gardens*, Orlando, FL: Harcourt, 1984.

_____. *The Temple of My Familiar*, Orlando, FL: Harcourt, 1989.

_____. *The World Has Changed: Conversations with Alice Walker*. Ed. Rudolph P. Byrd. New York: New Press, 2010.

Participant, Witness, Activist: Alice Walker's Novels in Historical Context

Donna Winchell

In the collection *The World Has Changed: Conversations with Alice Walker* (2010), editor Rudolph P. Byrd brings together in one convenient volume interviews with Walker ranging across time, from the well-known 1973 conversation with John O'Brien to Byrd's own 2009 "On Raising Chickens." In his introduction, Byrd also provides a useful way of looking at the change in Walker's novels over time. For him, a line can be drawn in 1983 between the works up to and including *The Color Purple* (1982) and the ones since the publication of that best known of Walker's novels. Byrd explains that "Walker is interested in exploring questions related to history, but in this second period her interest in history has been limited neither to the South nor the nation but rather encompasses the history of humankind in an effort to weave a narrative across millennia" (25–26).

An ambitious undertaking, certainly, and one that raises the question of how successful any writer can be in retelling the history of humankind through fiction. The single work in which Walker most directly undertakes this challenge is *The Temple of My Familiar* (1989), the first of Walker's novels published after Byrd's watershed date of 1983. Before that, she was satisfied in her first three novels to focus primarily on the history of the American South that she and her family were a part of.

Walker discusses often in her nonfiction and in interviews what life was like growing up in a family of Georgia sharecroppers. Her first novel, *The Third Life of Grange Copeland* (1970), is an indictment of the sharecropping system in the American South based on Walker's personal experience of moving from one shack in rural Georgia to another as a child in the 1940s and 1950s. Grange Copeland is caught up in the system that at that time kept black families in perpetual debt to the white man who owned the land they worked, and his son Brownfield follows in his footsteps to get trapped in the same cycle of despair. Both men are brutally violent and take out their frustration over their failures on their wives and children. The novel is, however, a study in contrasts between how the two men ultimately respond to a role in which so many African Americans found themselves in the middle of the twentieth century.

Walker has long been committed to the "survival and wholeness of entire people, male *and* female" (*Gardens* xi). The only one of Brownfield's children who survives whole is the third daughter, Ruth. Walker's original intent was to start with Ruth as a civil rights attorney in Georgia. Walker felt, however, that such a story would be "too recent, too superficial—everything seemed a product of the immediate present" (*Gardens* 256). By bringing in the grandfather, she gave the novel historical depth. It became Grange's novel not only in title but also in theme.

Grange ends his first "life" by abandoning his wife Margaret, son Brownfield, and the baby who is the product of one of Margaret's attempts to compete with Grange in his dissipation. When Margaret kills the baby and then herself, Grange doesn't even return for her funeral. He spends several years in the North and then returns a kinder and gentler version of his previous self. He has learned that black men cannot blame whites for all that is wrong with their lives:

By George, I *know* the danger of putting all the blame on somebody else for the mess you make out of your life. I fell into the trap myself! And I'm bound to believe that that's the way the white folks corrupt you even when you done held up before. 'Cause when they got you thinking that they're to blame for *every*thing they have you thinking they's some kind of gods! You gits just as weak as water, no feeling of doing *nothing* yourself. Then you begins to think up evil and begins to destroy everybody around you, and you blames it on the crackers. *Shit!* Nobody's as powerful as we make them out to be. We got our own *souls*, don't we? (207)

It is a lesson that Brownfield never learns. When his wife, Mem, proves herself more capable of taking care of the family than he is, he waits on the porch one Christmas Eve as she returns home from work and shoots her in the face.

Once Mem is dead and Brownfield is in jail for her murder, Grange supplements Ruth's inadequate public school education by teaching her the ways of the world. Grange would rather keep Ruth safe behind a barbed wire fence and guard her with his gun, but she wants a world broader than that. She believes that change is possible, and the novel ends at a time when major historical and social change is indeed coming. Together Ruth and her grandfather listen to Chet Huntley and David Brinkley discuss the civil rights movement on the nightly news. They listen to Dr. Martin Luther King Jr. on television, and she wonders, "Do you think he's got something going?" In their town, black and whites are marching together against racial inequality. Change is coming even to Green County, where the Copelands once lived and where blacks are starting to vote. Change is coming for Ruth, but Grange will not live to see it.

Walker based the name "Mem" on the French word meaning "the same," suggesting that the sort of violence perpetrated against her was not uncommon in the world in which Walker grew up. In an interview with William R. Ferris, she explains how the character was based on a woman in her community to whose murder Walker was a witness, not in the sense that she saw it happen, but in the sense that she felt compelled to bear witness for her:

> My first novel . . . grew out of the need to witness the murder of a woman when I was thirteen. There was a woman who was murdered by her husband as she came home on Christmas day with a bag of groceries that she had managed to buy. And I saw her body because my sister was the cosmetologist at the funeral home. . . . Who would know what this woman's life was, who would know that she had worked all that week as a maid for $7, that she had gone and tried to make Christmas for her children? And

here she comes with this little bag of food, and then she's met with this. And who would know, who would know about this, who would care? But in the role of storyteller and witness, years later, I had to learn to be able to tell her story. ("Giving Birth" 117)

Walker's second novel, *Meridian* (1976), is also about learning to tell the story. Parts of the novel are thinly disguised autobiography focusing on Walker's teenage and college years. American literature has offered no richer account of what it was like to be an African American college student during the civil rights movement. Inspired by teachers at Spelman College in Atlanta, Walker became involved in the movement there. Her beloved teacher Howard Zinn was fired for supporting Walker and others on the Student Nonviolent Coordinating Committee and in other civil rights organizations. In the novel, Spelman becomes the fictional Saxon College, and Walker writes of what it was like to be a Saxon "lady" during the day when you had spent the night before in jail after being arrested for protesting police brutality.

Where *The Third Life of Grange Copeland* focuses on the early days of the movement, Meridian as a college student must examine her beliefs at the point when the movement is shifting toward violence. In one key scene in New York, Meridian's friends try to get her to say that she would kill for the revolution. She knows that she would die for it, but she is shunned by the group when she cannot say that she would kill. To have violence done to her seems justified; to return violence for violence, however, threatens the world as she has known it: "When she was transformed in church it was always by the purity of the singers' souls, which she could actually *hear*, the purity that lifted their songs like a flight of doves above her music-drunken head. If they committed murder—and to her even revolutionary murder was murder—*what would the music be like?*" (28). At a time when nonviolent demonstrations and voter registration drives are becoming things of the past, she returns to the South to live among the people and assist them in any nonviolent way possible. She agonizes about her role in the revolution into the 1970s, when her former boyfriend Truman finally tells her that no one is asking those questions anymore.

Critic Greil Marcus, writing for the *New Yorker*, describes the novel as a "spiritual and political biography of a black woman who determines to live out the [civil rights] movement long after it has faded away." Gordon Burnside, writing for *Commonweal*, questions the book's coherence as a novel: "But if *Meridian* is a failure as a novel—and I think it is—it is also an extremely interesting historical document" (qtd. in White 292).

In *Meridian*, as in her first novel, Walker was writing about history that she had lived. She transferred from Spelman to Sarah Lawrence and then returned south to spend seven years in Mississippi. Initially her job was taking depositions from African Americans who had lost their homes because they had dared to try to register to vote. In the process she met Jewish lawyer Mel Leventhal, whom she soon married in New York and lived with in Mississippi at a time when cohabiting between races was illegal. In an atmosphere of racial tension and fear, she managed to find time and focus enough to write. At times she felt that she should be doing more for the movement. Eventually, though, she accepted that her role was to be the role of storyteller for a key era in American history.

In a pivotal scene in *Meridian*, the title character visits a church after not having attended any church for some time. As she looks around, she notices that it is no longer the church of her childhood. The stained glass window of Christ with a lamb has been replaced with one of jazz musician B. B. King with a bloody sword. Even the church building itself does not reach for the sky but is firmly planted on the ground. The music is martial music, and the sermon is political. Meridian walks out of the church and realizes that, yes, she is a failure as the type of revolutionary that her former friends in New York wanted her to be, but that there is a role for the artist in time of revolution:

It was this, Meridian thought, I have not wanted to face, this that has caused me to suffer: I am not to belong to the future. I am to be left, listening to the old music, beside the highway. But then, she thought, perhaps it will be my part to walk behind the real revolutionaries—those who know they must spill blood in order to help the poor and the black and therefore go right ahead—and when they stop to wash off the blood and find their throats too choked with the smell of murdered flesh to sing, I will come forward and sing from memory songs they will need once more to hear. (201)

The story that Walker has to tell in her third novel, *The Color Purple* (1983), is a story of the oppression of women, set in part in the American South. Here, however, she links the South to Africa through an exchange of letters and thus links the treatment of black women in the South to the treatment of women in Africa and to the treatment of Africans by the British. She is distancing herself from the South geographically. She distances herself in time as well by looking back to earlier generations in the life of her family and an earlier time historically.

The main character, Celie, is raped repeatedly as a teenager by the man she believes to be her father and bears two of his children before he finds a neighbor who needs a wife. Walker's own great-great-grandmother was raped and impregnated at the age of eleven by her master. Celie speaks in the voice of Walker's step-grandmother, Rachel. Like Grange and Brownfield Copeland—and like both of Walker's grandfathers when they were young—Celie's husband, Albert, is abusive. Celie finds Albert is much kinder to her when his lover Shug Avery lives with them, and she is happy with the arrangement because soon she too is in love with Shug. In her comprehensive biography of Walker, Evelyn White provides more of the story of the unorthodox relationship that existed among Walker's grandfather, his second wife, and his mistress, Estella "Shug" Perry. A single story that Walker had heard about those three, a true story in which Rachel, who didn't have pretty things, asked Shug for a pair of her "pretty pink panties" and got them, was the impetus for the novel. It also provides insight into how Walker looks at history. She once laughed to explain, "My 'history' starts not with the taking of lands, or the births, battles, and deaths of Great Men, but with one woman asking another for her underwear" (White 335).

That sort of detail makes the characters in Walker's first three novels come alive for her readers. She based her characters on people that she knew and her stories on events that she participated in, saw, or at least heard about from her parents or other relatives. She feels the presence of her ancestors with her as she writes, and the characters in *The Color Purple* were so real to her that she felt they came and talked to her. She has written and spoken about how these characters would visit her and even shaped the direction that the ending of the novel took. They led her to move from New York to California because they wouldn't speak to her in the city. She was so taken with these characters that some of them return in later novels.

Recurring characters help bridge the gap between Walker's earlier and later novels. As Byrd points out, so does Walker's belief in activism. She believes in the ability to bring about positive change. In her earliest volume of short stories, *In Love and Trouble* (1973), the women are just that—in love with men who are trouble. Some do not survive; most of the rest do not survive whole. In *The Third Life of Grange Copeland*, however, while Margaret and Mem do not survive, Ruth does. Meridian makes the decision not to be a martyr and chooses to just walk away. Celie breaks away from Albert to become her own woman and a businesswoman. These women are survivors, just as Walker's parents and most of her ancestors were. In her parents, in Howard Zinn, and in many others who nurtured her, Walker found the inspiration to activism, and her resistance to racial discrimination and sexual oppression laid a foundation for her to go on and champion other social causes beyond the South and beyond the country of her birth.

As Evelyn White reminds us, "the Pulitzer Prize is a notoriously difficult act to follow" (445). Walker's Pulitzer Prize for *The Color Purple* in 1983 brought her both fame and notoriety and left her audience eagerly awaiting what would come next. They had to wait seven years, and as White phrases it, *"The Temple of My Familiar* did not ring familiar at all" (445).

The new novel was advertised as "a romance of the last 500,000 years." Walker chose a drastically different approach to the whole subject of oppression. She wanted to tell in one novel the history of oppression of blacks in general and of black women in particular, and to do so, she created one character, Lissie, who has lived through it all. A sympathetic reading of the novel requires that a reader buy into the existence of transubstantiation of souls. Lissie's soul has existed in many bodies over many centuries. Few of her lives have been peaceful except the one that constitutes the novel's present. An old woman, Lissie was finally able to find happiness with two men, who together could meet her physical and spiritual needs. In her "marriage" both to Hal, her lawful husband, and Rafe, their friend who has recently died, Lissie found the perfect balance of body and soul. Rafe fulfilled her physical needs while Hal continues to fulfill the spiritual. In other lives she survived the horrors of a slave ship only to die after being caught in a bear trap while trying to escape, was burned at the stake as a witch, and was rejected by her new husband because he did not believe her truthful claim that she was a virgin, and thus died a prostitute. And these are just some of the lives that she remembers.

At first she tells her young friend Suwelo, Rafe's nephew, that she was fortunate to have lived all of her lives as a black woman, but later she admits that she was once a white man and another time a lion. Some readers who were willing to accept Lissie as an historical progression of black women drew the line at accepting her as a lion, and at least one rejected Lissie's claim that animals and humans once lived together in harmony as "ridiculous" (qtd. in White 447).

When Walker's readers picked up *The Temple of My Familiar*, they had become used to characters localized in time and place. Walker spoke through her characters in *The Third Life of Grange Copeland* and in *Meridian* about a world she knew firsthand and through *The*

Color Purple about a world that had been passed down to her through her family's stories. Lissie's stories are different even from Celie's sister Nettie's. Through Nettie's letters from Africa we get a detailed firsthand account of the death of a culture, which Nettie describes to Celie in letter after letter. Since we see Lissie only briefly in the contexts of which she speaks, the vignettes of women's suffering lack the realism and the impact of, for example, Mem's tragedy. Lissie's stories are also intertwined with other plot lines that make the book extremely complex. The unifying theme is that the younger generation—Suwelo and his peers—must discover for themselves that love needs to be a balance of the physical and the spiritual.

Where in *The Temple of My Familiar* Walker traces the history of the oppression of women back through time, letting Lissie represent many different women, in *Possessing the Secret of Joy* (1992) she focuses again on one woman's suffering. That one woman becomes a martyr and inspires others who are trapped in a culture that expects them to undergo a painful and dangerous procedure in the name of tradition.

In *The Color Purple* Walker mentions briefly that Tashi, an African friend of Celie's daughter Olivia and wife to her son Adam, had tribal scars inscribed on her face before they left Africa to show solidarity with her people, who were being pushed off their land by the British. She mentions only in passing that Tashi had another procedure as well. That procedure, female genital mutilation, became the subject of *Possessing the Secret of Joy*. It was also the subject of the documentary film *Warrior Marks* (1993) and the companion book *Warrior Marks: Female Genital Mutilation and the Sexual Blinding of Women* (1993), both of which Walker collaborated on with controversial British documentary filmmaker Pratibha Parmar.

Walker has said that she felt very much a witness once again in writing *Possessing the Secret of Joy* because she knew that something horrible was happening and she had to say something about it ("Giving Birth" 115). Millions of women, primarily in Africa, have had and still have some or all of their external sexual organs removed in a process

---

that is often carried out in the most unsanitary and painful of circumstances. Their families believe they will not be considered marriageable without the procedure. Writing *Possessing the Secret of Joy* was one means that Walker had of bringing this practice to the attention of the world. As years earlier she had wanted to bear witness to an anonymous black woman who was shot to death by her husband, she now wanted to show how the rest of a woman's life could be affected by a decision made for her when she was only a child for the sake of tradition.

The novel is a tale of both physical and psychological suffering. Her culture's tradition of "cleansing" left the formerly strong and proud Tashi initially too weak to walk and made consummating her marriage to Adam almost impossible. When, by some miracle, she managed to get pregnant, the difficult delivery left the baby with brain damage. Layered on top of all this is the fact that something from her childhood haunts Tashi. She seeks help from different psychiatrists to try to uncover what it is. Not until she meets a character that Walker based on psychiatrist Carl Jung does she break through to the memory that she has been suppressing. She is able to remember that her sister Dura died as a result of her "initiation." She sets off to Africa and calmly murders her sister's murderer, who ironically has become a national hero as a result of helping preserve her people's traditions. The African justice system cannot ignore the fact that Tashi has committed a murder, in spite of her reasons. The women who gather quietly around the courthouse with their infant daughters in support of Tashi cannot ignore it *because of* her reasons.

Working with Parmar on *Warrior Marks*, Walker traveled to Africa and interviewed girls and women who had undergone female genital mutilation, some of whom are now fighting to end it. She has lent her fame to the cause of ending the tradition worldwide, but not without having received some criticism for it. At one point in *The Temple of My Familiar*, Fanny's mother, Olivia, makes this statement about the white man: "He blocked the view between us and our ancestors, us and our ways; not all of them good ways, but needing to be changed according to our own light" (307). By taking on the whole issue of female genital mutilation, Walker was opening herself up to the charge that she was interfering with African people and their ancestors, between people and their ways. What right does she have, some have asked, to dictate someone else's cultural mores? Therein lies one danger in writing to advance a cause. Most people would agree with Walker that in the case of female genital mutilation, there is a clear wrong that needs to be eradicated. If her fame as a novelist helps her play a role in righting a wrong, Walker has said, "it pays the rent on being alive and being here on the planet" (" 'Writing to Save My Life' " 80).

In *Now Is the Time to Open Your Heart* (2004), Walker created a character, Kate Talkingtree, based on her paternal grandmother, who was murdered by a former lover. Walker dedicates this novel to her grandmother as a "memorial to the psychic explorer she might have become" (Preface). In the first portion of the novel Kate takes a rafting trip on the Colorado River with a group of other women. The river journey has long been symbolic of a journey within, and on the trip Kate journeys into her own psyche. She is trying to discover why the river that in her dreams represents her life has run dry. She returns home purged both physically and spiritually.

More relevant to Walker as historian, however, is Kate's second journey. She travels into the rainforest in South America with a group of other Americans to experiment with a drug called *yagé* as a means of psychic healing. Each is essentially seeking his or her own brand of personal healing. To do that, each must confront his or her own personal history. Kate has tried the drug before and realizes that it no longer has any effect on her, so she becomes the sounding board for the others in the group. Their conversations with Kate are, like Lissie's stories, a litany of wrongs. Lalika has been kept in a jail cell and raped repeatedly after having been arrested for shooting a policeman to keep him from raping her friend. Missy has been able to own the fact that she was molested by her grandfather almost from infancy but must also accept that she loved him anyway and missed him once he was gone. Rick is trying to purge himself of the guilty knowledge that his family has long been selling drugs to blacks in the ghetto. Hugh lives with the knowledge that his family has prospered because they stole their land from Native Americans.

In this novel, personal history reflects broader social and political issues: sexual abuse, incest, drug use, racism. This time, the storyteller is not necessarily the victim. Lalika is clearly a victim. Missy is a victim yet feels guilty for having loved her abuser. Rick has not sold drugs himself, but he can only fool himself for so long into thinking he does not know how his family makes its money. Hugh recalls being annoyed when his wealthy family's Thanksgiving dinner was interrupted by an elderly Indian coming to gather water at a sacred stream on their land, which clearly used to belong to his people. The story of the trip to the rainforest provides the frame for these individual stories of the demons that haunt people and the new understanding of themselves that frees them of their burdens.

In 2004, Walker commented, "Because my work is grounded in spirituality rather than in politics, I am able to follow my intuition and my sense of being one with other people much more easily than I ever thought possible" ("'I Know What the Earth Says'" 227). She has not given up her activism. In her novels, however, she does focus more now on the spiritual than on the political, less on attacking "the system" than on nurturing personal relationships. She no longer limits her setting to the American South or her theme to racial injustice, although there are hints of that still. In her early novels she was more concerned with what separates people than what draws them together. Her more recent "sense of being one with other people" includes people of all races, all religions, all sexual orientations, and all socio-economic groups. Rudolph Byrd refers to Walker's interest, after 1983, in the history of humankind. That is about as broad an historical context as an author can choose.

Works Cited

Walker, Alice. *By the Light of My Father's Smile*. New York: Random, 1998.

_____. *The Color Purple*. New York: Simon, 1982.

_____. "'Giving Birth, Finding Form: Where Our Books Come From': Alice Walker, Jean Shinoda Bolen, and Isabel Allende in Conversation from Creative Conversations Series (1993)." Byrd 93–123.

_____. "'I Know What the Earth Says': Interview with William R. Ferris from *Southern Cultures* (2004)." Byrd 225–38.

_____. *In Search of Our Mothers' Gardens*. San Diego: Harcourt, 1983.

_____. *Meridian*. New York: Simon, 1976.

_____. *Now Is the Time to Open Your Heart*. New York: Random, 2004.

_____. *Possessing the Secret of Joy*. New York: Harcourt, 1992.

_____. *The Temple of My Familiar*. San Diego: Harcourt, 1989.

_____. *The Third Life of Grange Copeland*. San Diego: Harcourt, 1970.

_____. *The World Has Changed: Conversations with Alice Walker*. Ed. Rudolph P. Byrd. New York: New Press, 2010.

_____. "'Writing to Save My Life': An Interview with Claudia Dreifus from *The Progressive* (1989)." Byrd 78–85.

_____, and Pratibha Parmar. *Warrior Marks: Female Genital Mutilation and the Sexual Blinding of Women*. New York: Harcourt, 1993.

White, Evelyn C. *Alice Walker: A Life*. New York: Norton, 2005.

Possessing the Secret of Metaphor: Alice Walker's Poetics of Self-Recovery _____

Opal Moore

I

"Resistance is the secret of Joy!"—Alice Walker, *Possessing the Secret of Joy*

In her novel, *Possessing the Secret of Joy* (1992), Alice Walker tells the story of Tashi, an Olinka woman tortured in her efforts to reconcile the demands of the self with the desire to belong to a people, a culture, and a tradition. The novel details the destructive consequences of her decision to affirm Olinka tradition—female genital cutting—persuaded by its illusory promises of belonging and completion as a woman, as an African, and as an Olinkan. Tashi's bitter struggle could be misinterpreted as the tragic story of a black woman's attempt to preserve a dying African culture *on her body,* or as a parable of the superiority of Western civilizations' democracy over "African savagery." Instead, I wish to frame this study of Walker's poetics, posing Tashi's story as metaphor—a figure of speech where the tangible *difference* provides the strategy for unveiling the intangible *likeness*. In other words, how could the story of a black African woman illuminate the struggles of black (and white) America? Or the universal struggles of humanity? Tashi's story can be viewed as a peculiarly American zen koan, a dialogue or question that seems to defy the constructions of a paradoxical "racial reasoning" or the "ethics" of historically gendered traditions, and rely instead upon intuition or feeling. Alice Walker, commenting on her processes, has said: "I am preoccupied with the spiritual survival, the survival *whole* of my people" (O'Brien 40). Walker has constructed her complex poetics, drawn from an eclectic mix of influences, not in pursuit of making poetry, but towards what Rudolph Byrd has called her "mission" as a writer and as a womanist (Gates 363).

What is a poet? Is writing poetry a calling or a profession? Poet Haki Madhubuti has said that the poet's work is not only to tell us *what is*, but also *what can be*. Walker, in her poetry and fiction, made a talking mirror for her people—a mirror that reveals our beauty, but also our terrible contradictions regarding sex, gender politics, and our systems of belonging that we call cultural tradition. She offers the black female body as both physical self (*her*story) and metaphor; it is the literal *figure* (or body) and a figure of speech. As both flesh and literary device, or metaphor, the black women of Alice Walker's stories are her improvisatory "changing same" (2). Or, to quote Toni Morrison, "to read imaginative literature by and about [black women] is to choose to examine centers of the self and to have the opportunity to compare these centers with the 'raceless' one with which we are, all of us, most familiar (qtd. in Wall 1). Morrison captures the peculiarity of Walker's proposition, and that of the black woman writer at large: that it is the blackness of this female body that allows the willing reader to escape "race" and find her own story thereby.

Alice Walker's long career as a writer begins in a lie, a lie of solidarity with her brother who had accidently shot a BB gun pellet into her eye. (*If you tell . . . we will get a whipping. You don't want that to happen, do you?*) In her essay "Beauty: When the Other Dancer Is the Self," Walker tells her memory of this bodily trauma, and her efforts at recovery. The injury resulted in the loss of sight in one eye (Walker 386). In her 1973 interview with John O'Brien, Walker talks about physical recovery as a process of discovering one's own strengths and capabilities. Walker recalls her fear that the injury had made her ugly. She became an introspective child, and "from [her] solitary, lonely position, the position of an outcast—[she] began to really see people and things . . . [and] relationships" (35).

Fundamentally, the work of the poet/artist is the work of seeing. What is resistance but the willingness to see things, not as they are presented in the grand cultural myths and romances, but as they *really are*?

Walker comments on the difficulty of seeing:

I think we are educated away from ourselves. I went to colleges for women, Spellman [sic] in Atlanta and Sarah Lawrence in New York. In each situation, I was aware of going through an educational process that was trying to develop me for whatever—job or life—but was not . . . able to deal with the self. . . . I don't think the self was very important [to the institutional aims] (Simon interview).

In a poem, "I, Too, for Freedom," published in the Spelman College student newspaper in 1963, the young Alice is already naming and writing her resistance:

> I push against the binds of assimilation
> I rebel against those ropes of hostile stares.
> Why must my hair be straight when its
> tendency to curl is my pride and joy?
> My song is like the beard of the maestro,
> It symbolizes my struggle for freedom— (1–6)

Walker links the personal—her natural hair as an extension of the self—to the political aims of liberation. Creating an implicit comparison between her hair and the "beard of the maestro" is brilliantly mischievous in its sacred and secular interpretive possibilities. As the poem continues, she travels from thesis question to humor to scorn to warning. The poem's title brings her reader into conversation with Langston Hughes ("I, Too Sing America / I am the darker brother") whose poem answered Walt Whitman ("I hear America singing / the varied carols I hear"). It also reveals a young woman who, even before she considered writing to be her "profession," was discovering the poem as a space of self-affirmation. In a later interview Walker considers the specific work of conserving and affirming "the dancer" as the self:

I grew up in a very large family; I was very lonely and we always lived in very poor and small housing. I needed to be outside of the house in order to think. My head became the only sacred safe place to be most of the time . . . So I think I carried over that need to make a space for myself, make a world for myself. I also used to talk to spirits. So that carried over; so that every crisis in my life as a child I met with some form of written creativity (Toms interview).

Walker has published several books of poems. The first four collections, *Once* (1968); *Revolutionary Petunias* (1973); *Goodnight Willie Lee, I'll See You in the Morning* (1979); and *Horses Make the Landscape Look More Beautiful* (1984), established her reputation as a poet. In her essay "Poetry as Preface to Fiction," critic Thadious Davis presents Walker as a fiction writer who uses poetry to prepare for her more sustained efforts in prose, and the works for which she is best known (275). Davis supports her assessment with Walker's comments to John O'Brien (1973) who has asked about her writing process:

The writing of my poetry is never consciously planned . . . Perhaps my unconscious begins working on poems from these emotions long before I am aware of it. I have learned to wait patiently . . . until a poem is ready to present itself. . . . There is a definite restlessness, a kind of feverish excitement that is tinged with dread. . . . I become aware that I am controlled by them, not the other way around. . . . I realize that while I am writing poetry, I am so high as to feel invisible, and in that condition it is possible to write anything (O'Brien 39, 40).

Walker's description of her process seems more akin to dream catching than poetry writing—a way of unleashing the powerful unconscious. She is not in control of this work—a claim that runs counter to the way that most poets describe their poetry-making.

Walker's process need not be understood as mysticism. She was a student of philosophy at Sarah Lawrence. Her process suggests the explorations of Carl Jung who believed that "the unconscious mind is capable at times of assuming an intelligence and purposiveness which are superior to actual conscious insight" (qtd. in Fromm 96). Psycho-analyst Erich Fromm said "in sleep the realm of necessity has given way to the realm of freedom in which 'I am' is the only system to which thoughts and feelings refer" (Fromm 27). The realm of dreaming, or unfocused meditation, is perhaps the place where Walker goes to disencumber her "self," a space of "I am" offering access to one's true self and meanings—a place to harvest difficult insights and knowingness. Speaking with Mary Helen Washington, Walker distinguishes her relationship to poetry and prose, insisting upon the involuntary or automatic quality of poetry versus the demands of planning and structure in fiction. She seems to be insisting that poems, or at least *her* poems, are not an art form, i.e., are not contrived:

> I hardly ever think about poetry, until it comes . . . I have no control over it when it comes. . . . Fiction I think about, stories I think about, but poems I know they're coming only by the discomfort I feel, and then usually I'll sit down and write all of them at once. I'll write 20 or 10 in one night, working from evening until dawn. I get them out of the way very quickly. (Interview MARBL).

Davis concludes that those who read only Walker's more celebrated fiction and essay collections will not unveil the "more organic and holistic" nature of Walker's canon. Walker's personal poetic praxis emerges in these works. Whether the work is "organic and holistic" in approach, or Walker is giving herself over to the possibilities of locating the free territories of dream, she reveals something of her efforts to enter the "dark interior," to summon the mysteries, to name the fears, to accept feelings of aloneness, to bring into speech all that is silenced and taboo to our public discourses, and uncover what may be veiled from our own self-censoring conscious mind.

However, Walker admits to cultivating a mystical persona, suggesting the intentionality behind her reports (as in her process of writing the *Color Purple*) of the visitations of spirits:

Oh well . . . of course [the voices] they're me, you know. It's like I love that Harriet Tubman and Sojourner Truth had this way of always saying, 'Well, God told me that I had to pack up and cross the river, and that if I would just take these slaves ten miles he would take them the rest of the way.' Every time I read those women I just love them more. *It also is sad, though, because you realize that the spiritual colonization of people is so intense that most people cannot take responsibility for their own desires and their own will.* . . . In the same way you have a dialogue with the imaginary, and that's what happens. *It's all you and you don't really forget that*, but there's that wonderful, playful quality of knowing that you have dreamed up people who are walking around and who have opinions (Hoy interview; emphasis mine).

Black women have needed rhetorical strategies to do their truth telling and their liberation work. Walker suggests that there have been few avenues for black women to do activist work in their own names.

Walker's first published collection of poems, *Once* (1968), offers a telescoping of her unfolding consciousness and career. In 1965, the year that Malcolm X was killed (catalyzing the Black Arts Movement), Walker was a senior at Sarah Lawrence College. In that year she would consider suicide as a solution to an unwanted pregnancy. Surviving that, she would complete the poems for her first book. The book would be published three years later, in the year that Dr. Martin Luther King Jr. and Robert F. Kennedy were killed. In the same year, revolutionary poet Larry Neal published an essay, declaring that the Black Arts Movement (BAM) would be "the aesthetic and spiritual sister of the Black Power concept" (Salaam 1995). Neal called for artistic purity, "a separate symbolism, mythology, critique, and iconology," declaring that the black artist's "primary duty is to speak to the spiritual and cultural needs of black people" (62). Amiri Baraka's (a.k.a. Leroi Jones) poem "Black Art" was considered by many to be the poetic manifesto for the Black Arts Movement. It was this determination to theorize and codify the movement's means and method that would inspire an analysis of the value of the African American cultural inheritance to the work of the creative artist.

The emergence of Walker's first book in that year of national trauma and creativity, her work as a civil rights activist in Mississippi, her race awareness, and her embrace of black identity and culture might tempt some to automatically locate her within the Black Arts/Black Power paradigm. It may be more accurate to say that she stood at that crossroad. Her artistic location is more complex, troubled. *Once,* as art, makes images of Africa and the American South that skim the undertow of racial violence. Walker's ideas do not enlist the verbal, performative brio of the movement. The brevity and heightened interiority of these poems summon an Eastern tradition of meditation and experiential attainment of personal enlightenment. They are spare and often elliptical, and tend to put ideologies under duress. Her brief vignettes juxtapose Africa and interracial lovers' trysts, and sometimes offer bright slivers of violence where race and sexuality intersect with politics.

The longish poem "Johann" offers a romantic argument on behalf of the possibilities of interracial love. The speaker is a black girl addressing her white German lover. The pair resist every imaginable racial prohibition regarding black women's sexual loyalties; the poem dares to idealize, rather than reject, the Aryan phenotype. The poem pushes histories of racial violence directed at Jews and Blacks into the background:

> Dare I kiss your German mouth?
> Touch the perfect muscles
> Underneath the yellow shirt
> Blending coolly
> With your yellow
> Hair?
> (*Her Blue Body* 127)

The speaker observes that "white . . . is the color / Of honest flowers, / And blue is the color / Of the sky" *(Her Blue Body* 127). These interracial fancies are leavened with poems of abortion and suicide. In "Ballad of the Brown Girl," the pregnant speaker dismisses the narrative of birth as mercy, duty, or redemption, asking: "did ever brown / daughter to black / father a white / baby / take—?" *(Her Blue Body* 136) In this room, birth is not a happy event; it is a violence visited upon the bodies of unruly (or unprotected) black girls. The organization of this first collection of poems from Walker's youth builds a narrative arc from the voice of a rather naïve girl who insists upon tigers in Africa to the girl who is "in love and in trouble." Walker's claim for sexual liberation of the black female, for her ownership of her own body, is indeed reaching toward "revolutionary" themes, but not those set forth by the articulators of the Black Arts Movement.

Once provides the first extended look at Walker's inclination to question social dictates and traditions of thought on race and sexuality, and to experiment with a formal poetics. Her later statements in interviews with O'Brien and Washington regarding her poetry process represent an evolving sensibility regarding the place of poetry in her writing life, perhaps as she discovered the prose form as more serviceable to her needs. But in these early works, and under the tutelage of poet/professor Muriel Rukeyser, Walker is striving for control of her form, her voice. She is shaping her ideas, her definitions, and her worldview.

Once did not garner any special attention. It was 1968, and the challenges Walker faced were not related to public reception of her fledgling poems, but to her life choices—her marriage to a white Jewish civil rights lawyer, Mel Rosenthal, and her participation in the voting rights actions intended to give black people back to themselves.

II

> because women are expected to keep silent about
> their close escapes I will not keep silent
> "On Stripping Bark from Myself," *Good Night Willie Lee* (23)

"Walker . . . has declared herself committed 'to exploring the oppressions, the insanities, the loyalties, the triumphs of black women'" (Washington 37). Her unequivocal embrace of feminism is better understood in her coining of the language of "womanism," and her authorizing of the term in her "dictionary" *In Search of My Mother's Gardens* (1983):

> **Womanist 1.** From womanish. (Opp. of "girlish," i.e., frivolous, irresponsible, not serious.) A black feminist or feminist of color. From the black folk expression of mothers to female children "You acting womanish" . . . Usually referring to outrageous, audacious, courageous, or *willful* behavior. . . . Interchangeable with another black folk expression: "You trying to be grown." (emphasis the author's; *Our Mothers' Gardens* xi).

Further on, Walker's definition affirms black women's community and sexual freedom of choice. With characteristic wit and impish humor, she provides a subtle re-visioning or linguistic herstory for black women who reject feminism as "a white women's thing." She neatly establishes the roots of black women's authority, autonomy, and agency in homegrown praxis (as with Tubman and Truth's assumption of God's voice to defy manmade barriers), and as a "given" in black women's rite-of-passage rituals and speech traditions. (Womanism is no second-hand legacy of Betty Friedan.) This more mature activist and writer seems to be relishing the work of inventing a useable language, authorizing her own story within the proper context for understanding, and freeing words and meanings from the traps and trappings of graven racial images and scripted notions.

Revolutionary Petunias (1973) and *Good Night Willie Lee, I'll See You in the Morning* (1979) are radically different from Walker's first work. These two volumes are closely aligned to one another in their tightly focused close-ups of black women's lives and spaces, the close questionings and muted celebrations. *Petunias* opens with a prefatory calling of names of the living and dead: George Jackson, Bob Moses,

Fannie Lou Hamer, and other artists, martyrs, and passionate workers for the movements. She offers a "libation" to these ancestors, those gone and those soon to go (*we are aware we did not make / ourselves)* (*Her Blue Body* 155). These two slim volumes are rueful; they acknowledge a passing of things we might have thought indelible. *Petunias* opens in the tones of requiem: "I shall write of the old men I knew" (156) and "The Old Men Used to Sing." Walker seems to be photographing the character of rural black community: "The old men . . . More awkward / With the flowers / Than with the widow / After they'd put the / Body in" (157). The women are described in monumental language: "They were women then /. . . Stout of / Step / With fists as well as Hands" (159). These word paintings are of mothers and uncles, of their peccadilloes ("They Take a Little Nip") and brilliant civilities. She captures, simply, these determined lives, unadorned. In the midst of this procession of the elders and ancestors appears the long poem "For My Sister Molly Who in the Fifties" about Molly who "found another world" and "Left us" (176–79). This traditional community sits at a crossroad of feeling. It is the locus of love and care; it also bears within it the contradictions of its own past and present.

In her title image of petunias, Walker captures a human paradox that is solved in nature. For the petunia, a simple flower, must bloom (change its aspect and its relation to the universe) even as it remains rooted in a homely soil. This blooming is not promised to the girl who remains rooted in her homely soil. What is solved in nature is a struggle for the black girls and women who populate Walker's source community, who may be judged hard for their blooming (O'Brien 53–55).

"Revolutionary Petunias . . . the Living Through," the volume's second section, captures the difficulty of dedicating one's life to the revolutionary work of love. The section opens with two pieces of stern advice: "Expect nothing. Live frugally / on surprise" (191), followed by "Be Nobody's Darling. Be an outcast. / Take the contradictions / Of your life / And wrap around / You like a shawl" (194). The closing lines surprise:

Be nobody's darling:
Be an outcast
Qualified to live
Among your dead. (194)

Revolutionary Petunias affirms love against a bleak landscape filled with misapprehensions and betrayal. And yet the contradictions are never fodder for despair; the volume ends declaring that "The Nature of This Flower Is To Bloom" (235).

The themes in *Revolutionary Petunias* continue in *Good Night Willie Lee I'll See You in the Morning* (1979). Her poem "On Stripping Bark from Myself," achieves the level of personal manifesto:

No, I am finished with living
For what my mother believes
For what my brother and father defend
For what my lover elevates
For what my sister, blushing, denies or rushes
To embrace

I find my own
Small person
A standing self against the world
An equality of wills (270–71)

Goodnight Willie Lee, seems to extend *Petunias,* or even complete that part of the story of black women's evolutionary consciousness— the journey from victim to rebel to self, where one's wholeness is adequate to achieve the leap of forgiveness. Again, Walker represents Everything We Know in the voice of her mother—that generation of women who knew how to struggle without, or perhaps through, hate on the way to something grand. The poem refrains from marveling at the simple matter-of-fact "civility" of her mother "Looking down into my father's / dead face" and opening the door to the "promise / of our return / at the end." Good Night, Willie Lee.

III

I heard the old songs from my grandmother's Hardshell Baptist Church ring out as the freedom songs they always were, I heard all the connectedness that racist oppression and colonial destruction tried to keep hidden. I heard the African beat, yes, and all the African tones. But I also heard the Native American "off the note" harmony that used to raise the hair at the back of my neck when my grandmother moaned in church. I heard the White words of the old, nearly forgotten hymns, and [felt] the irresistible need of Black people to give contemporary witness to struggle.

These songs . . . [urge] us to acknowledge suffering, yes, but to savor the beauty of life and the joy. Under this voice, the world begins to expand, and paradoxically, to grow smaller. . . . They show us the way home, which is the whole earth.

—Interview, Mary Helen Washington

Until I was nearly fifty, I barely thought of age. But now, as I approach becoming an elder, I find I want to give all that I know to youth. How are they to learn, otherwise?

—Simon, "An Intimate Conversation"

In 1984, the year following her receipt of the Pulitzer Prize and the National Book Award for *The Color Purple*, Walker published *Horses Make a Landscape Look More Beautiful*. The landscape, in this volume, has changed, reflecting Walker's move from New York to California. The voices in this work draw upon "many presences . . . . within my psyche as I was beginning to recognize in the world" (*Her Blue Body* 311). Ten years after the publication of *Horses*, and on her fiftieth birthday, Walker joined her great-grandmothers' names to her own—Tallulah, the name of her maternal great-grandmother, a Cherokee, and Kate, her paternal great-grandmother's name. This gathering of names,

Alice Tallulah-Kate Walker, is also a gathering of the stories that have shaped her continuing effort to locate her own spiritual wholeness. Walker has said that learning of the murder of Kate, and how she tended to be faulted for her own death by the retellers of her story, provided "the foundation of my womanism" (Simon 87/33).

In this volume, "recovery" assumes an alternate meaning. Here, Walker indicates her determination to claim all that has gone into her making and make up, including bloodlines to a rapist, her "white (Anglo-Irish?) / great-great-grandfather / on my father's side; / nameless / . . . whose only remembered act / is that he raped / a child" (*Horses* viii). In this introductory note, Walker recovers this genetic scraping—the fact of her eleven-year-old great-great grandmother—along with her Cherokee and African grandmothers, their labor and song, drawing these to and into her expanding psyche and "Self," gathering all of the discarded and disregarded parts of her story and family tree—victims, rapists, warriors, rebels, singers, dancers, artists, farmers, even (it seems) chickens. This ultimately is her claim and fleshy metaphor: female, revelatory, profound.

Walker published *Her Blue Body Everything We Know* in 1991, which included her complete corpus of poems and twelve unpublished new poems. In 2003, twelve years after *Her Blue Body* and nineteen years after *Horses*, two collections appeared in the same year, *Absolute Trust in the Goodness of the Earth,* and *A Poem Traveled Down My Arm.* In 2010, *Hard Times Require Furious Dancing* appeared.

It is wonderful to live long enough to learn from one's own life. Walker notes her own surprise at having lived long enough to become an optimist (*Her Blue Body* xv). In his review of *Her Blue Body,* Adrian Oktenberg calls Walker "both a mystic and a revolutionary poet, an apparent contradiction in terms but one that she exemplifies nonetheless" (24). Oktenberg notes that Walker's poetry has "not been taken as seriously as her novels and essays" perhaps because her poetry is more located in process than product, in questions rather than answers. He notes that Walker's regard as a poet suffers because her poetry defies categories, the containers for our ideas *about* or expectations *for* poetry. Walker, he notes, seeks revolutionary change through her own black body, "herself, used as a kind of laboratory in which possibilities for change are experimented with, charted and tested" (24).

Alice Walker came of age during the civil rights movement and Black Arts/Black Power movement—these were her emotional crucibles. But her poetry has always emerged from her highly personal engagement with the question of how to pursue revolutionary change in a way that allows us to love more, to become more human. Her pursuit of this question has engaged her lifetime pursuit of what critic Michael C. Cooke has called the achievement of intimacy: "If we consider not the question of images—how one is seen—but rather that of vision— what one encompasses when one sees—then the Afro-American scene becomes less bleak. . . . In vision, a quiet, deep growth continues" (134–35). Cooke defines intimacy as the "interpenetration of the One and the All."

Continuing, Alice Walker blogged (another evolution!) from the *Audacity of Hope*, the Freedom Flotilla II to Gaza, Palestine, in June of 2011. When asked why she was joining this effort to critique Israeli (and US) policy in Palestine, she replied,

> Why am I going on the Freedom Flotilla II to Gaza? I ask myself this, even though the answer is: what else would I do? I am in my 67th year. . . . It seems to me that during this period of eldering it is good to reap the harvest of one's understanding of what is important, and to share this, especially with the young. How are they to learn, otherwise? (*The Guardian* 2011)

Walker's poetry has evolved, and evolves. The laboratory remains open. Walker emerges from behind the Duboisian veil, again and again, positing the interpenetration of the One and the All. Perhaps this is the metaphorical difference in Tashi's death—the death of our precious rituals of death, a call for new rituals that teach us how to live.

"Resistance," Tashi Evelyn Johnson Soul calls back to us, as she approaches the edge of everything, "is the secret of Joy!" In other words:

> do not
> be
> like
> cows
>
> grazing
>
> watching
> the
> butcher
> (*A Poem Traveled Down My Arm* 144)

Works Cited

Byrd, Rudolph P. "Spirituality in the Novels of Alice Walker: Models, Healing, and Transformation, or When the Spirit Moves So Do We." *Wild Women in the Whirlwind: Afra-American Culture and the Contemporary Literary Renaissance*. Eds. Joanne M. Braxton and Andree McLaughton. Piscataway, NJ: Rutgers UP, 1989. 363–78.

Cooke, Michael G. *Afro-American Literature in the Twentieth Century: The Achievement of Intimacy*. New Haven: Yale UP, 1984.

Davis, Thadious. "Poetry as Preface to Fiction." *Alice Walker: Critical Perspectives Past and Present*. Eds. Henry Louis Gates Jr. and K. A. Appiah. New York: Amistad, 1993. 275–83.

Oktenberg, Adrian T. "Revolutionary Contradictions." *The Women's Review of Books* 9.3 (1991):24–25.

Salaam, Kalamu ya. "The Black Arts Movement." *The Oxford Companion to African-American Literature*. Eds. William L. Andrews et al. New York, Oxford: Oxford UP, 1997. 70–74.

Walker, Alice. *Absolute Trust in the Goodness of the Earth*. New York: Random 2003.

_____. "Alice Walker, an Intimate Conversation: My Life as Myself." Interview by Tammy Simon: MARBL Papers: Box 87, Folder 33. 1995. TS and transcript.

_____. "Alice Walker: Why I'm Joining the Freedom Flotilla to Gaza," *The Guardian*. Guardian News and Media, 25 June 2011. Web. 12 Mar. 2012.

_____. *Good Night, Willie Lee, I'll See You in the Morning*. New York: Harcourt, 1979.

———. *Hard Times Require Furious Dancing*. Novato, CA: New World Lib., 2010.

———. *Her Blue Body Everything We Know*. New York: Harcourt, 1991.

———. *Horses* Make *a Landscape Look More Beautiful*. New York: Harcourt, 1984.

———. "I, Too, for Freedom." *Focus Magazine*. Ed. Chantal James. Atlanta, GA: Spelman College, 2007. 10.

———. *In Search Of Our Mothers' Gardens*. New York: Harcourt, 1983.

———. "Interview with Alice Walker." By Mary Helen Washington. MARBL Papers: Box 87, Folder 23.1973. TS.

———. "Interview with John O'Brien from *Interviews with Black Writers* (1973)." *The World Has Changed: Conversations with Alice Walker*. Ed. Rudolph P. Byrd. New York: New Press, 2010. 35–57.

———. Papers. Subseries 2.4D: Interviews, 1973–2006. Manuscript, Archive, and Rare Book Library (MARBL)–Emory University Lib., Atlanta, GA.

———. *A Poem Traveled Down My Arm*. New York: Random, 2003.

———. *Possessing the Secret of Joy*. New York: Simon, 1992.

———. "The Richness of the Very Ordinary Stuff." Interview by Jody Hoy. MARBL Papers: Box 87, Folder 32. Oct. 1994. TS.

Wall, Cheryl A., ed. *Changing Our Own Words: Essays on Criticism, Theory, and Writing by Black Women*. New Brunswick: Rutgers UP. 1991.

Euterpe's Daughter: Ecological/Political/Sociological Poetics of Alice Walker_____

Gerri Bates

In Greek mythology, nine lovely, violet-wreathed daughters of Zeus and Mnemosyne are the patronesses of the arts and distributors of creative inspiration and intellectual pursuit collectively referred to as Muses. One of the sisters, Euterpe, whose name means "she who gladdens," is the Muse of lyric poetry. She is also a constant nurturing presence, a mother figure, in the lives of her anointed poets. Her goal is to inspire lyric poets to best use the creativity that she places at their disposal. Originally introduced through the oral tradition of storytelling, immortal Euterpe works her magic consistently and effectively over time, pouring out the gift of poetic ability cautiously, selectively, and discriminately. Euterpe, invading the consciousness of the youngest female sibling of an impoverished sharecropper family in Eatonton, Georgia, prepared the youngster to give the gift of poetry to a world that was not yet aware of her creative energy.

Influences
Along the journey to becoming an acclaimed poet, developing a loyal and committed readership and audience, Walker discovered other poets who left indelible impressions on her. The common thread of these poets is simplicity of style and the ability to observe and analyze societal surroundings. Most are not just poets, but Walker focuses on their poetic contributions. Among her favorites are Catullus (84–54 BCE), a Roman poet known for writing about everyday existence and for romantic love poems; Ovid (43 BCE–17), a Roman poet who penned the *Metamorphoses*; and Li Po (701–62), a popular Chinese poet of the Tang Dynasty who produced poetry about nature, solitude, and friendship.

Walker is also influenced by Emily Dickinson (1830–86), who, like Walker, rebelled against her father's strictness and refrained from a total commitment to Christianity. William Carlos Williams (1883–1963), an advocate of free verse, native experience, and sensitivity toward the disadvantaged, was another influence on Walker, as well as Edward Estlin Cummings (1894–1962), better known as e. e. cummings, who deviated from the established poetic traditions by eschewing capital letters, using ungrammatical constructions, and experimenting with letter placement on the page.

Jean Toomer (1894–1967) authored the critically successful *Cane* (1923), a collection of prose and poetry. Breaking from the protest tradition in African American literature, *Cane* elucidates the importance of Southern soil, a discovery Toomer made while working in rural Georgia. In an interview, Walker states, "[W]hen reading Toomer's 'Song of the Son' it is not unusual to comprehend—in a flash—what a dozen books on black people's history fail to illuminate" (*World Has Changed* 46). Anna Akhmatova (1889–1966), a witness to Russia's pre- and post-revolutionary periods, wrote poetry that reflects the anguish of living in tragic times. Walker has said of Akhmatova, "She's typical of the Russians in that she has passion and political sensibility" (*World Has Changed* 231).

Langston Hughes (1902–67), a poet of the African American experience, wrote about it in lucid poetic language. Walker became his biographer when she wrote *Langston Hughes, American Poet* (1974). Arna Bontemps (1902–73) is another influence. Walker says of Bontemps, "The passion and compassion in his poem 'A Black Man Talks of Reaping' shook the room I was sitting in the first time I read it . . . I changed. Became someone the same, but different" (*World Has Changed* 46). About Gwendolyn Brooks (1917–2000), recipient of a 1950 Pulitzer Prize for Poetry for *Annie Allen* (1949), Walker comments, "If there was ever a born poet, I think it is Brooks. Her natural way of looking at anything, of commenting on anything, comes out as a vision, in language that is peculiar to her" (*World Has Changed* 46). Okot p'Bitek (1931–82), a Ugandan poet, writes about the preservation of culture, as well as economic, political, religious, and social issues. Walker states, "[he] has written my favorite modern poem, 'Song of Lawino'" (*World Has Changed* 47). Walker also prefers poets who demonstrate the "care" factor, as she believes these poets understand and are sensitive to the individual and social needs of the underserved. This nonexhaustive list of Walker's favorite poets exemplifies her preference for poems that are accessible in form but complex in content and message.

Poetry Oeuvre

Walker has written eight volumes of poetry to date. Her poetry, like most poetry, has a strong musical foundation. In a conversation with John O'Brien, discussing *Revolutionary Petunias*, she reminds him that the blues and jazz musicians bloomed because they made the best of the worst of the South. Walker explains to O'Brien, "poetry is more like music—in my case, improvisational jazz, where each person blows the note that she hears . . . Whether lines are long or short depends on what the poem itself requires. Like people, some poems are fat and some are thin. Personally, I prefer the short thin ones" (*World Has Changed* 56). Indeed, Walker's preference for "short thin" poems is clear in the lyrical sound as well as the visual presentation of her poems.

Walker structures her poems in free verse, preferring white space, brevity, and mixed constructions of sentences of few words and one-word lines. The use of white space allows a framing of the poem on the page. Her most recent volumes contain drawings, extensions of her signature in the text. Although she refrains from conventional meter or metrical versification, she achieves balance in her syntactical patterns. Stanzas may or may not be present, or units may be divisible by lower- or uppercase roman numerals. Incorporated in chapter or section divisions are titles and introductions of quoted text. The developmental plan determines the rhythm of the poetry rather than the counting of syllables or feet. Some poems have dedications to specific individuals or allude to specific events. Interspersed within the volume may be quotes from writers whom Walker believes make statements that have an impact. On rare occasions, Walker includes poetry that takes the form of a narrative.

The overwhelming tone of Walker's poetry is conversational instruction, which often blends humor, intimacy, playfulness, seriousness, spirituality, and whimsy but never condescension. Readers come away with historical reflection and revelatory comprehension. Walker's poetry provides a deeper exploration or reexamination of the world and its regions, especially the South and Africa. Through her poetic teachings, readers may realize the possibility of a better world, one that provides space for all inhabitants—humans, flora, and fauna. Walker, in her optimistic poetry, provides refuge or solace from a polemical society. She sees beyond the immediate and takes readers on a journey with her, as if she is saying "come up here; let us explore and examine together"—a very compelling invitation. She provides the perfect instructional tone, one that is meditative, personal, and reflective.

Walker's ecological themes are pervasive in her poetry, yet are subtly implied rather than overtly stated. Walker's poetry considers the impact of humanity on the earth. Searching for solutions to global ecological issues, some of her poems encourage waste management, healthier edibles, and environmental stewardship. Furthermore, sociological themes are pertinent to Walker's poetry, and she presents them in a sociological context. In a subtle way, she responds to social situations, commenting on their existence and significance. In like manner, Walker addresses politics thematically; she makes references to social movements and advocates political empowerment as a means to oppose the domination of cultural groups.

Once (1968)

Walker's first poetry collection, *Once*, established her as a significant presence in the literary community of writers and scholars. The publication contains a heightened poetic diction in free verse. Walker comments, "*Once* is what I think of as a 'happy' book, full of the spirit of an optimist who loves the world and all the sensations of caring in it;

it doesn't matter that it began in sadness" (*World Has Changed* 50). This book is the genesis of Walker's inclusion in anthologized texts as one of the emerging African American women poets in the English tradition.

Walker's book dedications are as intriguing as her content. *Once* begins with "For Howard Zinn," a dedication to her professor and mentor at Spelman College, and follows with a quote from Albert Camus's *De l'envers et l'endroit*. With this first publication, the selection of Camus's quote reveals the depth of her thoughts, her sensitivity to conditions of poverty, and the impact of place in a carefully contrived universe. The compilation of the text, twenty-seven poems hurriedly written and slid under the office door of Muriel Rukeyser, center on Africa, suicide, love, despair, civil rights, and the South. Writing in the *Christian Science Monitor*, Sam Cornish explains that the poems in *Once* "are pictures of Africa's landscapes, the harshness of the early civil rights movement, and portraits of friends and lovers . . . they show rather than tell of an immediate experience" (B1). Mary C. Williams in a similar manner writes, "*Once* reveals her desire to know her heritage and be close to it but also her feelings of separation from it. In the poems . . . about a trip to Africa she is somewhere in between ordinary tourists and the Africans themselves" (44).

Form and diction, innovative subject matter, and experimentation inform her poetic achievement in this volume. "African Images: Glimpses from a Tiger's Back" has forty-five stanzas that play on the unrhymed verse form of Japanese haiku. "Karamojans" has nine stanzas, mostly three syllables per line, and is the subject of homage to a nearly extinct African people. "Once," the title poem, is a fourteen-stanza exposé on racism in the American South, those who challenge the system, and hope. "Chic Freedom's Reflection," "They Who Feel Death," and "On being asked to leave a place of honor for one of comfort" are poems that acknowledge those who persevered against great odds. "Hymn" is a satirical but humorous examination of Black music and the antics that often accompany it. There are also poems about love, "real and imagined." "To the Man in the Yellow Terry" is the result of the influence of Robert Graves. "Johann" explores an interracial relationship between a German man and an African American woman, unaware that their love is inordinate.

Metonymy, a substitution that uses an aspect of an experience to represent the whole experience, is the literary focus in "South: The Name of Home." In this case, the unnamed specific geographical location of home represents all Southern states. The first stanza (lines 1–11) has a first-person speaker. The key word in the first line is "night," symbolically the absence of light. The second line reveals that the narrator "prayed for eyes to see again." These are not literal eyes but the desire to be able to have a new outlook. This assertion is apparent because the next six lines (3–8) indicate that the last image the speaker remembers of home was "a broken bottle" that was clenched "in a racist fist"—an image that perhaps the speaker wishes to forget. The last three lines (9–11) are a prayer for "trees to plant," something that "hands and eyes" can appreciate. The stanza begins and ends with a prayer. Repetition of the word "eyes" displays different uses in the beginning (new outlook) and the end (caressing). Internal rhyme with the words "night" and "sight" reveals a transformation from darkness to light. The shortest word in the stanza is "fist," an image with a very negative connotation. Thus, the narrator desires to move beyond such a negative memory.

Walker's style, unpretentious diction, and expressive beauty drew readers to her poetry. This first publication also exhibited Walker as a complex thinker, providing the scholarly and lay communities with renewed aesthetic appreciation.

Revolutionary Petunias and Other Poems (1973)

Revolutionary Petunias and Other Poems won the Southern Regional Council's Lillian Smith Award in 1973 and was nominated for a National Book Award in 1974. While *Revolutionary Petunias* focuses on the themes of revolution and love, it also expands upon and advances the themes of civil rights, black power, black arts, and Africa found in *Once*. In short, the second volume is a compilation of two types of poems: validation poems and love poems.

Walker also expanded the dedication from a single listing in *Once* to a group listing in this second volume, including a descriptive account of the group's signature societal contributions. A Soledad Brother who adopted revolutionary philosophy and armed struggle ideology, George Jackson receives the first dedication; his face described by Walker as "determined, unconquered, and sweet." The dedication to SNCC (Student Nonviolent Coordinating Committee) "heroes, heroines, and friends" follows. Next, Walker makes a dedication to the legend of Bob Moses (activist and organizer) in the Mississippi Delta. She then acknowledges the "strength and compassion" of Winson Hudson and Fannie Lou Hamer (civil rights activists) and the sky paintings of Charles Merrill (artist activist). Her final dedication is to Mel—civil rights attorney and activist Melvyn R. Leventhal, Walker's husband from 1967 to 1976—for fighting and loving daily. With this book, critics and readers began to scrutinize and analyze Walker's dedications; in this instance, Walker gives personal and public recognition to individuals she felt were instrumental in the struggle for civil rights, particularly in Mississippi. Thus, Walker's dedication proceeds from revolution to love, the primary order of the content of *Revolutionary Petunias*.

Structurally, *Revolutionary Petunias* is a five-part division that functions as the macrocosm, with each division containing introductory quotes. Groups of poems that function as the microcosm comprise each division. "In These Dissenting Times . . . Surrounding Ground and Autobiography" includes commendable poems, such as "For My Sister Molly Who in the Fifties," a poem about the intellectual pursuits of a sister held in high esteem by her less knowledgeable but appreciative family who later felt separated from and deserted by her. In the section titled "Revolutionary Petunias . . . the Living Through," the title poem "Revolutionary Petunias" elucidates the rebellious nature of a woman whose lack of sophistication prohibits her from realizing her horrific crime. She feels justified in taking the life of the white man who took the life of her husband and becomes a legend. As the authorities take her to death row, she instructs her loved ones to water her flowers, something not on the agenda of real revolutionaries. Also, "Be Nobody's Darling" recommends taking the low road as an outcast rather than the high road of acceptance. The section "Crucifixions" includes the poem "Lost My Voice? Of Course," which expresses dislike for writing only of revolution and never of love and flowers. "Mysteries . . . the Living Beyond" includes "Mysteries." The attraction of the dark center, a point of knowledge, is more compelling than the full blooming petals. Acquisition of the knowledge that the center holds requires the poem's persona to keep that knowledge a secret. Finally, "The Nature of This Flower Is to Bloom" contains "While Love Is Unfashionable," a poem dedicated to love despite its odds.

"Women" is a heroic poem, an examination of the relationship between the characters and their actions. Praising and defining the actions of a generation of women, this twenty-six-line poem commemorates their deeds and performances. With no punctuation marks (except for dashes) until the period at the end of the last line, the poem is also a twenty-six-line sentence. Its characters function as a unified whole. Free verse gives the poem grace and rhetorical balance. The poem is political commentary on a unique fighting force engaged in both covert and overt encounters.

Lines 1–4 give the poem's subject a gender, a description, and an identity. They are women of stoic quality and are referred to collectively rather than individually. The word "step" on line 4 implies unified marching, in time and on time. Lines 5–6 highlight the physicality of the group, their use of "fists" and "hands" as they "step." Lines 7–8 reflect their ability and willingness to demolish anything that hinders or restricts them, i.e., doors of segregation or doors of opportunity. This action incorporates, as well, the "fists" and "hands." Then the poem makes an about-face in lines 9–11 with its mention of domestic responsibilities, which the women do not forsake as they fight on other fronts. It returns to the militaristic symbolism in lines 12–18, commenting on the women's actions as generals. They are "headragged" generals, not attired in the customary one-to-five-star uniform headdress of traditional military personnel. However, they perform actions often associated with traditional military officers, leading armies "across mined fields" and "booby-trapped ditches," which are, in actuality, hindrances to equal access to education. Successful military action leads to discovery, indicated in lines 19–26. Symbols of education are "books" and "desks." The women's action is not in vain, for they discover educational tools and the path to literacy, an avenue for future generations—their children. Not only do they discover a place for their children but also a place for themselves. Their discovery comes from sheer gut instinct and determination, not from prescriptive techniques of a text.

"Women" is a tribute to a generation of women with revolutionary tendencies that dismantled barriers, ironed shirts, and demanded education for the next generation. They are generals par excellence, who fought to keep future generations from the double attack of marginalization and scapegoating.

Good Night, Willie Lee, I'll See You in the Morning (1979)

Six years later, Walker published *Good Night, Willie Lee, I'll See You in the Morning*, a book of poems that did not win the critical reception or awards of the previous volumes. Thematically, the book abandons the heroics of sacrificial lambs and turns to love, forgiveness, and transformation. Poems within this volume reveal Walker's genius for female gender emphasis and psychological catharsis as poetic expression. The interconnectedness of humanity, relationship changes, societal transformation, and self-preservation and progress are the distinguishing elements of this volume.

Again, Walker creates an interesting dedication, one that exemplifies the criteria of allegory and parable. The story is illustrative and didactic, as well as functions as a prologue to the poetic content. Beginning with a folktale formula, "many years ago," similar to "once upon a time," a young woman embarks on a journey to collect the last vestiges of the characteristics of a people. Discovering that previous visitors had already usurped the ideal that she sought, she becomes less enthusiastic about her search, but would preserve in a "notebook" the escaped faces containing the "saltysweet drops of sweat." The legend of a highly educated "quiet man" came to her attention, enticing a vigorous search. Although he was erudite, she questioned his wisdom, for his education was from white ivory towers. Everywhere she went, she heard the legend that the quiet man always proposed that the people should be the decision-makers and always aligned himself with the wishes of the people. Later she learned that the quiet man left the land, changed his name, took his mother's name, and returned to his mother's native land of Africa. He became symbolic of a collective unconscious. Whether the quiet man was real or imagined, she desired to believe in his existence. Then Walker dedicates this book of poetry to the "quiet man," her "five fine brothers," her "friend Gloria," and the "memory of [her] father's shining eyes." The lesson of the story is to choose faith over doubt in the search for the ideal.

The search for the ideal way to love is a compilation of poems as a quintessential five-fold path. The initial path is "Confession," which includes "Did This Happen to Your Mother? Did Your Sister Throw Up a Lot?" This poem's narrator undergoes the torture of love's disappointment, a relationship that is pathological. It results in vowing to retain pride by not revealing true feelings to the lover. The next path is "On Stripping Bark from Myself" where the poetic voice examines the needs of the internal rather than the external self. Included in this section is the poem "Janie Crawford," a commemoration of women who become independent and free thinkers, branching out for experiences that do not limit. "Early Losses: a Requiem" follows this section. The title poem is an examination of love in a historical context. The poem's narrator recollects life in Africa before the arrival of colonizers and enslavers. Memories become the love of homeland, freedom, and the voice of the mother who witnesses the enslavement of the girl child. The memories command forgiveness of the violators, therefore making future love possible. The fourth path is "Facing the Way," which focuses on the way of escape from imposition and the development of the right mind to proceed. Included in this section is the poem "(in answer to your silly question)," an exposé of the many ways in which people unite. The reality is acknowledgment of adoration for the people. The final path is "Forgiveness," the beginning of wisdom, understanding, and knowledge. In the accomplishment of the final path, optimal love at all levels becomes possible—eros, philia, and agape. "Your Soul Shines" is the poem in this section that awaits, invites, and welcomes love again.

"Good Night, Willie Lee, I'll See You in the Morning," the title poem, is a lyric poem that merits examination as a sonnet in free verse. Deviating from the rigidity of convention, it is nonetheless within the tradition. Lines 1–3 introduce the reader to the burden of death through a look, a stare, or a reflection. Lines 4–6 indicate the unemotional approach to the burden—with no "tears," "smiles," or "regrets." Then a change in the situation occurs with the word "but"; lines 7–9 articulate the change. Although the preparation to speak begins in lines 4–6, the actual speaking occurs in lines 7–9. The speech is "with civility," an expression made in courtesy and politeness—"Good night, Willie Lee, I'll see you in the morning." Lines 10–15 drive home the narrative through an observation and a comment on the actions of the previous nine lines. The narrator realizes that forgiveness is the impetus to the healing process of effectual change or transformation, as well as the promise of resurrection.

Throughout *Good Night, Willie Lee* Walker repeatedly uses the words "heart" and "soul." This repetition indicates an in-depth exploration of the emotional and moral nature of humanity, an integral component required for the path to forgiveness. The empathy and compassion that flow through the book make it a powerful contribution to literature. With this volume, Walker amends a cycle of attention to primarily social and political poetry and begins to incorporate themes of nature in her poetry.

Horses Make a Landscape Look More Beautiful (1984)

This volume of poetry marks the beginning of Walker's second period, in which her poetry focuses on nature and Native American and Anglo heritage. The dedication in this volume is a poem that appeals to African, Native American, and Anglo ancestry to rest peacefully together as the meaning of their existence unfolds through their descendant. A quote from Lame Deer follows the dedication, a comparison of the gifts of whiskey and the horse from the "white man": the gift of the horse almost makes up for the gift of whiskey because "horses make a landscape look more beautiful." In addition, the explanation for the recreational decimation of bison comes in another quote from Black Elk. As a food source, the bison were of no value to the "Wasichu"— "he who takes the fat" in the Sioux language (*Horses* 47)—but as a commodity, the bison were invaluable, even their bones.

Walker's "No One Can Watch the Wasichu" is free verse with some of the musical characteristics of the villanelle and the ballad. The narrative presents a group identified as the "Wasichu" with whom the narrator is familiar. Instructional in approach, the story-song provides information about a group that is aggressive or threatening. Repetition in each of the five stanzas is at the beginning followed by detailed reasons for no longer watching the Wasichu. The incidents or infractions committed by the Wasichu are against ordinary, defenseless individuals or against the earth itself. These repetitions are also examples of anaphora, where the beginning lines repeat the sound. The summary section indicates that the presence of the Wasichu is so pervasive that any attempt not to watch is in vain.

Her Blue Body Everything We Know: Earthling Poems 1965–1990 Complete (1991)

This publication is an anniversary issue covering twenty-five years of poetic expression. It includes volumes previously published with new introductions and a new section of uncollected and unpublished poetry. The dedication is a brief, simplistic poem: "Always to You / Beautiful

One / From whom / I have come. / And to whom / I shall happily / Return." Walker's tribute is to the earth, an adaptation of Genesis 3:19, "for dust thou art, and unto dust shalt thou return."

Walker's poem "We Have a Beautiful Mother" offers a romantic view of the physical world. Walker personifies Earth through a series of metaphors that support the poem's premise that the planet is our "beautiful mother" (1–2). In the second stanza, Walker uses a paired metaphor in which Mother Earth's "oceans" are not just *like* wombs, they *are* wombs—and vice versa (9–12). In the third stanza the personification continues with the Earth's vegetation and minerals rendered as comely human characteristics, as in "the summer / grasses / her plentiful / hair" (18–22). The final stanza pairs the colors of Earth with references to physical characteristics that are not just female, but maternal. Mother's lap is green and "immense" as a child would find it; her embrace is brown and "eternal" suggesting a mother's unconditional love; and her body is not only blue with fertile oceans/wombs but is also "everything we know" (25–31) as her offspring.

From 2003 to the Present

Following *Her Blue Body*, Walker published three volumes of poetry: *Absolute Trust in the Goodness of the Earth* (2003); *A Poem Traveled Down My Arm* (2003); and *Hard Times Require Furious Dancing* (2010). Walker's pagan pleasures and practices produced the inspiration for *Absolute Trust in the Goodness of the Earth*. The dedications in this volume acknowledge feminine energy and its importance in the making of a world. *A Poem Traveled Down My Arm* is a collection of Walker's golden nuggets, her philosophy of life that was personal but has become public. At the request of her editor to pre-sign hundreds of sheets for the new volume, Walker's hand became fatigued and her signature illegible. To improve upon this task, she decided to make her signature a design by personalizing her signature with drawings, poems, sayings, and expressions, whatever came to mind. Walker's latest volume presents the poet as public servant to the masses, as one on a journey from chaos to peace.

Some critics have reacted indifferently to Walker's craftsmanship. They find her use of language stilted and her message as fused with a kind of naïveté. They seem to want her to be more grand and eloquent; simplicity to them is ineffective. However, Walker's poetry covers more than four decades of devotion to free verse. Her poetry underscores many of the complexities of life. She not only writes love poetry but also composes poetry with ecological, social, and political themes, demonstrating a humanely noble approach to her aesthetics. Skillfully exhibiting an ability to write about complex topics using clear, simplistic syntax, Walker demonstrates that she embraces the energy gifted to her as Euterpe's daughter.

Works Cited

Cornish, Sam. "Alice Walker: Her Own Woman." *Christian Science Monitor* 76.49 (1984): B1.

Walker, Alice. *Absolute Trust in the Goodness of the Earth*. New York: Random, 2003.

_____. *Good Night, Willie Lee, I'll See You in the Morning*. New York: Dial, 1979.

_____. *Hard Times Require Furious Dancing*. Novato, CA: New World Lib., 2010.

_____. *Her Blue Body Everything We Know*. New York: Harcourt, 1991.

_____. *Horses Make a Landscape Look More Beautiful*. New York: Harcourt, 1984.

_____. *Once: Poems*. New York: Harcourt, 1968.

_____. *A Poem Traveled Down My Arm*. New York: Random, 2003.

_____. *Revolutionary Petunias and Other Poems*. New York: Harcourt, 1973.

_____. *The World Has Changed: Conversations with Alice Walker*. Ed. Rudolph P. Byrd. New York: New Press, 2010.

Williams, Mary C. "The Poetic Knife: Poetry by Recent Southern Women Poets." *The South Carolina Review* 11.1 (1978): 44–54.

Alice Walker's Essays, Speeches, and Conversations _____

Donna Akiba Sullivan Harper

Before she ever published her first book, Alice Walker had won national recognition for her essay writing. In 1967 "The Civil Rights Movement: What Good Was It?" was published in *The American Scholar,* the journal of the Phi Beta Kappa honor society. From that auspicious beginning until now, Alice Walker has spoken out in a nonfiction voice that is poignant, powerful, and unflinching. While readers can observe her proud and confident transition from young writer into the status of "elder" in the more than four decades of her essay and interview comments, Walker remains consistent is the expression of key values of her ethos: openness, love, and truth-seeking—even when it hurts.

Before tracing these key values in her essays, speeches, and interviews (or conversations, as they are called), it may be useful to review the chronological record of her extensive work as an essayist. As noted above, in 1967, just a year after earning her BA degree from Sarah Lawrence College, Alice Walker won a first-prize cash award of $300 for her essay, "The Civil Rights Movement: What Good Was It?" She reprinted that essay along with others in her first volume of essays, *In Search of Our Mothers' Gardens: Womanist Prose by Alice Walker* (1983). In this volume she also published her often-quoted and often-discussed definition of "womanist." Included in the four parts of her definition were these descriptions: "A black feminist or feminist of color. From the black folk expression of mothers to female children, 'You acting womanish,' i.e., like a woman," (xi) and "womanist is to feminist as purple is to lavender" (xii). Walker invigorated the women's movement with her definition, inviting women of color to engage fully in what had previously been labeled a movement for white women only. In a 2006 conversation with Marianne Schnall of Feminist.com, Walker embellished her term "womanist," insisting first of all "it's feminist."

Womanism comes, though, from Southern African American culture because when you did something really bold and outrageous and audacious as a little girl, our parents would say, "You're acting womanish." It wasn't like in white culture where that was weak—it was just the opposite. And so, womanism affirms that whole spectrum of being which includes being outrageous and angry and standing up for yourself, and speaking your word and all of that. ("Conversation with Schnall," 288–89)

In Search of Our Mothers' Gardens also provided a convenient location for readers to understand Walker's admiration for Zora Neale Hurston. In her 1976 essay, "Saving the Life That Is Your Own: The Importance of Models in the Artist's Life," Walker shares some of the origins and inspirations for her short story, "The Revenge of Hannah Kemhuff," which was included in *Best Short Stories of 1974*. If Zora Neale Hurston's work had not been available to Alice Walker when she sat down to write this story, it "might never have been written, because the very bases of its structure, authentic black folklore, viewed from a black perspective, might have been lost" (13). She elaborates on the connections between Hurston's ethnographic writing and her own writing in a 1979 essay, "Zora Neale Hurston: A Cautionary Tale and a Partisan View." Specifically praising *Mules and Men*, Hurston's 1935 collection of folk tales and hoodoo experiences, Walker says that her own family, whom she calls "typical black Americans" (*In Search* 84) read the book aloud and experienced "joy over who she [Hurston] was showing them to be: descendants of an inventive, joyous, courageous, and outrageous people; loving drama, appreciating wit, and, most of all, relishing the pleasure of each other's loquacious and *bodacious* company" (85). Walker further relished the "racial health" she observed in Hurston's work. When so many educated African Americans "were still infatuated with things European," Walker writes, "Zora was interested in Africa, Haiti, Jamaica, and—for a little racial diversity (Indians)—Honduras" (85). The cautionary tale Walker derives from Hurston's life is that "without money of one's own in a capitalist society, there is no such thing as independence" (90). Walker admonishes, "*A people do not throw their geniuses away*. And if they are thrown away, it is our duty *as artists and as witnesses for the future* to collect them again for the sake of our children, and, if necessary, bone by bone" (*In Search* 92).

As part of her self-appointed duty to collect Hurston's memory, Walker visited a Fort Pierce, Florida, cemetery in 1973 searching for Hurston's unmarked grave. Walker details this journey in her 1975 essay, "Looking for Zora." She recalls her first time visiting Eatonville, lying to folks about being Zora Neale Hurston's niece—a lie that seems quite appropriate in pursuit of a woman who lied about so many things and who cherished the folk tales folks called "big old lies." Repeatedly, Walker returns to the events that led to her efforts to revive the memory and the works of Zora Neale Hurston.

Her second collection of her own essays, *Living by the Word: Selected Writings, 1973–1987,* was published in 1988. Already having won both the Pulitzer Prize and the National Book Award for her 1982 novel *The Color Purple*, and having seen her novel reach the big screen as an Academy Award–nominated film, Walker writes in the preface of her collection that *Living by the Word* is less a deliberate book than it is "a map of my journey and my discoveries" through what she conceived of as "a new age of heightened global consciousness" (xx). The collection includes numerous journal entries; speeches delivered in various public venues (The Atlanta Historical Society in 1981 and Founders' Day at Spelman, 1987, for instance); a tribute to a Native American "big brother," Bill Wahpepah; a response to a publisher about the origins of her first published short story ("To Hell with Dying"), which was reborn as a children's book; reflections and observations from her travels (including China and Bali); and her responses to various news events (including the MOVE massacre in Philadelphia in May 1985). Also included was the essay "Am I Blue?" which will be discussed below. Many of these essays are deeply personal, including her discovery that her "friend hair" did not like being oppressed by mechanical straightening or even by orderly braiding, and her initiation into eating raw seaweed. Yet even within those deeply private and introspective lines are the clarion calls to honor and respect all humans, to value the lives of other animals—since she repeatedly reminds readers that humans are animals, too—and to cherish and protect Mother Earth.

Her 1996 volume, *The Same River Twice: Honoring the Difficult*, focused upon the work of translating *The Color Purple* into film. A second volume published in 1996, *Alice Walker Banned*, evaluated Walker's short story "Roselily" and her essay "Am I Blue?" and the decision of the California State Board of Education to ban those works from their 1994 California Learning Assessment System test. "Roselily," the introspective story of a black single mother who seeks to escape some of her financial difficulties by marrying a Black Muslim from Chicago, was initially published in one of the earliest issues of *Ms.* Magazine. It subsequently appeared as the opening story in Walker's first short story collection, *In Love and Trouble* (1973). "Am I Blue?" (included in *Living by the Word*) patiently takes readers into the expressions one can read—if one takes the time to do so—in the eyes of a horse. The protagonist, a white horse named Blue, reminds Walker of "the depth of feeling one could see in horses' eyes" (4) and "that human animals and nonhuman animals can communicate quite well" (5). Through Blue's treatment, Walker traced brutality to humans who were considered to have been savages or beasts, and she ends the essay unable to eat steak. *Alice Walker Banned* includes transcripts from the public hearing in which people responded to the decision of the California State Board of Education to ban those works from the test. Arguments for and against banning are included, as a testimony to Walker's own sense of balance.

A year later, in 1997, *Anything We Love Can Be Saved: A Writer's Activism* used essays and photographs to capture Walker's passionate adoration of creations and creativity. Her "saving" in this volume returns to Zora Neale Hurston and reaches toward Cuba and Fidel Castro. By the time Alice Walker addressed the First Annual Zora Neale Hurston Festival in Eatonville, Florida, on January 26, 1990, she knew that all her early efforts had been successful. Thus, while she had wanted in 1973 "to mark Zora's grave so that one day all our daughters and sons would be able to locate the remains of a human mountain in Florida's and America's so frequently flat terrain" (*Anything* 47), she also appreciated the ultimate fate of all living things—to return to the earth. Thus, she announced that "it matters little . . . where our bodies finally lie, and how or whether their resting places are marked" (47). The true marker, she realized was something not physical, not tangible, and not engraved into stone. "Love and justice and truth are the only monuments that generate ever-widening circles of energy and life. Love and justice and truth are the only monuments that endure, though trashed and trampled, generation after generation" (48).

With regard to Fidel Castro and Cuba, Walker connects some of her fondness for that nation with some of her observations during her visit. Her own experiences in her youth made her see life for Cubans in a specific light.

> Since I was born into the poorest, least powerful, most despised population of the United States and was spoken to as if I were a dog when I asked to use a library or eat in a restaurant, the revelation that people of color, who make up between 40 and 60 percent of Cuba's population, and women, who make up half, can share in all the fruits of their labors was a major gift Cuba gave to me—a major encouragement to struggle for equality and justice, and one I shall never forget. (*Anything* 194)

Walker also details the day she actually met Fidel Castro, shared her books (translated into Spanish) with him, and relished his confession that he is weary of reading government reports and actually enjoys reading novels (*Anything* 204).

In "Getting as Black as My Daddy: Thoughts on the Unhelpful Aspects of Destructive Criticism," Walker shares her own vulnerability to "battering" criticism. Recalling a black woman critic from *The Village Voice* and *The Washington Post* who "declared that although my political writing was banal, my writing about my spiritual development was simply of no interest" (156), Walker expresses sympathy for that critic. "What is truly banal is to think writers write books to please critics," Walker asserts. Yet perhaps inhibited by that critic who wanted Walker to "shut up," Walker refused to provide details about her own discovery about her skin. "I end the essay here, not telling you the particulars, as a demonstration of what, because of battering rather than constructive criticism, is sometimes lost" (157).

In 2001, Walker offers a fifty-seven-page volume giving her early response to September 11, 2001: *Sent by Earth: A Message from the Grandmother Spirit after the Attacks on the World Trade Center and Pentagon.* Her epigraph for the first essay in the book is one she also used to preface her first novel, *The Third Life of Grange Copeland* (1970): "The Great danger in the world today is that the very feeling and conception of what is a human being might well be lost," words from Richard Wright to Jean Paul Sartre in the 1940s. Addressing the Midwives Alliance of North America on September 22, 2001, Walker asserts, "There is not a midwife in this room who would bomb a baby or a child or a pregnant woman. Perhaps in this particular room there is not one person who would do so. And yet, that is the position we find ourselves in" (18). Consistently, Walker envisions herself in the place of the people who are usually depicted as "others." She leads her readers and her audiences to erase the boundaries and walls that would allow us to only see "us" opposed to "them." Her slim volume reaches to international sources for peacemaking and reconciliation strategies.

In 2006, Walker published essays and talks in *We Are the Ones We Have Been Waiting For: Inner Light in a Time of Darkness.* This volume led Walker to a different publisher, the New Press, since her regular publisher, Random House, could not decide what to do with the book. In her acknowledgments, Walker thanks her agent, Wendy Weil, "for finding just the right publishing house for a book that contemplates, on a deep, often intimate level, the spiritual trials and practical requirements of this quite alarming period we are living in" (xi). In a

2006 interview with David Swick, Walker elaborated that she intended this book as a way to help readers respond to "the most dangerous, frightening, unstable time that the earth has known and that human beings have ever known." She says she tried to explain to Random House:

> We live in a time when things are so dire, and politics especially. The political discussion is so discouraging that people need a book that is political but is at the same time infused with spirituality. They need a book that instructs them to step back and meditate, sit and contemplate, rather than dissolve into despair. (*World* 309)

Her reflections in these dire times are decorated with poems, since she refers to poetry as her first love. Yet the most gripping statistic in the volume is one that she both quotes and reiterates. It comes from a speech by Fidel Castro, President of Cuba, delivered March 21, 2002. He said, "The assets of the three wealthiest persons in the world amount to the GDP of the forty-eight poorest countries combined" (112–13). When she repeats this statistic, she contextualizes both the words and the reception of such words, given the "actual situation of the peoples of the earth":

> We are starving, we are illiterate, our environment is polluted almost beyond bearing, we are dying of all kinds of diseases, not just cancer and AIDS; we are running out of water, air, land. . . . And it is getting worse. However, when voices are raised to make this reality plain, and when people actually risk their lives to change the bad plan the masters of the world have laid out for us, they are in danger of being labeled "terrorists" or . . . made to feel vulnerable, threatened, and alone. (*We Are the Ones* 115–16)

Further in this same essay, Walker suggests that "[a]ll the taboos set in place over the last six thousand years must be carefully brought to light, inspected in council, and probably broken, if we are to move further along our evolutionary path" (127). Certainly, Walker makes many readers review things they have always been taught.

In 2009, Walker responded to the genocide in Rwanda with *Overcoming Speechlessness: A Poet Encounters 'The Horror' in Rwanda, Eastern Congo, and Palestine/Israel*. This slim and powerful volume will be discussed below, since it epitomizes the truth-seeking that Alice Walker embodies.

Most recently, in 2010, Rudolph P. Byrd edited and introduced the first collection of interviews (called conversations) with Alice Walker: *The World Has Changed: Conversations with Alice Walker*. One of the earliest interviews dates back to 1973 with John O'Brien. The most recent one in that collection is a 2009 interview with Rudolph Byrd himself.

Evident in the large number of essays, speeches, and conversations she has published, Alice Walker has much to say that she does not need to distill into poetry or embellish with fiction. Courageously and intentionally, she reveals her own autobiographical insights and her keenly-felt exhortations. Thematically, many concepts return throughout these essays, journal entries, speeches, and conversations. Let us focus upon these three: openness, love, and truth-seeking.

Closed minds never appealed to Alice Walker. Her academic matriculation at Spelman College ended when she felt that her mentor, Howard Zinn, had been dismissed from the college in a manner that contradicted the liberal arts education she sought. Her editorial writing in the Spelman college newspaper also revealed that even as a teenager, she was alert to injustices.

Walker's openness is evident in her discussions about religious beliefs. She embraces the beliefs and practices from several religions or cultures, including Buddhism, the *I Ching*, the Tao, meditation, and yoga ("Swick" 306–7). There are things she loves about Jesus, for example, because "like Fidel Castro, Gandhi, Martin Luther King Jr., and especially Che Guevara" he "never abdicated his responsibility to the suffering, the dispossessed and the poor" ("I Call That Man Religious,

We Are the Ones 118). Nevertheless, she abhors the depiction of Jesus on the cross, wishing instead that he could be represented as is the Buddha, smiling and happy. She readily identifies herself as an animist ("everything has spirit") and a pagan ("I worship nature and the spirit of nature"), but she insists that she is "enchanted with wisdom wherever it is found" ("On Raising Chickens," *The World Has Changed* 316).

Alice Walker advocates love. The two great loves for her are love and appreciation for the original African ancestor, the mother of all humans, and devoted love and care for Mother Earth. These loves and her resolute refusal to be closed-minded have allowed her to transgress against society's restrictions in her choice of lovers and to embrace all creation as worthy of our appreciation and protection.

> In the Sixties I found it possible to love a man of European descent. Against the laws and attitudes of my country, I married him. Thirty years later I found myself deeply loving a black, black woman of African descent. Both these relationships were, in a very real sense, taboo. However loving is nothing if it is not an education, and through the relationship with the Euro-American man I learned that all white men are not racist, are not shut down, closed off, from the life of others who appear different from themselves. (*We Are the Ones* 125)

Moreover, Walker names love as the source of her energy ("Conversation with Marianne Schnall," *World Has Changed* 296) and as the force that allowed her to heal from and deal with the injury to her right eye when she was a child ("Walker and Jefferson" 251–52). As one of her volumes of essays clearly states, *Anything We Love Can Be Saved* (1997). Walker seems to love all creatures, all of the earth. Thus, she advocates saving us all—especially from the hatred, fear, ignorance, and violence that injure us physically and psychologically. She has campaigned for most of her life to reveal these hurtful practices and to encourage people to treat each other and the world with kindness and respect.

An important aspect of her revelations about hurtful behaviors and beliefs is her own quest to discover the truth. Truth-seeking can be painful. Yet Walker insists that alert humans persist in finding out what is happening to other humans and to the earth we inhabit. Even if gaining knowledge about the horrors people inflict upon each other or upon the planet might be painfully depressing, "have the courage to be more depressed," she urges ("Swick" 309). For her, ignorance is the opposite of bliss. In her first major essay, she praised "knowledge of my condition" as a lasting benefit of the "freedom movement" of the civil rights period. This knowledge was decidedly "better than un-awareness, forgottenness, and hopelessness" (*In Search* 121). The epi-graph for *Overcoming Speechlessness: A Poet Encounters 'the Horror' in Rwanda, Eastern Congo, and Palestine/Israel* comes from Buddha: "Three things cannot be hidden: the sun, the moon, and the truth." That slim volume embodies the most depressing depths of discover-ing truth. Working with Women for Women International—of which Walker is an honorary cofounder—Walker visited maimed and bru-talized women in Rwanda who had survived, healed, and were deter-mined to live. The speechlessness that Walker overcame to produce the book certainly strikes the reader, unwilling to grasp the descriptions of murder, mutilation, and rape that survivors shared with her.

Walker writes in *Overcoming Speechlessness* that she required a healing after seeing and hearing first-hand accounts of maiming and murder in Rwanda. Yet she insists, "[W]hatever has happened to hu-manity, whatever is currently happening to humanity, it is happening to all of us" (17). Her empathy extends to the people of Palestine, who are bombed, Walker says, with weapons provided by US taxpayers. She traveled to Gaza with CODEPINK, seeking to convey that "not all Americans are uncaring, deaf and blind, or fooled by the media" (21). Walker feels passionately that "Americans have been deliberately mis-led by our government and by the media about the reality and *meaning* of events in the Middle East" (21).

Just as her first major essay in 1967 insists that the civil rights movement had illuminated us and had made a lasting difference, so too her conversation with Rudolph P. Byrd in 2009 insists, "With the election of a black man to the presidency of the United States, the world *has* changed" (311). She began her website and blog in 2008 on the day when Barack Obama won the election (312, 320.) Readers can explore Walker's most up-to-date observations on her website Alicewalkersgarden.com. In the changing world, readers are fortunate to have the forthright voice of Alice Walker, bringing to our attention transgressions against humanity or against the earth that we all should recognize and purposefully act to stop.

Works Cited

Walker, Alice. "Alice Walker and Margo Jefferson: A Conversation from LIVE from the NYPL" (2005). *World* 239–67.

_____. *Alice Walker Banned.* San Francisco: Aunt Lute, 1996.

_____. *Anything We Love Can Be Saved: A Writer's Activism.* New York: Random, 1997.

_____. "A Conversation with David Swick from *Shambhala Sun*" (2006). *World* 303–10.

_____. "A Conversation with Marianne Schnall from feminist.com" (2006). *World* 285–302.

_____. *In Search of Our Mothers' Gardens: Womanist Prose by Alice Walker.* New York: Harcourt, 1983.

_____. *Living by the Word: Selected Writings 1973–1987 by Alice Walker.* New York: Harcourt, 1988.

_____. "On Raising Chickens: A Conversation with Rudolph P. Byrd" (2009). *World* 311–22.

_____. *Overcoming Speechlessness: A Poet Encounters 'The Horror' in Rwanda, Eastern Congo, and Palestine/Israel.* New York: Seven Stories, 2009. Kindle.

_____. *Sent by Earth: A Message from the Grandmother Spirit after the Attacks on the World Trade Center and Pentagon.* Open Media Pamphlet Series. New York: Seven Stories, 2001. Kindle.

_____. *We Are the Ones We Have Been Waiting For: Inner Light in a Time of Darkness.* New York: New Press, 2006.

_____. *The World Has Changed: Conversations with Alice Walker.* Ed. Rudolph P. Byrd. New York: New Press, 2010.

RESOURCES

Chronology of Alice Walker's Life _____

1944	On Wednesday, February 9, Alice Malsenior Walker is born the eighth child and third daughter of Minnie Lou Grant Walker and Willie Lee Walker in Eatonton, Georgia.
1948	Walker enters the first grade at East Putnam Consolidated School.
1952	Walker suffers what she will later call a "patriarchal wound." Her brother Curtis shoots her in her right eye with his BB gun during a game of cowboys and Indians. The incident leaves her blind in the injured eye.
1957	Walker enters the racially segregated Butler-Baker High School in Eatonton, Georgia.
1961	Prom queen and class valedictorian, Walker graduates from high school and wins a scholarship to Spelman College in Atlanta, Georgia.
1962	Walker travels abroad to Helsinki, Finland, as a delegate to the World Festival of Youth and Students.
1963	Involved with the civil rights movement, Walker attends the March on Washington.
1964	Dissatisfied with the restrictions at Spelman College, Walker transfers to Sarah Lawrence College in Bronxville, New York.
1965	Travels to Kenya, East Africa, as a student in the Experiment in International Living program. Walker returns from Kenya pregnant and has an illegal abortion.
1966	Graduates from college with honors. Her thesis on Albert Camus, "Albert Camus: The Development of His Philosophical Position as Reflected in His Novels and Plays," is directed by her adviser, Helen Lynd. Moves to New York City and works for the welfare office. Spends the summer in Jackson, Mississippi, working with the NAACP Legal Defense Fund. Meets Melvyn Leventhal, a civil rights attorney.

1967	Marries Leventhal in New York City and they return to Mississippi where their interracial marriage is illegal. Walker wins first prize and $300 for her *American Scholar* essay, "The Civil Rights Movement: What Good Was It?" Meets Langston Hughes, to whom Muriel Rukeyser has sent Walker's short story, "To Hell with Dying." Hughes includes the story in his edited volume, *The Best Short Stories by Negro Writers*.
1968	Walker's first poetry collection, *Once,* is published and she becomes writer-in-residence at Jackson State College. On April 4, Rev. Martin Luther King Jr. is assassinated. Walker, who is pregnant, miscarries days later after walking in the funeral processional.
1969	On November 17 Walker gives birth to her daughter and only child, Rebecca Grant Leventhal.
1970	*The Third Life of Grange Copeland* is published by Harcourt Brace Jovanovich. She is writer-in-residence at Tougaloo College. Begins to research the works of Zora Neale Hurston. Awarded the Radcliffe Institute Fellowship.
1972	Becomes a lecturer in the Department of English at Wellesley College and at the University of Massachusetts, Boston.
1973	Her father, Willie Lee Walker, dies. *In Love and Trouble: Stories of Black Women* is published. *Revolutionary Petunias*, a poetry collection, is published and wins the Lillian Smith Award.
1974	Walker moves to New York City and becomes an editor at *Ms.* Magazine. Her biography of Langston Hughes, *Langston Hughes: American Poet*, is published.
1976	Walker and Mel Leventhal divorce. *Meridian* is published.
1977	Wins a Guggenheim Fellowship. Tries to begin work on her third novel but is distracted by the city.
1978	Leaves New York for San Francisco, California. Begins writing *The Color Purple*. Travels to Cuba.

1979	*Good Night Willie Lee, I'll See You in the Morning* is published. *I Love Myself When I Am Laughing . . . and Then Again When I'm Looking Mean and Impressive: A Zora Neale Hurston Reader,* a volume of Hurston's writings edited by Walker, is published
1981	*You Can't Keep a Good Woman Down* is published.
1982	The novel, *The Color Purple,* is published. Walker becomes the Fannie Hurst Professor of Literature at Brandeis University in Waltham, Massachusetts.
1983	Walker is awarded the Pulitzer Prize and the National Book Award for *The Color Purple. In Search of Our Mothers' Gardens* is published.
1984	Walker, her companion Robert Allen, and friend Belvie Rooks establish Wild Trees Press. *Horses Make the Landscape Look More Beautiful,* her fifth volume of poetry, is published.
1985	The motion picture version of *The Color Purple* (Steven Spielberg's film adaptation) is released.
1986	*The Color Purple* is nominated for eleven Academy Awards, but does not win. Walker receives the O. Henry Award for her short story "Kindred Spirits."
1988	Walker closes Wild Trees Press. The short story "To Hell with Dying" is published as a children's book. The essay collection *Living by the Word: Selected Writings 1973–1987* is published.
1989	*The Temple of My Familiar* is published.
1991	*Finding the Green Stone* and *Her Blue Body Everything We Know: Earthling Poems 1965–1990* are published.
1992	*Possessing the Secret of Joy* is published.
1993	On September 10 Walker's mother, Minnie Tallulah (Lou) Grant Walker, dies. The documentary film and book *Warrior Marks: Female Genital Mutilation and the Sexual Blinding of Women* are released.

1994	Walker changes her name to Alice Tallulah-Kate Walker as a tribute to her maternal great-grandmother, Tallulah Calloway, and her paternal grandmother, Kate Nelson. *Alice Walker: The Complete Stories* is published.
1996	Walker's brother, William (Bill) who had paid for her eye surgery to remove the unsightly scar tissue when she was fourteen, dies. *The Same River Twice: Honoring the Difficult* is published.
1997	The Alice Walker Literary Society is formed as a joint effort between Spelman College and Emory University's James Weldon Johnson Institute. Walker attends the chartering. *Anything We Love Can Be Saved: A Writer's Activism* is published.
1998	*By the Light of My Father's Smile*, Walker's sixth novel, is published.
2000	*The Way Forward Is with a Broken Heart* is published.
2001	After the September 11 attacks, Walker publishes *Sent by Earth: A Message from the Grandmother Spirit after the Attacks on the World Trade Center and Pentagon*.
2002	Walker's brother James (Jimmy) Walker dies.
2003	Walker publishes two books of poetry: *Absolute Trust in the Goodness of the Earth: New Poems* and *A Poem Traveled Down My Arm: Poems and Drawings*.
2004	*Now Is the Time to Open Your Heart: A Novel* is published. *The Color Purple* musical, produced by Scott Sanders, premiers in Atlanta, Georgia. Walker becomes a grandmother when Rebecca gives birth to a son, Tenzin.
2005	*The Color Purple* musical opens in New York on Broadway.
2006	The musical, *The Color Purple,* wins a Tony Award. Walker is inducted into the California Hall of Fame. *We Are the Ones We Have Been Waiting For: Inner Light in a Time of Darkness: Meditations* and *There Is a Flower at the Tip of My Nose, Smelling Me* are published.

2007	The twenty-fifth-anniversary edition of *The Color Purple* is published. Walker places her archive at Emory University in Atlanta, Georgia. *Why War Is Never a Good Idea* is published.
2008	Walker's sister Annie Ruth Walker Hood dies. Alice Walker's Garden (Alicewalkersgarden.com), Walker's official website, is published online.
2009	The Walker archive at Emory University opens on April 24. Walker attends the symposium and exhibit titled "A Keeping of Records: The Art and Life of Alice Walker." Walker receives the James Weldon Johnson Medal for Literature awarded by the James Weldon Johnson Institute of Emory University. *Overcoming Speechlessness: A Poet Encounters the Horror in Rwanda, Eastern Congo, and Palestine/Israel* is published.
2010	*Overcoming Speechlessness: A Poet Encounters the Horror in Rwanda, Eastern Congo, and Palestine/Israel, The World Has Changed: Conversations with Alice Walker*, and *Hard Times Require Furious Dancing* are published.
2011	Walker publishes *The Chicken Chronicles*, a collection of writings from her Internet blog.

Works by Alice Walker

Long Fiction

The Third Life of Grange Copeland, 1970
Meridian, 1976
The Color Purple, 1982
The Temple of My Familiar, 1989
Possessing the Secret of Joy, 1992
By the Light of My Father's Smile, 1998
Now Is the Time to Open Your Heart: A Novel, 2004

Short Fiction

In Love and Trouble: Stories of Black Women, 1973
You Can't Keep a Good Woman Down, 1981
The Complete Stories, 1994
Alice Walker Banned, 1996 (stories and commentary)
The Way Forward Is with a Broken Heart, 2000

Poetry

Once: Poems, 1968
Five Poems, 1972
Revolutionary Petunias and Other Poems, 1973
Good Night, Willie Lee, I'll See You in the Morning: Poems, 1979
Horses Make a Landscape Look More Beautiful, 1984
Her Blue Body Everything We Know: Earthling Poems, 1965–1990 Complete, 1991
A Poem Traveled Down My Arm: Poems and Drawings, 2003
Absolute Trust in the Goodness of the Earth: New Poems, 2003
Hard Times Require Furious Dancing: New Poems, 2010

Nonfiction

In Search of Our Mothers' Gardens: Womanist Prose, 1983
Living by the Word: Selected Writings, 1973–1987, 1988
Warrior Marks: Female Genital Mutilation and the Sexual Blinding of Women, 1993
    (with Pratibha Parmar)
The Same River Twice: Honoring the Difficult—A Meditation on Life, Spirit, Art,
    and the Making of the Film, The Color Purple, *Ten Years Later*, 1996
Anything We Love Can Be Saved: A Writer's Activism, 1997

Sent by Earth: A Message from the Grandmother Spirit after the Attacks on the World Trade Center and Pentagon, 2001

Pema Chödrön and Alice Walker in Conversation: On the Meaning of Suffering and the Mystery of Joy (with Pema Chödrön), 2005

We Are the Ones We Have Been Waiting For: Inner Light in a Time of Darkness, 2006

Overcoming Speechlessness: A Poet Encounters the Horror in Rwanda, Eastern Congo, and Palestine/Israel, 2010

The World Has Changed: Conversations with Alice Walker, 2010 (Rudolph P. Byrd, editor)

The Chicken Chronicles: Sitting with the Angels Who Have Returned with My Memories: Glorious, Rufus, Gertrude Stein, Splendor, Hortensia, Agnes of God, the Gladyses, and Babe: A Memoir, 2011

Edited Text(s)

I Love Myself When I Am Laughing . . . and Then Again When I Am Looking Mean and Impressive: A Zora Neale Hurston Reader, 1979

Children's Literature

Langston Hughes: American Poet, 1974
To Hell with Dying, 1988
Finding the Green Stone, 1991
There Is a Flower at the Tip of My Nose Smelling Me, 2006
Why War Is Never a Good Idea, 2007

Bibliography

Allan, Tuzyline Jita. *Womanist and Feminist Aesthetic: A Comparative Review.* Columbus: Ohio UP, 1995.

Awkward, Michael. *Inspiring Influences: Tradition, Revision, and Afro-American Women's Novels.* New York: Columbia UP, 1991.

Banks, Erma Davis, and Keith Byerman. *Alice Walker: An Annotated Bibliography 1968–86.* New York: Garland, 1989.

Bates, Gerri. *Alice Walker: A Critical Companion.* Westport, CT: Greenwood, 2005.

Bell, Bernard. *The Afro-American Novel and Its Tradition.* Amherst, MA: U of Massachusetts P, 1987.

_____. *The Contemporary African American Novel: Its Folk Roots and Modern Literary Branches.* Amherst, MA: U of Massachusetts P, 2005.

Bloom, Harold, ed. *Alice Walker.* New York: Chelsea, 2007.

_____. *Alice Walker: Major Novelists.* New York: Chelsea, 1999.

Brogan, Jacqueline Vaught. "Hemingway Talking to Walker Talking to Hemingway." *Hemingway Review.* 30.1 (2010):122–28.

_____. "The Hurston/Walker/Vaughn Connection: Feminist Strategies in American Fiction." *Women's Studies* 28.2 (1999): 185–200.

Butler-Evans, Judith. *Race, Gender, and Desire: Narrative Strategies in the Fiction of Toni Cade Bambara, Toni Morrison, and Alice Walker.* Philadelphia: Temple UP, 1989.

Byrd, Rudolph P. "Shared Orientation and Narrative Acts in *Cane, Their Eyes Were Watching God,* and *Meridian.*" *MELUS: Journal for the Study of Multi-Ethnic Literature of the United States* 17. 4 (1991–92): 41–46.

_____. "Spirituality in the Novels of Alice Walker: Models, Healing, and Transformation, or When the Spirit Moves So Do We." Eds. Joanne M. Braxton and Andree McLaughlin. *Wild Women in the Whirlwind: Afra-American Culture and the Contemporary Literary Renaissance.* New Brunswick, NJ: Rutgers UP, 1990. 363–78.

Marín Calderón, Norman David. "The Female Signs in Celie's Discourse of Desire: A Psychoanalytic Reading of Alice Walker's *The Color Purple.*" *Káñina.* 31.2 (2007): 49–58.

Christian, Barbara, T., ed. *Alice Walker: Everyday Use.* New Brunswick, NJ: Rutgers UP, 1994.

Dieke, Ikenna, ed., *Critical Essays on Alice Walker.* Westport, CT: Greenwood, 1999.

Duck, Leigh Anne. "Listening to Melancholia: Alice Walker's *Meridian.*" *Patterns of Prejudice.* 42.4/5 (2008): 439–64.

Fabi, Giulia M. "Sexual Violence and the Black Atlantic: On Alice Walker's *Possessing the Secret of Joy. Black Imagination and the Middle Passage.*" Eds. Maria

Diedrick, Henry Louis Gates Jr., and Carl Pedersen. New York: Oxford UP, 1999. 228–39.

Ferris, William R. "Alice Walker: "I Know What the Earth Says." *Southern Culture.* 10.1 (2004): 5–24.

Fitzgerald, Stephanie. *Alice Walker: Author and Social Activist.* Minneapolis, MN: Compass Point, 2008.

Gates, Henry Louis, and K.A. Appiah, eds. *Alice Walker: Critical Perspectives Past and Present.* New York: Amistad, 1993.

George, Olakunle. "Alice Walker's Africa: Globalization and the Province of Fiction." *Comparative Literature.* 53.4 (2001): 354–72.

Greenwood, Amanda. "The Animals Can Remember: Representations of the Non-Human Other in Alice Walker's *The Temple of My Familiar.*" *Worldviews: Environment Culture Religion.* 4.2 (2006): 164–78.

Harris, Melanie. *Gifts of Virtue: Alice Walker and Womanist Ethics.* New York: Palgrave , 2010.

Harris, Trudier. "Folklore in the Fiction of Alice Walker: A Perpetuation of Historical and Literary Traditions." *Black American Literature Forum.* 11 (1977): 3–8.

_____. On *The Color Purple,* Stereotypes, and Silence." *Black American Literature Forum.* 18.4 (1984): 155–61.

_____. "Our People, Our People." *Alice Walker and Zora Neale Hurston: The Common Bond.* Ed. Lillie P. Howard. Westport, CT: Greenwood, 1993. 31–42.

_____. *Saints, Sinners, Saviors: Strong Black Women in African American Literature.* New York: Palgrave, 2001.

_____. *South of Tradition: Essays on African American Literature.* Athens, GA: U of Georgia P, 2002.

Hite, Molly. *The Other Side of the Story: Structures and Strategies of Contemporary Feminist Narratives.* Ithaca: Cornell UP, 1989.

Hooker, Deborah Anne. "Reanimating the Trope of the Talking Book in Alice Walker's 'Strong Horse Tea.'" *Southern Literary Journal.* 37.2 (2005): 81–102.

Howard, Lillie P., ed. *Alice Walker and Zora Neale Hurston: The Common Bond.* Westport, CT: Greenwood, 1993.

Johnson, Ellen. "Geographic Context and Ethical Context: Joel Chandler Harris and Alice Walker." *Mississippi Quarterly.* 69.2 (2007): 235–55.

Kerr, Christine. *Bloom's How to Write About Alice Walker.* New York: Chelsea, 2008.

Kramer, Barbara. *Alice Walker: Author of the Color Purple.* Berkeley Heights, NJ: Enslow, 1995.

Lagrone, Khevin. *Alice Walker's The Color Purple.* New York: Rodopi, 2009.

Lauret, Maria. *Alice Walker.* New York: St. Martin's, 1999.

_____. *Alice Walker.* 2nd ed. New York: Palgrave, 2011

Lazo, Caroline Evensen. *Alice Walker: Freedom Writer.* Minneapolis, MN: Lerner, 2000.

Mosely, LaReine-Marie. "The Future of Womanist Theology and Religious Thought." *New Theology Review.* 24.1 (2011): 65–68.

Plant, Deborah G. *"Inside the Light": New Critical Essays on Zora Neale Hurston.* Santa Barbara, CA: Praeger, 2010.

Razak, Arisika. "Her Blue Body: A Pagan Reading of Alice Walker Womanism." *Journal of the Britain and Ireland School of Feminist Theology.* 18.1 (2009): 92–116.

Robinson, Cynthia Cole. "The Evolution of Alice Walker." *Women's Studies.* 38.3 (2009): 293–311.

Royster, Philip. "In Search of Our Fathers' Arms: Alice Walker's Persona of the Alienated Darling." *Black American Literature Forum* 20.4 (1986): 347–70.

Simcikova, Karla. *To Live Fully, Here and Now: The Healing Vision in the Works of Alice Walker.* Plymouth, UK: Lexington, 2007.

Strong-Leek, Linda. *Excising the Spirit: A Literary Analysis of Female Circumcision.* Trenton, NJ: Africa World, 2009.

Warren, Nagueyalti. "Beyond the Peacock: Psychosexual Symbolism in Flannery O'Connor and Alice Walker's Southern Landscape." *Flannery O'Connor Review* 6 (2008): 59–70.

_____. "Resistant Mothers in Alice Walker's *Meridian* and Tina McElroy's *Ugly Ways. Southern Mothers: Fact and Fictions in Southern Women's Writing.* Eds. Nagueyalti Warren and Sally Wolff. Baton Rouge: Louisiana State UP, 1999. 182–203.

Warren, Nagueyalti, and Sally Wolff. "Like the Pupil of an Eye: Sexual Blinding of Women in Alice Walker's Works. *Southern Literary Journal* 31.1 (1998): 1–16.

White, Evelyn C. *Alice Walker: A Life.* New York: Norton, 2004.

Willis, Susan. "Alice Walker's Women." *New Orleans Review* 12.1 (1985): 33–41.

Yeo. Jae-Hyuk. "Alice Walker: Community, Quilting and Sewing." *Studies in Modern Fiction* 8.2 (2001): 111–35.

CRITICAL
INSIGHTS

About the Editor_____

Nagueyalti Warren, PhD, is senior lecturer and director of undergraduate studies in the Department of African American Studies at Emory University in Atlanta, Georgia. She is a founding member of the Alice Walker Literary Society. A former associate dean of Emory College (1988–2005), Warren has taught an undergraduate seminar on Alice Walker's works for almost twenty years. She is coeditor of *Southern Mothers: Fact and Fictions* with Sally Wolff and contributed the chapter titled, "Resistant Mothers in Alice Walker's *Meridian* and Tina McElroy Ansa's *Ugly Ways*." She is editor of the poetry anthology *Temba Tupu! (Walking Naked): Africana Women's Poetic Self Portrait* (2008). Warren is a Cave Canem fellow and received an MFA from Goddard College in 2005. Her second volume of poetry, *Margaret*, won the Naomi Long Madgett Poetry Award (2008) and her third collection, *Braided Memory* (2011), has won the Violet Reed Hass Prize for Poetry. Warren is the recipient of fellowships to the Fine Arts Center in Provincetown, MA, and the Idyllwild Arts Center in Idyllwild, CA. *Grandfather of Black Studies: W. E. B. Du Bois* (2011) is her latest monograph.

Contributors _____

Paula C. Barnes is an associate professor of English at Hampton University where she teaches the survey course in African American Literature. In addition to an article on the autobiographical essays of Alice Walker in *African American Autobiographers: A Sourcebook*, Dr. Barnes has published in varied reference works, journals, and books such as *Magill's Survey of Long Fiction, The Oxford Companion to African American Literature, Belles Lettres, Obsidian: Literature of the African Diaspora, Forum on Public Policy: A Journal of the Oxford Round Table*, and *Arms Akimbo: Africana Women in Contemporary Literature*. With Australia Tarver, she coedited *New Voices on the Harlem Renaissance: Essays on Race, Gender, and Literary Discourse* in 2006.

Gerri Bates is associate professor of English, Africana literature, and women's literature at Bowie State University in Bowie, Maryland, and coordinator of Africana Literature and Interactive Writing. She is the author of *Alice Walker: A Critical Companion, The Color Purple: Character Studies* (2007), as well as critical articles on literature and education. Her research interests are Africana literature and women's literature. She is a founding member of the Middle Atlantic Writers Association.

Antoinette Brim is professor of composition and African American literature at Capital Community College in Hartford, Connecticut. She is the author of *Psalm of the Sunflower* (2009). Her poetry has appeared in various journals and magazines including *Reverie Midwest African American Literature, The November 3rd Club, Tidal Basin Review*, and anthologies including *44 on 44: Forty-Four African American Writers on the 44th President of the United States, In Our Own Words: A Generation Defining Itself, Not a Muse*, and *Just Like a Girl: A Manifesta*. She is an Assistant Editor of the NAACP Image Award–nominated *Surviving and Thriving: 365 Facts in Black Economic History* by Dr. Julianne Malveaux, a Cave Canem Foundation fellow, and a Harvard University W. E. B. Du Bois fellow of the National Endowment of the Humanities Summer Institute. A former guest host of Patrick Oliver's Literary Nation Talk Radio (KABF 88.3, Little Rock), she interviewed a variety of entertainers, literary figures, political pundits. and community developers.

Rudolph P. Byrd (1953–2011) was the Goodrich C. White Professor of American Studies in the Graduate Institute of Liberal Arts and the Department of African American Studies at Emory University. He wrote widely on the subject of American literature with special emphasis on African American authors including Jean Toomer, James Weldon Johnson, and Alice Walker. He played an instrumental role in Emory's acquisition of the Alice Walker papers in 2008–2009. Dr. Byrd was the founding director of the James Weldon Johnson Institute at Emory. His books included a new edition of *Cane* coedited with Henry Louis Gates Jr. (2011), and he was editor of Alice Walker's collected interviews, *The World Has Changed: Conversations with Alice Walker* (2010).

Shirley Toland-Dix is assistant professor of English at the University of South Florida, Tampa, where she teaches African American and Anglophone Caribbean literature. She has published articles in the journals *Small Axe* and *Studies in the Literary Imagination* and in edited volumes that include *Just Below South: Intercultural Performance in the Caribbean and the U.S. South, The Caribbean Woman Writer as Scholar: Creating, Imagining, Theorizing,* and *The Inside Light: New Critical Essays on Zora Neale Hurston.* She has also completed a book manuscript entitled *"Half the Story Has Never Been Told": Black Atlantic Women Novelists, History and Imagined Community.*

Carmen Gillespie is a professor of English, director of the Griot Institute for Africana Studies, and university arts coordinator at Bucknell University. In addition to article and poem publications, Dr. Gillespie is the author of *A Critical Companion to Toni Morrison* (2007), *A Critical Companion to Alice Walker* (2011), and the editor of *The Clearing: Forty Years with Toni Morrison, 1970–2010* (2011). She has published a poetry chapbook, *Lining the Rails* (2008) and a poetry collection, *Jonestown: A Vexation*, which won the 2011 Naomi Long Madgett Poetry Prize. Dr. Gillespie's awards include an Ohio Arts Council Individual Artist Fellowship for Excellence in Poetry and grants from the NEH, the Mellon Foundation, the Bread Loaf Writer's Conference, and the Fine Arts Work Center in Provincetown. She is a Cave Canem fellow and a Fulbright scholar. *Essence* named her one of its forty favorite poets in commemoration of the magazine's fortieth anniversary.

Donna Akiba Sullivan Harper, the Fuller E. Callaway Professor of English at Spelman College, was educated at Hampton University, Oberlin College (BA), and Emory University (MA and PhD). A founding member and past president of the Langston Hughes Society, she authored *Not So Simple: The "Simple" Stories by Langston Hughes* (1995) and edited four collections of short fiction by Hughes. She has published numerous articles and book reviews and has given lectures and conference presentations throughout the United States and in special presentations in Wuhan, China (2007), and Turkey (2010). She is a life member of the College Language Association and a past member of the Executive Committee of the Association of Departments of English of the Modern Language Association. Passionately committed to increasing the ranks of the professoriate, she coordinates the UNCF-Mellon Undergraduate Fellowship Program at Spelman and directs the UNCF-Mellon Summer Institute at Emory University.

Lillie P. Howard is professor emeritus of English at Wright State University in Dayton, Ohio, where she had a long and distinguished career as a professor and university administrator. Dr. Howard's scholarly works on Zora Neale Hurston and Alice Walker have been well-received nationally and internationally, and include *Zora Neale Hurston* (1980), *Alice Walker and Zora Neale Hurston: The Common Bond* (editor, 1993), book chapters, and numerous articles on African American literature. In 2007, Dr. Howard was inducted into the Ohio Women's Hall of Fame, and has been the recipient of a number of other honors and awards. A native of Alabama, Howard has always felt a special kinship with Hurston, Walker, and other writers whose works capture the beauty and the pain, the challenges and triumphs of the Deep South. Howard is the mother of two children, Kimberly and Benjamin Kendricks.

Nagueyalti Warren is senior lecturer and director of undergraduate studies at Emory University in the Department of African American Studies. For seventeen years Warren worked in the Office for Undergraduate Education at Emory College, serving first as assistant dean and then as associate dean. Her appointment to the core faculty in African American studies took place in 2005. Her teaching and research specialties are African American literature, specifically women's fiction, creative writing (mainly poetry), and W. E. B. Du Bois's contribution to the field of African American studies. Dr. Warren's current projects include research for a book on the writings of Alice Walker. Her recent publications include an edited anthology of poetry by black women from throughout the Diaspora titled *Temba Tupu! (Walking Naked): Africana Women's Poetic Self-Portrait* (2008); *Margaret,* a persona poem and winner of the 2008 Naomi Long Madgett Poetry Award; *Braided Memory* (2011), winner of the Violet Hass Reed Poetry Award; and *Grandfather of Black Studies: W. E. B. Du Bois* (2011).

Sally Wolff King is adjunct professor of English in the Department of English at Emory University where over the last twenty-years she has also served as assistant and associate dean in the College of Arts and Sciences and as an assistant vice president. Her book, *Ledgers of History: William Faulkner, an Almost Forgotten Friendship, and an Antebellum Diary* (2010), has been called "one of the most exciting literary finds in recent history" and "a major discovery in Faulkner scholarship." Dr. Wolff King has coedited with Gary S. Hauk a new Emory history book titled *Where Courageous Inquiry Leads: The Emerging Life of Emory University* (2010). She is also the author of *Talking about William Faulkner* (1996) and coeditor of *Southern Mothers: Fact and Fiction in Southern Women's Writing* (1999).

Karla Kovalova is assistant professor of American literature in the Department of American and British Studies, University of Ostrava, Ostrava, Czech Republic. She holds a PhD in modern history and literature with emphases on African American and African studies and women's studies from Drew University in Madison, New Jersey. She is the author of two books (published under the name Karla Simcikova), *To Live Fully Here and Now: The Healing Vision in the Works of Alice Walker* (2006) and *European Scholars Teaching African American Texts* (2007), as well as numerous articles on African American literature. She was the chief editor of *Studia Anglica* and currently serves on the editorial board for *The Ostrava Journal of English Philology.* Her research interests include black studies, particularly black feminism/womanism, slavery, and spirituality, and more recently, representations of children in literature. She is currently completing her next book on contemporary slave narratives.

Ciara Darnise Miller currently teaches GED Jobs for Youth in Chicago. She was born and raised on the West Side of Chicago. After becoming a *Louder Than a Bomb* poetry slam champion, she performed at various high schools and colleges throughout the United States, including Lane Tech, North Side Prep, Berkeley High, Chicago Academy of the Arts, Marymount Manhattan College, Milliken University, and Sarah Lawrence College. She has been a featured performer at the Nuyorican Poets Cafe and has been published in various Young Chicago Authors anthologies, *StarWall Paper*, *What I Know Is Me—Black Girls Write about Their World*, and *The SLC Review*. She also published a chapbook entitled *Black Dorothy*. She is a Cave Canem fellow, a graduate from Sarah Lawrence College, a lyricist/rapper (when rhymes are the best way to express herself), playwright, and a graduate fellowship MFA candidate at Indiana University. She approaches writing by taking influences from any speck of truth she can find.

Opal Moore is an associate professor of English; she teaches fiction and poetry writing, and African American literature at Spelman College. Ms. Moore is the author of *Lot's Daughters* (2005). Her fiction and poetry have appeared in journals and anthologies, including *Callaloo, Connecticut Review, The 100 Best African American Poems, Honey, Hush! An Anthology of African American Women's Humor, Homeplaces: Stories of the South by Women Writers,* and elsewhere. Ms. Moore was a Fulbright Scholar, a Cave Canem fellow, a DuPont scholar, and Bellagio fellow. She served as the 2008 McEvers Chair in Creative Writing at the Georgia Institute of Technology.

Deborah G. Plant is an associate professor of Africana studies at the University of South Florida, in Tampa, Florida. Her research and publications focus on African, African American, and Afro-Caribbean writers. She is the author of several articles, two monographs, and one edited volume on Zora Neale Hurston: *Every Tub Must Sit on Its Own Bottom: The Philosophy and Politics of Zora Neale Hurston; Zora Neale Hurston: A Spiritual Biography;* and *The Inside Light: New Critical Essays on Zora Neale Hurston.* Dr. Plant's current work is focused on author and activist Alice Walker.

Napolita Hooper-Simanga is an associate professor of English at Georgia Perimeter College. Dr. Hooper-Simanga is a poet, playwright, and educator. Her work has appeared in several anthologies, including *Temba Tupu! (Walking Naked): Africana Women's Poetic Self-Portrait* (2008); *Crux: Conversations in Words and Images from South Africa to South USA* (2008); *The Ringing Ear: Black Poets Lean South* (2008); *Gathering Ground: A Reader Celebrating Cave Canem's First Decade* (2006); and

Role Call: A Generational Anthology of Social and Political Black Literature and Art (2005). She is the author of two chapbooks, *Legacy* and *Perspectives*, and a critical biography, *Art of Work: The Art and Work of Haki Madhubuti* (2006). She is a coeditor of *44 on 44: Forty-Four African American Writers on the Election of the 44th President of the United States* (2011). Her collection of poems *Thunder in Her Voice: The Narrative of Sojourner Truth* was recently published in 2010.

Donna Haisty Winchell recently retired as professor of English from Clemson University in South Carolina, where she taught writing and ethnic American literature, with an emphasis on African American women novelists. She is the author of the Twayne book on Alice Walker and the editor of a special edition of the *Mississippi Quarterly* on history and the African American voice. She lives in Clemson with her two sons and regularly updates her argumentation textbook *Elements of Argument* (with Annette Rottenberg).

Toni Wynn is an arts educator, poet, museum professional, and creative nonfiction writer at Hampton University. Ms. Wynn creates collaborations that encourage learning through the arts. She designs and facilitates both formal and informal arts education experiences for learners of all ages. Her museum projects address history and culture, and she collaborates with visual artists and book-art artisans, publishing limited-edition broadsides and books of poetry. Her work is featured in anthologies and journals such as *Black Nature* and *The International Review of African American Art*. She is a Cave Canem graduate fellow and a member of the Squaw Valley Community of Writers. Ms. Wynn is on the project team of Spark!, an arts + STEM education initiative based at Hampton University. She once lived in San Francisco down the hill from Alice Walker and would wave as Walker strode by en route to BART.

Brenda Young is a professor of English at Georgia Perimeter College in Atlanta where she teaches academic writing. She received her degree in African American studies from Emory University in Atlanta, Georgia. She loves teaching students, undergraduate or graduate, because it allows her to have some influence over who they will ultimately become. Dr. Young is the general editor of *Fracturing the Canon: An Interdisciplinary Humanities Reader* (1999), which was meant to help students, particularly the disenfranchised, find themselves in a canon created by cultural gatekeepers and not intended to be inclusive.

Index

Eleandra (*Temple of My Familiar*), 213
Eleanora (*Temple of My Familiar*), 213
Elly. *See* Eleandra
Elsley, Judy, 189
Emory University, 26
Equal Rights Amendment, 69
Estes, Clarissa Pinkola, 167
Euterpe (Greek mythology), 250
"Everyday Use" (Walker), 175

Fanny (*Possessing the Secret*), 8
Fanny (*Temple of My Familiar*), 209,
    211, 215, 216, 219
Fat Josie (*Third Life*), 96, 100
Feather Mae (*Meridian*), 113, 114
Female genital mutilation, 72, 229, 230,
    234
Feminist movement, 68–69
Fifteenth Amendment, 61
Finding the Green Stone (Walker), 26
Flower imagery, 113, 123, 132, 135,
    161, 178, 180, 181–82, 184, 209,
    212, 216, 241, 243, 257
"Flowers, The" (Walker), 173–85
Folklore
    Meridian, 50–51
Forgiveness theme, 7, 8, 49, 168, 202,
    260
Fourteenth Amendment, 61
Freedom Flotilla II, 26, 247
Friends of the Children of Mississippi,
    21

Gaza, 170
Gender
    deity, 134
    norms, 47
    oppression, 77
    race and, 143
    roles, 83
    theory of, 99–100

George (*Mama Day*), 132
Georgia
    history of, 158
"Getting as Black as My Daddy:
    Thoughts on the Unhelpful Aspects of
    Destructive Criticism" (Walker), 268
Ghost Dance movement, 112
God
    depiction of, 126, 133–39. *See also*
        Color Purple, The; Creation story;
        "Gospel According to Shug, The";
        Mama Day; Spirit/Love; *Their
        Eyes Were Watching God*
*Good Night, Willie Lee, I'll See You in
    the Morning* (Walker), 23, 244–45,
    258–60
"Gospel According to Shug, The"
    (*Temple of My Familiar*), 170
Grandmother (*Now Is the Time to Open
    Your Heart*), 111
Guber, Peter, 25
Guggenheim Fellowship, 23

Hal (*Temple of My Familiar*), 9, 210,
    212, 218, 228
Harcourt Brace Jovanovich, 35
Hard Times Require Furious Dancing
    (Walker), 262
Harpo (*Color Purple*), 79, 163
Haverstock, Mary Ann (*Temple of My
    Familiar*), 213
Healing theme, 15
Held, Truman (*Meridian*), 34, 115
Her Blue Body Everything We Know
    (Walker), 26, 40, 246, 261
Hill, Meridian. *See* Meridian (*Meridian*)
Hogarth Press, 25
Holmes, Ernest
    philosophy of, 14
*Horses Make a Landscape Look More
    Beautiful* (Walker), 25, 245, 261

yurt, 215
Their Eyes Were Watching God (Hurston), 124
  depiction of God, 133
Thich Nhat Hanh, 167–68
Third Life of Grange Copeland, The (Walker), 7, 12, 13, 22, 52, 58, 93–106, 166, 167, 168, 221, 227, 228
  inspiration for, 93–94, 223
  sharecropping system in, 100
"To Hell with Dying" (Walker), 13, 21, 35
Toomer, Jean, 251
To Secure These Rights (Committee on Civil Rights), 62
Tree symbol, 7, 136–38
Truman, Harry S., 62
Truth-seeking theme, 273
Tsunga, 8, 193, 194, 195

"Unglamorous But Worthwhile Duties of the Black Revolutionary Artist, Or of the Artist Who Simply Works and Writes, The" (Walker), 149

Vision/blindness theme, 9, 63, 151, 175, 191, 194, 195. *See also* Walker, Alice: eye injury of

Wade, Sapphira (*Mama Day*), 125, 134, 135
Walker, Alice
  abortion procedure, 21
  activism of, 71–72, 74, 108–10, 114, 155, 157–59, 170, 227, 230, 232
  ancestry of, 33, 158
  archive of, 26
  autobiographical works of, 11–13
  birth of, 19
  career of, 22–26, 35, 70–74, 156, 235
  childhood of, 8, 12, 19–20, 60, 64

civil rights work, 21, 65
critical reception of, 15, 31–44, 187, 263, 268
divorce from Mel Leventhal, 23
education of, 19, 20–21
eye injury of, 7, 8, 19–20, 63, 151, 175, 235
family of, 63, 64, 160, 246
fiction of, 40
folk traditions, use of, 10, 57–58
impact of, 54, 58
influences on, 12, 14, 35, 145, 149, 250–52
literary periods of, 32–34, 37, 107
literary themes of, 35, 37, 54, 118, 121, 187, 232, 271
Lyme disease, 33
marriage to Mel Leventhal, 21
name change of, 245
nonfiction of, 44, 264–74
philosophy of, 3–4, 155, 156, 167–68
poetics of, 38–40, 234–48, 252, 252–63
Southern writer, 10
spiritual beliefs of, 3, 5, 32, 33, 108–110, 111, 122, 167, 271
vegetarianism, 15
writing process of, 237–39
Walker, Curtis Ulysses (brother), 19
Walker, Henry Clay (grandfather), 20, 24, 226
Walker Hood, Annie Ruth (sister), 63
Walker, James Thomas (brother), 19
Walker, Minnie Tallulah (Lou) Grant (mother), 19, 25, 60, 72, 159
  gardening of, 55, 182
Walker, Rachel (step-grandmother), 20, 24, 226
Walker, Rebecca Grant (daughter), 68
  birth of, 22

Walker, Robert Louis (brother), 19

Walker, Willie Lee (father), 19, 22, 63, 64, 159

Wards Chapel, 19, 20, 63

Warrior Marks (film), 26, 72, 229, 230

Warrior Marks (Walker and Parmar), 72, 229, 230

Watch for Me in the Sunset (Walker), 70

Way Forward Is with a Broken Heart, The (Walker), 12, 31

We Are the Ones We Have Been Waiting For (Walker), 108, 122, 169, 269

Weil, Wendy, 269

Wellesley College, 22

What the Negro Wants (Logan), 61

Whitman, Walt, 236

Wild Trees Press, 7, 25

Wile Chile (*Meridian*), 47, 49, 51

Williams, William Carlos, 251

Willow Springs (*Mama Day*), 132

Winchell, Donna Haisty, 38

Winfrey, Oprah, 60

Womanism, 70, 141–52, 189, 242, 265

Womanist, 32
  definition of, 70, 141, 242, 264

World Has Changed, The (Walker), 107, 221, 271

World War II, 60, 61

Wright, Richard, 156

X, Malcolm, 239

Yaddo, 23

You Can't Keep a Good Woman Down (Walker), 23

Zedé (*Temple of My Familiar*), 9, 210, 213

Zinn, Howard, 224, 271

"Zora Neale Hurston: A Cautionary Tale and a Partisan View" (Walker), 147, 265

Zora Neale Hurston Festival, 267